STUDENT'S GUIDE TO LANDMARK CONGRESSIONAL LAWS
ON YOUTH

D0103125

STUDENT'S GUIDE TO LANDMARK CONGRESSIONAL LAWS ON YOUTH

KATHLEEN URADNIK

STUDENT'S GUIDE TO
LANDMARK CONGRESSIONAL LAWS
John R. Vile, Series Editor

Greenwood Press
Westport, Connecticut • London

Library of Congress Cataloging-in-Publication Data

Uradnik, Kathleen Ann.
    Student's guide to landmark congressional laws on youth / Kathleen Uradnik.
      p.   cm.—(Student's guide to landmark congressional laws, ISSN 1537–3150)
    Includes bibliographical references and index.
    ISBN 0–313–31461–6 (alk. paper)
    1. Children—Legal status, laws, etc.—United States. 2. Youth—Legal status, laws,
etc.—United States. I. Title: Landmark congressional laws on youth. II. Title.
III. Series.
    KF3735.U73 2002
    346.7301'35—dc21   2001055613

British Library Cataloguing in Publication Data is available.

Library of Congress Catalog Card Number: 2001055613
ISBN: 0–313–31461–6
ISSN: 1537–3150

First published in 2002

Greenwood Press, 88 Post Road West, Westport, CT 06881
An imprint of Greenwood Publishing Group, Inc.
www.greenwood.com

Printed in the United States of America

∞™

The paper used in this book complies with the
Permanent Paper Standard issued by the National
Information Standards Organization (Z39.48–1984).

10 9 8 7 6 5 4 3 2 1

For Sona and Maya

Contents

Series Foreword

Most of the Founding Fathers who met at the Constitutional Convention in Philadelphia in the summer of 1787 probably anticipated that the legislative branch would be the most powerful of the three branches of the national government that they created. For all practical purposes, this was the only branch of government with which the onetime colonists had experience under the Articles of Confederation. Moreover, the delegates discussed this branch first and at greatest length at the convention, the dispute over representation in this body was one of the convention's most contentious issues, and the Founding Fathers made it the subject of the first and longest article of the new Constitution.

With the president elected indirectly through an electoral college and the members of the Supreme Court appointed by the president with the advice and consent of the Senate and serving for life terms, the framers of the Constitution had little doubt that Congress—and especially the House of Representatives, whose members were directly elected by the people for short two-year terms—would be closest to the people. As a consequence, they invested Congress with the awesome "power of the purse" that had been at issue in the revolutionary dispute with Great Britain, where the colonists' position had been encapsulated in the phrase "no taxation without representation." The framers also entrusted Congress with the more general right to adopt laws to carry out a variety of enumerated powers and other laws "necessary and proper" to the implementation of these powers—the basis for the doctrine of implied powers.

Wars and the threats of wars have sometimes tilted the modern balance of power toward the president, who has gained in a media age from his position as a single individual. Still, Congress has arguably been the most powerful branch of government over the long haul, and one might expect its power to increase with the demise of the Cold War. Especially in the aftermath of President Franklin D. Roosevelt's New Deal and President Lyndon B. Johnson's Great Society program, the number and complexity of laws have increased with the complexity of modern society and the multitude of demands that citizens have placed on modern governments. Courts have upheld expansive interpretations of federal powers under the commerce clause, the war-powers provisions, and the power to tax and spend for the general welfare, and in recent elections Democratic and Republican candidates alike have often called for expansive new federal programs.

It has been noted that there are 297 words in the Ten Commandments, 463 in the Bill of Rights, 266 in the Gettysburg Address, and more than 26,000 in a federal directive regulating the price of cabbage. Although the U.S. Constitution can be carried in one's pocket, the compilation of federal laws in the *U.S. Code* and the *U.S. Code Annotated* requires many volumes, not generally available in high-school and public libraries. Perhaps because of this modern prolixity and complexity, students often consider the analysis of laws to be the arcane domain of lawyers and law reviewers. Ironically, scholars, like this author, who focus on law, and especially constitutional law, tend to devote more attention to the language of judicial decisions interpreting laws than to the laws themselves.

Because knowledge of laws and their impact needs to be made more widely accessible, this series on Landmark Congressional Laws presents and examines laws relating to a number of important topics. These currently include education, First Amendment rights, civil rights, the environment, the rights of young people, women's rights, and health and social security. Each subject is a matter of importance that should be of key interest to high-school and college students. A college professor experienced in communicating ideas to undergraduates has compiled each of these volumes. Each author has selected major laws in his or her subject area and has described the politics of these laws, considering such aspects as their adoption, their interpretation, and their impact.

The laws in each volume are arranged chronologically. The entry on each law features an introduction that explains the law, its significance, and its place within the larger tapestry of legislation on the issues. A selection from the actual text of the law itself follows the introduction. This arrangement thus provides ready access to texts that are often difficult for students to find while highlighting major provisions, often taken from literally hundreds of pages, that students and scholars might spend hours to distill on their own.

These volumes are designed to be profitable to high-school and college students who are examining various public policy issues. They should also help interested citizens, scholars, and legal practitioners needing a quick, but thorough and accurate, introduction to a specific area of public policy-making. Although each book is designed to cover highlights of the entire history of federal legislation within a given subject area, the authors of these volumes have also designed them so that individuals who simply need to know the background and major provisions of a single law (the Civil Rights Act of 1964, for example) can quickly do so.

The Founding Fathers of the United States devised a system of federalism dividing power between the state and national governments. Thus, in many areas of legislation, even a complete overview of national laws will prove inadequate unless it is supplemented with knowledge of state and even local laws. This is duly noted in entries on laws where national legislation is necessarily incomplete and where powers are shared among the three layers of government. The U.S. system utilizes a system of separation of powers that divides authority among three branches of the national government. Thus, while these volumes keep the focus on legislation, they also note major judicial decisions and presidential initiatives relating to the laws covered.

Although the subjects of this series are worthy objects of study in their own right, they are especially appropriate topics for students and scholars in a system of representative democracy like the United States where citizens who are at least eighteen years of age have the right to choose those who will represent them in public office. In government, those individuals, like James Madison, Abraham Lincoln, and Woodrow Wilson, who have acquired the longest and clearest view of the past are frequently those who can also see the farthest into the future. This series is presented in the hope that it will help students both to understand the past and to equip themselves for future lives of good citizenship.

This editor wishes to thank her friends at Greenwood Press, her colleagues both at her own university and at other institutions of higher learning who have done such an able job of highlighting and explaining the laws that are the focus of this series, and those students, scholars, and citizens who have responded by reading and utilizing these volumes. When the Founding Fathers drew up a constitution, they depended not only on a set of structures and rights but also on the public-spiritedness and education of future citizens. When Benjamin Franklin was asked what form of government the Founding Fathers had created, he reportedly responded, "A republic, if you can keep it." When we inform ourselves and think deeply about the government's role in major areas of public policy, we honor the faith and foresight of those who bequeathed this government to us.

John R. Vile
Middle Tennessee State University

Acknowledgments

This book is the result of combined efforts, and I have many people to thank. I'm grateful to my series editor, John Vile, for giving me this project and for making the final product better. His unfailing support during the writing meant a lot to me. Thanks go as well to Kevin Ohe and Jane Lerner at Greenwood Press, who were patient with deadlines as well as with my questions and who offered helpful insights about the text along the way. My husband, Tad, was loving and supportive as usual.

There are two inspirations behind this book. First, I owe much to my students. I teach both high school and college students in my American Government courses, and I've written this book with them in mind. It's often a challenge to get students excited about anything these days, particularly about American government and politics. But that's the fun of it. I enjoy trying to make American government interesting to young people or, failing that, at least understandable and relevant. I have always felt that the key to gaining students' attention is to repeatedly demonstrate that this seemingly boring stuff is, in fact, highly relevant to their lives. As I tell them often, the mere fact that many of them don't know or care about American government is a powerful testament to its success. How lucky we are to have a government that we can take for granted. Ultimately, however, we all must accept the responsibilities of citizenship. To that end, this book emphasizes the impact these laws have had and will have on young people and strongly encourages them to become active to preserve the ones they like and change the ones they don't. Students should find this book both readable and understandable; if they do not, I have let them down.

The second inspiration behind this book is my professor, mentor, and friend, Sandy Muir. The University of California, Berkeley, has never had a professor who cared more about his students and about his country than Sandy. As anyone who knows him can attest, Sandy's optimism about both is permanent and infectious. To the extent that this book sounds too positive about Congress and American government, you can blame me. But I got that attitude from Sandy, and neither one of us is going to apologize for it.

Finally, I would like to thank Google.com and Ben and Jerry's, both of which greatly facilitated the completion of this project.

Timeline for Enactment of Laws

1862   **Morrill Act**. President Lincoln rewarded states that stayed in the Union during the ongoing Civil War with gifts of federal land that they could use to fund the development of public colleges and universities. Over seventy "land-grant" institutions were created under this law, which is sometimes called the "First Morrill Act."

1868   **Fourteenth Amendment**. One of the three "Civil War Amendments," the Fourteenth Amendment extended citizenship rights to all persons born or naturalized in the United States. Thus, any child born in this country, even if born to illegal aliens, is a citizen of the United States.

1890   **Second Morrill Act**. Congress amended the original act to make historically black colleges and universities eligible for its benefits.

1935   **Social Security Act**. This act was Congress' first major undertaking to protect children through a federally operated and funded national welfare program. The original legislation offered four specific types of assistance: aid to dependent children, aid for maternal and child health, aid to disabled children, and aid to children at risk.

1938   **Fair Labor Standards Act (FLSA)**. In addition to establishing the first federal minimum wage and setting maximum working hours, this groundbreaking legislation outlawed most forms of child labor and placed restrictions on the rest.

1944   **The G.I. Bill**. Through this legislation, Congress provided extensive student financial aid to veterans returning from World War II. The G.I. Bill not only sent millions of veterans to college, it opened the door to higher education to middle- and lower-class Americans.

1946   **National School Lunch Act**. Passed originally to protect national security, the act provides free or reduced cost lunches to millions of underprivileged schoolchildren across the nation.

1965   **Head Start**. The Head Start program offers a comprehensive set of services to underprivileged children from birth to age five, including medical and dental care, psychological counseling, social services, and educational instruction.

1965   **Elementary and Secondary Education Act (ESEA)**. Now nearly forty years old, this Great Society legislation has been expanded significantly over the years. It provides extensive federal aid to elementary and secondary schools through dozens of federal programs. The act covers virtually every aspect of elementary and secondary school education, from teacher training to family literacy, and from magnet schools to drug-free schools.

1965   **Higher Education Act (HEA)**. This act contains a number of federal programs to assist students, educators, and institutions of higher education. Title IV provides for numerous types of financial aid to students, including Pell Grants and student loans.

1965   **Medicaid**. Congress expanded the Social Security Act to include this sweeping new program that makes medical insurance and services available to low-income families.

1966   **Child Nutrition Act**. This act complements the National School Lunch Act by, among other things, creating a school breakfast program, a national fluid milk program, and a program of supplemental nutritional assistance for pregnant women, infants, and young children.

1967   **Early and Periodic Screening, Diagnosis, and Treatment for Children (EPSDT)**. To supplement Medicare, Congress provided this specialized medical benefit package to Medicaid-eligible children. Originally the states had the option of offering EPSDT services; today they are required to do so.

1971   **Twenty-sixth Amendment**. This amendment lowers the voting age of American citizens to eighteen. It was passed largely in response to the protests of young people, who argued that they were old enough to be drafted for the Vietnam War, but were not old enough to vote in federal elections.

1973   **Rehabilitation Act of 1973**. The Rehabilitation Act forbids many forms of discrimination against the disabled. Section 504, in particular, prohibits discrimination by any institution, program, or activity that receives federal funds. Section 504, then, applies to virtually every college and university in the nation.

1975   **Education for All Handicapped Children Act**. Following up on the Rehabilitation Act, Congress sought to assist state and local governments in providing educational services to disabled children. This act was renamed the "Individuals with Disabilities Education Act" in 1983.

1980   **Military Selective Service Act**. All men age eighteen through twenty-five are required to register with the Selective Service. Their names are kept on a list for use in case of a future military draft. Females do not have to register.

1983   **Individuals with Disabilities Education Act (IDEA).** This act, the expanded and renamed Education for All Handicapped Children Act, requires that disabled children receive a "free and appropriate" public school education. It calls for educators, in consultation with parents, to prepare an "individualized education plan" (IEP) for each disabled child and for these children to be educated in regular classrooms whenever possible. The act was significantly amended in 1997.

1984   **Uniform Drinking Age Act.** In this classic "carrot and stick" legislation, Congress called for states to raise their legal age for consumption of alcohol to twenty-one. States that did not comply faced the loss of federal aid, specifically federal highway funds. All states have complied.

1986   **National Childhood Vaccine Injury Act.** The purpose of this act is two-fold: first, it seeks to ensure the continued research and development of vaccines to combat childhood diseases; second, it establishes a compensation system for victims of the side effects of vaccines.

1988   **Fair Housing Act Amendments.** These amendments extend the protections of the original Fair Housing Act to families with children and to the disabled. The amendments also provide important new enforcement measures to combat housing discrimination.

1989   **Early and Periodic Screening, Diagnosis, and Treatment for Children (EPSDT).** Through this amendment, Congress required that states provide under Medicaid extended diagnosis and treatment services to eligible children, even if they do not make the same services available to adults. States must provide treatment to children whenever medically necessary to correct their physical or mental illnesses.

1990   **Americans with Disabilities Act (ADA).** Taken together, the Rehabilitation Act of 1973, the IDEA, and the Americans with Disabilities Act constitute a three-pronged attack on discrimination against disabled children and provide the legal basis for protecting and educating them.

1990   **Clean Air Act Amendments.** The original Clean Air Act was a sweeping law designed to improve air quality throughout the nation. The 1990 amendments reauthorized the act. The amendments are included here because they required the elimination of lead from gasoline and in so doing removed a major health threat to children.

1992   **Residential Lead-Based Paint Hazard Reduction Act.** This act is one of several congressional measures to protect children from the health risks posed by the ingestion of lead. The act focuses on federal and privately owned homes that may contain lead-based paint.

1994   **School-to-Work Opportunities Act.** Recognizing that most high school graduates do not attend college, this act seeks to prepare these students to obtain meaningful employment upon graduation. It does so by promoting and funding cooperative efforts between high schools and employers to create and implement broad-based, educationally focused job-training programs.

1995   **Federal Zero Tolerance Law**. A complement to the Uniform Drinking Age Act, this law again uses the threat of the loss of federal highway funds to encourage the states to adopt a "zero tolerance" alcohol policy for drivers under age twenty-one.

1996   **Safe Drinking Water Act Amendments**. These amendments require the Environmental Protection Agency, in regulating contaminants in drinking water, to consider the health risks posed to certain groups, including pregnant women, infants, and children.

1996   **Food Quality Protection Act**. This act requires that children's health be the benchmark for setting acceptable regulatory levels of toxins in food.

1997   **State Children's Health Insurance Program (CHIP)**. In response to the fact that millions of American children were and are uninsured, Congress created this comprehensive program to provide health insurance and treatment to children from families that have incomes too high to qualify for Medicaid, but too low for them to purchase private health insurance.

2000   **Child Citizenship Act**. This act grants citizenship automatically to foreign children adopted by American parents.

2000   **Intercountry Adoption Act**. In passing this law, the United States joined approximately forty countries around the world to protect adopted children by following uniform adoption procedures.

2002   **No Child Left Behind Act**. The 2002 Reauthorization of the ESEA.

Introduction: What Has Congress Done for YOUth Lately?

A NEW LEGISLATURE FOR A NEW NATION

How should we govern ourselves?

The framers of the Constitution faced this fundamental question when they assembled in Philadelphia in the summer of 1787 to confront the crisis created by the fact that their first attempt at government, the Articles of Confederation, had ended in failure. Now, as they met to revise the Articles, the future of the United States hung in the balance. If they could not create a central government strong enough to unify the states, the nation would be lost. But if they created too powerful a central government, the continued existence of the states could be in doubt.

When it started, no one really knew what to expect from the Constitutional Convention. The framers did agree to discard the Articles and start from scratch; after that they had a hard time agreeing on anything. As they met and debated the role and structure of government, no one was certain that an agreement would be reached, let alone a successful one. But the framers must have done something right, because the outcome of their struggles—the United States Constitution—remains in effect today, more than two hundred years after it was drafted. Indeed, the U.S. Constitution is the longest continuously operating written constitution in history.

But the work of the framers, and indeed of the American people, did not start and end in Philadelphia. The framers knew that that Constitution would be an evolving document and would have to be adjusted by the citizenry to meet its ongoing needs. They provided an amendment process just for that purpose; it has been used twenty-seven times since the Constitution's adoption. But more fundamentally, the framers knew that the business of government was not fully contained in the Constitution. Indeed, one of the striking aspects of the document is its generality. The Constitution provides an overarching framework for American government. It outlines the basic structures of government, the roles of each branch of government, and the rights of American citizens. It does not, however, provide very many details about how government should operate and what it should do. That is left to the citizens and to their elected officials.

In creating this general framework, the framers not only hoped that future generations would be active in government, but ensured that they would have to be active. They strongly believed in democracy, the notion that free citizens should govern themselves, but they knew that a direct democracy was not practical, for even at its founding America had far too many citizens for direct participation and decision making by all of them. More workable was the "republic," a form of democratic government where citizens elect representatives to act on their behalf. At the time this notion of a representative republic was rather new, and many people were justifiably skeptical. But the framers, led perhaps most ardently by James Madison, argued that this form of government would best meet the needs of the disparate states and people within them. He insisted in Federalist Paper No. 10, for example, that the republic would not only best represent the wishes of the people, but also control "factions" or dissenters who might seek to undermine the nation. A large, representative republic, he concluded, would ensure that all voices would be heard and that no one voice would become too powerful. This approach promised a government that was elected by and responsive to its people, but insulated from their foibles.

The citizens of the United States, therefore, would always have a say in electing their representatives. *But representatives to what?* What sort of body would do the people's bidding? The framers were well familiar with political philosophy and history and with the various forms of government that had been adopted in the past. They knew that governments of all types basically shared the same three roles: one part, or branch, of government must make the laws that the citizens live by ("legislate"); a second branch must implement and enforce those laws ("execute"); and a third branch must review the creation, implementation, and enforcement of the laws, to ensure that they are in keeping with what the government has been authorized to do ("adjudicate"). From the beginning of the convention, the framers probably expected that they would end up with three branches in their new government. After all, the Articles of Confederation lacked a judiciary, did not really have a chief executive, and provided at best for a weak legislature. The framers learned from their mistakes and weren't going to repeat them.

After much discernment and compromise, the framers did indeed settle on a tripartite system of government: a congress, a president, and a supreme court. The drafters of the Constitution chose a president rather than a monarch or council of elders to lead the executive branch. They created a single court, known as the Supreme Court, to head the judicial branch. And, when it came time to negotiate the structure of the legislative branch, they ultimately decided on a congress, consisting of two houses, the House of Representatives and the Senate.

A congress is not the most common choice of legislature for people who live in democracies. Far more common is the "parliament," an approach to governing where the legislature is elected and then its members choose the nation's chief executive, often called the "prime minister." Typically, the winning political party or coalition of parties in the legislature will select its own leader to become prime minister. Therefore, in a parliamentary democracy, the legislative branch and the executive branch work together as one. Cooperation is more than expected; it is virtually assured. The legislators and their prime minister work to implement the agenda that they presented to the voters during the election. Thus, in casting a vote in a parliamentary democracy, a citizen essentially knows what "package" he or she is going to get: the legislator, the prime minister, and that party's agenda or platform are all reflected in each vote cast.

But our framers chose a congress instead. Its members are elected by district or state and serve their district's needs, their state's needs, and the needs of the nation. The members of the U.S. Congress may or may not cooperate with the president, who is separately elected. They may or may not pledge loyalty to a political party and vote as that party dictates. Instead, each member of Congress is expected independently to propose, write, debate, and pass legislation and to participate in other legislative functions, such as overseeing or investigating the performance of the rest of the government.

To many Americans today, the choice of a congress over a parliament might seem unfortunate. Instead of having a neat package to select on election day, an American votes three times to choose national leaders: once for the House of Representatives, once for the Senate, and once again for president. Since voters separately elect the legislative and executive branch officials, it is possible— even likely—to have a Congress led by one political party and a president who belongs to another party. Or, to confuse things a bit further, it's possible to have one house of Congress dominated by one party and the other house of Congress dominated by another. The president, for his part, may not get along with either of them. This phenomenon is called "divided government," and it is responsible for much of the criticism of Congress today. Critics allege that Congress, in part because it has divided party loyalties, works very slowly and doesn't accomplish very much.

Did the framers make a bad choice? Wouldn't a parliamentary system like England's be more efficient and effective? To answer these questions is not a simple task. It requires an examination of the framers' purposes and values in creating a new system of government for the nation. The framers knew that this government must be made stronger; but they also feared making it too strong. They despised tyranny and recognized that it could come in many forms. The executive could prove tyrannical, for example, as King George III had shown during the American Revolution a decade earlier. A legislature could become tyrannical. A majority or a minority of the citizenry could become tyrannical too. Any one of these forms of tyranny could destroy the liberty of the people and with it the soul of the new nation.

Consequently, in a concerted effort to avoid tyranny, the framers included a number of structural safeguards in the Constitution. These safeguards, often referred to as "checks and balances," would help to ensure that each branch of government performed its duties and stayed within its proper bounds. Thus, it was not enough simply to give lawmaking power to the Congress or executive power to the president. The framers made the branches dependent on each other by mixing the powers that each branch possessed. For example, the framers decided that Congress cannot pass a law on its own; for a bill to become law, the president must sign it, or the

Congress must muster enough votes to override the president's veto. The president, similarly, cannot simply implement a budget or program for the nation. He must obtain a sponsor for his budget or program in Congress and ask for funding. Moreover, the president cannot appoint just anyone to the Supreme Court; all of his major appointments—Supreme Court justices, most federal judges, ambassadors, and even his own Cabinet members—have to be approved by the Senate. The Senate, for its part, cannot act alone when it comes to spending federal funds. All funding bills, including all of the bills that fund the programs discussed in this book, must originate in the House of Representatives.

These are but a few examples from a long list of checks and balances implemented by the framers. Their innovation—to not only separate powers among the branches, but to mix them—set the government of the United States apart, both at that time and now. By spreading power among the branches and therefore requiring their cooperation with each other, the framers sought to ensure that no one branch of government or any single official would become too powerful. This process of spreading power out among the branches (and indeed, to the states as well) is sometimes called "decentralization." So while the framers succeeded in creating a stronger central government, they also succeeded in decentralizing its power too. In disbursing power among the branches and between the central government and the states, they walked a very fine line indeed.

When they developed the U.S. Congress, the framers knew that some of its lawmaking power would be shared with the president and the Supreme Court. But they perceived that most of the work of government would still be done by the legislature, as it was chosen by the people and remained closest to them. The issue of how the citizens would actually choose their representatives was one of the most difficult faced by the framers. The debate over representation was perhaps the most wrenching and became the most famous contest of the Constitutional Convention. Framers from large states naturally tended to support a Congress that would be elected based on a state's population. Framers from small states wanted equal representation with the larger states, so that they would not be overpowered and, as some feared, overrun by their larger neighbors. This dilemma threatened the success of the entire convention. It was resolved by a compromise, aptly referred to as the "Great Compromise." Under this compromise the members of the House of Representatives would be chosen by district, with the total number of representatives from a state based on its population. The larger, more populous states were happy with this result. The members of the Senate, to the contrary, would be set at two per state, regardless of the state's geographic size or population. Small states would therefore have an equal voice with larger ones in the Senate.

In striking this obvious but ingenious compromise, the framers divided legislative power into two houses, making the legislature "bicameral." They also provided for different types of representation and different approaches to electing our representatives. The members of the House of Representatives serve two-year terms, and the entire House is up for reelection every two years. Senators serve six-year terms, and one-third of the Senate is up for reelection every two years. Originally senators were selected by the method approved by each state's legislature (and often by the state legislature itself); since passage of the Seventeenth Amendment in 1913, voters directly elect their senators.

After debate, negotiation, and compromise, the framers created the U.S. Congress and empowered it with general and specific lawmaking duties as outlined in Article I of the Constitution. The institution it constructed would become the most powerful legislature in the world, but it also had constitutional limits. The two houses of the Congress would have to work with each other and with the president before any law could be made. The members within each house would have to work with each other and find some way to overcome their political, philosophical, cultural, and regional differences while still serving the voters who elected them.

Thus the Congress did not end up as a neat "package" for efficient lawmaking. One might even argue that it was designed for inefficient lawmaking. But it was also designed for lawmaking that reflected the framers' fear of abuse of power and consequently stressed the values of representation, interdependence, and compromise.

Today our elected representatives and senators continue to reflect the values that the framers built into the Constitution. But they are also expected to be active and independent. Each member of Congress is expected to adopt and promote his or her own legislative agenda and to write or sponsor legislation in keeping with that agenda. The member is expected to represent his or her home state or district and to lobby in Congress to ensure that the voters back home receive their fair share of federal funds and programs.

Members constantly deal with the demands of their individual constituents, whether it is to find out why a Social Security check is late, to arrange for a Washington internship for an outstanding local student, or to attend a hometown barbecue. In short, a member of Congress is pulled in many directions. The representative or senator must serve his or her constituents, political party, congressional caucuses, the institution of Congress itself, and the nation as a whole.

These multiple responsibilities and the multiple loyalties they require, combined with the structural checks placed on Congress' design, make it difficult for any one member, let alone the entire Congress, to function gracefully. Congress is not a graceful place. The House, for example, is frenetic—a beehive of activity, with 435 members broken into various topical committees and subcommittees, each member with his or her own staff, and each committee and subcommittee with a staff. It needs a host of rules to keep its members in line and to ensure that everyone has a chance to speak. The Senate, although smaller at 100 members, is also divided into committees and subcommittees and participates in joint committees with the House. And senators are spread rather thin, as they represent all the people of their home states, rather than simply those of local districts.

It should not be surprising, therefore, that Congress moves slowly on legislation. The slow pace of Congress, its alleged inability to "get things done," is perhaps the most common criticism of that body today. A look at the numbers supports this criticism: Of all the bills that are introduced by various legislators, only a very few ever become law. Indeed, there is plenty of opportunity for legislation to die, including important legislation that the people want and that their representatives may agree upon in principle. And a law that is passed often bears little resemblance to the bill that was first introduced, having been edited and amended numerous times as it made its way down the legislative path.

Americans sometimes pay a high price for a slow Congress, when the legislation that they want and need arrives in a watered-down version after a long wait. On the other hand, legislation that is approved has been subject to the input of countless individuals and groups, all who have an interest in it and an opinion about it. Indeed, Americans remain active in self-government not only by electing their legislators, but also by constantly telling them what to do. The role of an active citizen is not limited to voting, but includes joining interest groups; contacting elected officials to praise or complain; working in elections; participating in political, religious, or civic groups; or volunteering for community or public service. Congress was designed to be responsive to the American people, and many Americans take full advantage of that fact.

MAKING YOUNG PEOPLE A POLITICAL CONSTITUENCY

The danger in any self-governing nation is that some of its citizens may not be able to participate and, consequently, may not be heard. America is not immune from this danger; indeed, it has a number of constituencies that have a limited ability to influence public policy. Prisoners who committed felonies and illegal aliens, for example, do not have the right to vote. They are cut off from the greater society and have limited ability to express their views. They can be shunned by elected officials, who are busy representing the needs of their more mainstream and vocal constituents. But both prisoners and illegal aliens have rights under the Constitution and laws of the United States and are entitled to the protections they afford. It is often a challenge for Congress, and for the state governments as well, to recognize and act on their responsibilities to groups at the margins of society. Often these groups find representation only through political or social interest groups that champion their causes.

There's another disfranchised group in America, one that also needs advocates in order to be heard: America's young people. Children cannot vote; they cannot easily contact elected officials; they cannot protest. Even teenagers, who have greater ability to influence government, still find themselves restricted, unable to enjoy the full array of citizens' rights until they become adults. America's children have often been a forgotten constituency because of their inability to speak for themselves and to participate in American democracy.

And, in fact, Congress has not always acted favorably toward America's children. For the first 110 years of our nation's history, it really didn't act at all. Congress did not deal extensively with social issues and programs, believing them to be better left to state governments or, more commonly, to private charitable organizations. Examples of governmental efforts on behalf of needy citizens can be found—many of the colonies provided some measure of

care for the poor—but the role of government during the eighteenth and nineteenth centuries did not encompass the type of social welfare programs that are familiar today.

Thus, throughout the eighteenth and nineteenth centuries, social services were considered largely a private matter. To the extent
they existed, charitable undertakings were sponsored by religious
or civic organizations. In serving the needs of poor people, these
groups commonly made a distinction between the "deserving poor"
and the "undeserving poor." The deserving poor, it was thought,
included persons who were not responsible for their condition, and
thus merited charity. The deserving poor commonly included wid-
ows with young children and orphans. Often, orphaned children
were institutionalized, as were disabled or mentally impaired children—such was the extent of social services back then.

But these private endeavors, even if better than nothing, rarely
proved adequate to meet the needs of underprivileged children,
and many were forced to fend for themselves. Child labor was common and legal in the nineteenth century, not just on family farms,
but in the factories and mines developing in response to the Industrial Revolution. Children worked long hours for meager wages;
the money they earned generally went to support their families.
Schooling was not offered or required, or it was stopped at an early
age so that children could work.

The notion of civil rights for children would be long in coming.
Indeed, as late as the 1930s, Congress had not passed a constitutional ban on child labor; the Supreme Court, now often considered the champion of civil rights, led the way in striking down
Congress' attempts to do so. The idea that children possess rights
independent of their parents was and is a controversial one. American culture is quite deferential to the role of parents and guardians
and grants them significant latitude in determining how to raise
their children. Thus, if Mr. Dagenhart wished to have his youngsters
work in the North Carolina textile mills, the Supreme Court was
not going to stand in his way. (See *Hammer v. Dagenhart, infra* page
35.) The Constitution, after all, never expressly mentions children
and historically was not interpreted as providing explicit rights or
protections to them. Even after the passage of the Fourteenth
Amendment, which purported to clarify the rights of persons in the
United States as extending beyond white males, Americans did not
view young people as separately entitled to constitutional rights.

Eventually, the amendment would be used to some extent to protect the nation's children, but not until late in the twentieth century.

How, then, did the nation change its views toward children, to the point that "family values" and "protection of our most precious resource, our children" have become the buzzwords of seemingly every contemporary American politician? Several factors explain the nation's slow change of heart. First, perhaps, was the Progressive Movement (also called the Progressive Era), a grassroots social and political movement that emerged in the late 1890s to call for social change and, among other things, to fight against the excesses of industrialization. The Industrial Revolution was beginning to make America prosperous, but many Americans were suffering its ill effects. Laborers toiled for long hours and days on end, often for very low wages. Protections we take for granted today, such as the forty-hour work week and the minimum wage, were only distant dreams (and, in fact, were ruled unconstitutional by the Supreme Court). Conditions in the nation's factories and mines were dangerous; the federal government had yet to regulate them. American consumers faced dangers as well, as food and water were not regulated to ensure their safety. The nation's major cities were growing rapidly, but sanitation systems were often nonexistent. Housing for the poor or displaced, or for the nation's new wave of immigrants, was hard to come by. Disease spread through tightly packed urban communities, yet there was little or no available public health care.

The followers of the Progressive Movement advocated a greater role for both state and federal governments to deal with these and other growing problems. In addition, the movement called for politics to be made more open and democratic by, for example, extending the franchise to women, protecting the civil rights of minority groups, permitting the direct election of senators, and implementing other election reforms. At the same time, the union movement took hold in America, and union activists demanded changes in salaries and working conditions for their members, often through direct political action.

Across the nation citizens' perception of the role of government slowly began to change. Increasing numbers of people saw a benefit to having government improve the safety of working conditions and common products through regulation and inspection. As Americans began to consider using some of their new-found prosperity to better their living conditions, children quickly became the beneficiaries of this new attitude. Opponents of child labor argued that a civilized nation should not subject its children to work, particularly in the deplorable conditions many of them faced. They pointed out that the United States lagged behind many other European nations in outlawing this practice.

Congress took note and in 1912 established the Federal Children's Bureau, an agency located within the Department of Labor. The Children's Bureau was given general statutory authorization to investigate issues pertaining to the welfare of children, including child labor. The bureau's work was largely research based: It cooperated extensively with other public and private organizations to document the plight of the nation's children and to propose solutions to the problems they faced. The bureau's research and advocacy proved crucial not only to placing children's issues on Congress' legislative agenda, but also in ensuring passage of the Fair Labor Standards Act of 1938, which outlawed child labor once and for all.

The Progressive Movement succeeded in making Congress, and particularly state governments, more aware of and responsive to the needs of children. During the period between 1910 and 1929, many states began to adopt laws for the protection of children, including restrictions on child labor, funding for orphans, and the establishment of juvenile courts. States expanded the availability of public school education and began to make it mandatory. It is fair to say that, at least until the Great Depression, the states, not Congress, led the way in meeting the needs of young people.

The stock market crash of 1929 and the Great Depression that followed plunged America into great economic despair. This depression, which lasted throughout the 1930s, was the worst our country had ever experienced. Millions of people lost their jobs. Thousands of family farms failed. Even local governments went bankrupt. At the height of the depression, nearly one-quarter of Americans were unemployed. Children, who were still allowed at that time to work in factories and mines, lost their jobs as employers searched for ways to employ adults. Many families that depended on their children's wages suffered; indeed, the whole nation suffered from the collapsed economy. Many people were homeless, and many more were hungry. Vulnerable groups—the elderly, single mothers, and young children—suffered the most.

America's dire economic condition only strengthened public calls for greater governmental action to fix the nation's economic, political, and social problems. President Franklin Delano Roosevelt, who was elected in 1932, promised to rescue America from the Great Depression. During his famous "First 100 Days" in office, he introduced sweeping legislation designed to put the country back on its feet. As his first term progressed, Roosevelt and the Congress, which was controlled by Democratic party members who had been elected with him, continued to introduce measures aimed at fixing the broken economy and improving the living conditions of Americans. Collectively these measures became known as the "New Deal."

The New Deal faced early obstacles, in large part because the Supreme Court ruled many pieces of legislation unconstitutional. Eventually, however, revolutionary new laws were put into place, including, for example, the Social Security Act and the Fair Labor Standards Act (FLSA), both of which are discussed in this book. The Social Security Act was a national program designed to provide benefits to retired workers; in addition, however, it contained provisions protecting needy children. The FLSA outlawed child labor. These two provisions and others signaled a new role for the federal government in providing basic social services to Americans. The government took an active, unprecedented role in securing employment, undertaking public works projects, and providing for the underprivileged. The New Deal was, in many ways, the culmination of years of efforts by progressive reformers, many of whom now worked in Roosevelt's administration and who were forced to act swiftly to overcome the crisis of the depression.

The next major burst of legislative activity on behalf of children came not out of depression, but out of prosperity. America emerged from World War II a stronger nation. American servicemen and servicewomen returned from overseas and went back to work. Millions of veterans in the 1940s and 1950s went to college on the G.I. Bill. The economy burgeoned. Economic prosperity again encouraged Americans to consider what the government, and indeed private citizens as well, could do to help people in the nation to live a better life. At his 1961 inauguration President John F. Kennedy's famous words, "ask not what your country can do for you, ask what you can do for your country," seemed to resonate with the American people and their legislators. Kennedy saw the potential for additional governmental action to ensure that the basic needs of Americans were being met and that their rights were being upheld.

But Kennedy's tenure proved to be a short one. After Kennedy's assassination in 1963, President Lyndon B. Johnson continued and expanded the late president's efforts. Like Roosevelt before him, Johnson proposed a series of monumental, government-sponsored programs aimed at improving the welfare of Americans. Collectively, this legislation and Johnson's overall public policy agenda is referred to as "the Great Society." The Great Society introduced many laws and programs that we are well familiar with today, including the Civil Rights Act of 1964, the Voting Rights Act, Medicare and Medicaid, an enhanced Social Security program, numerous pieces of legislation providing federal aid to education, grants to struggling urban areas, and a host of social welfare programs to fight the "War on Poverty." This undertaking included a number of laws targeted specifically at helping children and young people; many Great Society laws are discussed later in this book.

The 1960s also saw the rise of the Civil Rights Movement, where disfranchised African Americans struggled to obtain equal rights under the Constitution. The movement used a variety of methods to achieve this goal, including protesting, lobbying state and federal governments for legislation, and litigating its grievances in court. The Civil Rights Movement made several contributions to American politics, too many to detail here, but two in particular must be mentioned. First, it included major, nationwide efforts on behalf of African-American and other minority children in seeking desegregated schools and enhanced educational opportunities for all students. Second, it paved the way for advocacy by other groups seeking civil rights, including women, the disabled, other racial and ethnic minorities, and, finally, children. Indeed, the Civil Rights Movement caused concerned Americans to perceive the plight of these and other groups as a struggle for equal rights, and advocates employed many of the same tactics used by the NAACP (National Association for the Advancement of Colored People) and other African-American civil rights groups to make the needs of their own constituencies known.

Still, the process of recognizing children as a political constituency remained a slow one. Other more vocal groups came first. The Women's Rights Movement, for example, took off in the early 1970s on the heels of the Civil Rights Movement. At the same time, members of the Disability Rights Movement began to lobby and protest actively. The mid- to late-1970s saw major pieces of legislation adopted to protect and enhance the lives of children, but there was no equivalent "Children's Movement." Many of the important laws that were passed by Congress during this period benefited children, but were not specifically targeted toward them. For example, the major environmental protection legislation that was adopted at this time (the Clean Air Act, the Clean Water Act, and so forth) sought to improve health and safety for Americans, but did not initially take into account the special hazards pollution posed to children. In later years Congress would come to revise many pieces of legislation, instructing federal regulatory agencies to investigate whether children were being adequately protected. Where deficient, the agencies were required to strengthen their regulations on children's behalf.

The 1980s and 1990s saw the interests of children take on new meaning and new urgency. The plight of children had become a worldwide issue by this time. In 1989, for example, the United Nations adopted the Convention on the Rights of the Child, a document detailing the basic human and civil rights to which every child is entitled. These rights include among other things the right to life, to survival and development, to protection from all forms of discrimination, to have their best interests taken into account during governmental decisionmaking and resource allocation, to live with their natural families, and to participate in the fundamental decisions that affect their lives. This document stands as perhaps the most comprehensive statement ever developed outlining how governments should treat their youngest citizens. It recognizes that young persons are full-fledged individuals and should by virtue of their humanity alone enjoy all of the rights to which they are entitled.

The rights of children have been expressed in other significant ways as well. Many organizations promote various versions of a "Children's Bill of Rights." American divorce and family law attorneys, for example, advocate a model Bill of Rights for children embroiled in family disputes, and several states have adopted all or part of it in the provision of child and family services. Newer groups such as the Children's Defense Fund (founded in 1973) have emerged to advocate on behalf of children, and established groups such as UNICEF have grown in size and power as the issue of children's rights has gained popularity over the past two decades.

It is probably fair to say that children's rights became an actual political movement in America during this time. The reasons for the coalescence of efforts and resources on behalf of children are complex, but a number of factors seem to have played a part. First,

Americans, drawing from other social movements, began to view children not as the possessions of their parents, but as a large group of people sharing similar needs and interests. Second and relatedly, Americans recognized that children have basic human, civil, and political rights apart from their parents. Although people continue to disagree on the extent of those rights, there was and is agreement that these rights at least in part had been historically overlooked. Third, numerous new advocacy groups emerged, both in this country and internationally, as powerful forces for the protection of children. Fourth, the Women's Movement changed American's perceptions about the role of women. As more women entered the workplace, the nation was forced collectively to rethink not only their role, but the role of the family generally. The definition of a "family" and how the family and the nation should care for its children became and remain major policy issues. They are a continuing source of rancorous debate, not only in Congress, but in the state legislatures, in school boards, in the media, and indeed everywhere people gather to discuss the welfare of our nation's children.

Fifth, the Great Society programs of the 1960s matured. By the 1980s Americans and their elected officials were ready to review the Great Society's successes and failures and to make needed changes in the way its programs were carried out. Welfare reform became politically popular, but perhaps harkening back to the early days of the "deserving poor," even the most ardent reformers did not want their efforts to hurt children (or, more cynically, to be perceived as hurting children), who were, after all, the innocent victims of poverty. National legislative reforms therefore had to take children into account. Sixth, as America entered into the ongoing Technological Revolution, advances in scientific and medical research provided new information to make us more aware of the effects of many national policies on the health and well-being of children, causing changes in these policies as a result. Finally, the same revolution made access to information easier for adults and children, facilitating political advocacy by individuals and interest groups alike. Indeed, one popular version of the "Children's Bill of Rights" was drafted by young people from around the world and is now posted on the Internet for all to see.

These factors all contributed to the development of young people as a separate and distinct political constituency. Young people have emerged out of the shadows and entered into mainstream political life. Advocates for children's issues now routinely testify before and propose legislation to Congress and make the same demands that any constituency group would. They use the same tactics, too: lobbying, advertising, direct mail solicitation, fundraising, media presentations, and, of course, voting and other forms of political action. In large part, these ongoing political efforts on behalf of children have paid off. Congress, government in general, and the American people have never been more aware of the needs of children or more supportive of those needs.

THE FUTURE OF YOUNG PEOPLE'S RIGHTS

Although tremendous progress has been made in advocating for the rights of children and young adults both in this country and abroad, much work remains to be done. Recent federal legislation, such as the Children's Health Insurance Program, has great promise, but is still in the early stages of implementation. Many children have yet to receive that program's benefits. Other laws, such as the Individuals with Disabilities Education Act, have been around long enough now that Congress is being asked to consider their efficacy and, if necessary, make substantial changes in the benefits they deliver and in the methods of implementation they employ. Still other laws, like the one granting federal student loans, are always on the "chopping block" in some legislators' minds.

Members of Congress, advocates for children, and indeed all Americans continue to debate the best way to provide for young people's basic needs. Should we adopt universal health insurance, at least for children? Should the federal government remain involved in education or leave that responsibility entirely to state and local governments? Should we employ national standardized tests for all elementary and high school students? Are school vouchers a good idea? What is the best way to educate disabled children? To provide for day care? How can we protect children from the dangers of the Internet—and should we? How can we best address the serious issues that our teenagers face, including sexuality, violence, substance abuse, and suicide? How can we ensure that college student bodies remain racially and ethnically diverse? What, in short, can we do to make America more understanding of and responsive to the plight of its youth?

These are important questions. More significantly, they are important *unanswered* questions. Reasonable people disagree on how best to approach these difficult and sensitive issues. But this is not a problem; rather, it is an opportunity. There is always room in a democracy for additional voices as we struggle collectively to resolve the issues that divide us. High school and college students are directly affected by each of the political debates listed above. Like it or not, politics is relevant to young people. Shouldn't young people, therefore, have a say in the development of the policies to which they will be subjected? Young persons need not be passive onlookers in the legislative process; even those too young to vote can advocate in other ways for what they believe. Today's youth should be emboldened by the accomplishments of students of the past, particularly those from the antiwar and free speech movements of the 1960s. Whether or not one agrees with the philosophical origins of these undertakings, they nonetheless serve as examples of successful student advocacy on a national scale. Young people have made and can continue to make their voices heard in significant ways.

This book provides a sampling of important legislation that has already been implemented on behalf of youth. Each entry features at least one law that has affected young adults. Every eighteen-year-old male, for example, will have the privilege or the burden of registering with the Selective Service. Every eighteen-year-old female will not. Readers should consider each law and the philosophy behind it, think about whether they agree or disagree with it and, after that, plan what they can do to keep the law or change it. Students can debate it with their classmates, discuss it with their parents, and send an e-mail to their senators or representatives. They can make Congress listen to them and work for them. That is in large part what the framers designed the Constitution for. Young people should remember that self-government begins and ends with the governed. The first words of the Constitution—"We the People"—include them.

METHODOLOGY FOR LANDMARK CONGRESSIONAL LAWS ON YOUTH

The laws included in this book are in part a testament to the fact that democracy works. They are the products of concerned citizens and legislators who are committed to meeting the needs of an important constituency that this nation cannot afford to ignore: its young people. The laws in this book constitute a sampling of Congress' most significant efforts in the twentieth century on behalf of youth. The entries were selected for a variety of reasons, including historical importance, overall contribution to the protection of children's health or rights, and relevance to today's youth.

The book is divided into three parts—health and welfare laws, citizenship and democratic participation laws, and education laws. The laws included here are by no means an exhaustive list of major contributions, but rather are representative examples of how Congress can affect the lives of this nation's children in direct and substantial ways. In many cases, initial pieces of legislation on a particular issue, such as childhood disabilities, have been excluded in favor of a discussion of a piece of major legislation that represents the culmination of years of legislative struggle over that issue. Where possible, the legislative origins of these entries have been discussed to provide background for the reader. Where there has been extensive legislative activity, such as in the areas of child health care and safety, an attempt has been made to select laws that are representative and that have had the greatest impact in improving child welfare. Many of the laws in this book are relatively recent, and their full effects have yet to be measured. But congressional boldness and comprehensiveness counts for something, and certain laws, such as the Children's Health Insurance Program, merit inclusion even if they are too new to be fully evaluated or are still works in progress. The text avoids well-known social welfare laws such as the Food Stamp Program and the Supplemental Food Program for Women, Infants, and Children (WIC) in favor of laws that address children directly, such as the National School Lunch Act.

The focus here is on laws that today's youth will find highly relevant, such as the federal educational grant and loan programs upon which so many college-bound students rely. The Uniform Drinking Age Act and the Selective Service Act, again, are discussed in an effort to demonstrate that youth who do not agree with actions taken on their behalf have not only the right, but also the responsibility, to make their voices heard.

With regard to the editing of these laws, it was of course a challenge to express the laws in a clear and concise manner. Most of these entries have been judiciously edited to their significant portions for ease of use of the reader. In the case of sweeping legislation like the Social Security Act, only those parts most relevant to young people, as described in the introduction to each law, have

been included. For the most part, the laws are arranged chronologically within each part of the book. From time to time, however,
closely related laws with different enactment dates are addressed in
a single entry to help the reader understand the nature and extent
of Congress' work on that particular issue. The timeline represents
a complete chronological listing of all the entries offered here, plus
a few significant additional laws that appear within the discussion.
Placing an exact date on a law can be problematic. Almost all of
the laws in this book have been repeatedly and significantly
amended over the years. (Some have even undergone name
changes.) The laws are organized within each part by the year they
were first passed, but with the exception of the Social Security Act,
which appears in its original 1935 form, recent versions of the laws
are presented, as they are the most relevant to today's reader. Constitutional amendments are listed by their ratification dates. "Author's Notes" define key words or concepts in these texts.

Changes to internal punctuation were commonly made to make
the laws more readable and understandable, but always with the
goal of preserving context and meaning. Occasional spelling and
grammatical errors are corrected, but Congress' inconsistencies in
capitalization may remain. Internal codification marks from Congress are often deleted (all of those roman numerals and section
and subsection indicators, whether letters or numbers). Congress
is not very consistent in the way it codifies its laws or even in the
way it writes them. (Interested readers are encouraged to look up
these laws and read them in their original form; this undertaking
is an education in itself.) Sometimes, for the sake of clarity and
brevity, parts of a law are paraphrased. These paraphrases are indicated by brackets [ ]. Major paraphrases are noted after the original text as "Author's Restatements." I used ellipses (. . .) to denote
major textual omissions when presenting the laws; however, to use
ellipses for all gaps was impractical, lest this volume be taken over
by them. Footnotes and citations may be omitted without notice.
Congressional statutes can be unwieldy, and even the best editing
cannot contain some of them. Therefore, for more information
about a law or for fuller understanding of its language and com-
plexities, the reader again is encouraged to refer to the actual statute. The appendix includes the legal citations for all of the laws
and court cases discussed in this book.

PART I

HEALTH AND WELFARE LAWS

1

Social Security Act

1935

When most people hear the term "Social Security," they think of the huge federal government program that provides retirement benefits to older Americans. Working teens notice that there's a significant deduction from their paychecks for this program and know that they won't see that money again until they retire. But Social Security is not just an insurance program for retirement. Since its inception, Social Security has provided much-needed benefits to young people as well.

Before Social Security was adopted in 1935 the federal government played a limited role in providing assistance to needy Americans, including needy children. But changing American attitudes toward social services, coupled with the economic upheaval caused by the stock market crash of 1929 and the Great Depression, prompted President Franklin Delano Roosevelt (F.D.R.) and the Congress to act.

When F.D.R. was elected in 1932, America was experiencing an economic catastrophe that came to be known as the "Great Depression." This depression, which lasted throughout the 1930s, was the worst our country had ever experienced. Millions of people lost their jobs. Thousands of family farms failed. Even local governments went bankrupt. At the height of the depression nearly one-quarter of Americans were unemployed. Children, who were allowed at that time to work in factories and mines, lost their jobs as employers searched for ways to employ adults. Many families that depended on their children's wages suffered; indeed, the whole nation suffered from the collapsed economy. Many people were homeless, and many more were hungry. Vulnerable groups—the elderly, single mothers, and young children—suffered the most.

President Roosevelt promised to rescue America from the Great Depression. During his famous "First 100 Days" in office, he introduced sweeping legislation to put the country back on its feet. As his first term progressed Roosevelt and the Congress, which was controlled by Democratic party members who had been elected with him, continued to introduce measures aimed at fixing the broken economy and improving the living conditions of Americans. Collectively, these measures became known as the "New Deal."

In 1934 Roosevelt offered perhaps the most important, and certainly the most famous, New Deal proposal: a system of social insurance to provide income to Americans in their old age. These payments would be funded by a mandatory tax on almost all American workers and their employers. The workers' tax money would be deducted automatically from their paychecks and placed into a fund managed by the government. The employers' tax money would be collected and placed into the fund as well. Upon retirement those who had paid into the system would be able to draw from it, ensuring that all Americans had a basic, yet stable, source of income. This program became known as "Social Security," and it still exists—in an even more expansive form than Roosevelt and his supporters could have envisioned.

But Social Security was not and is not simply about the aged. From its inception Social Security sought to provide benefits to other vulnerable groups of citizens, including children. The original legislation, excerpted below, offered four specific kinds of funding for children: aid to dependent children, aid for maternal and child health, aid to disabled children (who were called "crippled children" in the original legislation), and aid to children at risk.

The provision for aid to dependent children called for each state to create a program to assist needy dependent children. Each state that did so was eligible for federal funds of up to one-third of the amount it spent on the program. Under the original legislation dependent children included those under the age of sixteen who did not have support because of the death, incapacity, or absence of a parent. The original sum allocated for support of these children was $24.75 million—a significant sum for that time.

To receive their one-third contribution from the Social Security program, the states had to follow a number of steps. They were required to offer aid to children statewide. They were also required to prepare written reports that documented their activities and kept track of the number of dependent children in the state and the amount of money spent on them. The federal government limited the states' ability to set residency requirements for children, and it required states to grant a hearing to any child denied aid under the program.

The second component of Social Security's protection for children called for each state to promote the health of mothers and children, especially those "in rural areas and in areas suffering from severe economic distress." To this end the federal government pledged $3.8 million dollars in its original allocation of funds, to be distributed to states in basically the same manner as described above. The act called for the states' health care agencies to work with local agencies, as well as with medical, nursing, and welfare groups, to extend health services to needy mothers and children. The federal government would reimburse the states in an amount up to one-half of their expenditures for this part of the program.

Finally, Social Security provided financial assistance to disabled children. (In the original version of the act included below, note that Congress first described these children as "crippled children." This unfortunate term has been replaced in modern times, most commonly by the phrase "children with disabilities.") The act called for identifying these children and providing medical care, including surgical and corrective care if possible. It also called for the states to create facilities to diagnose and treat disabled children. In addition, the act provided funds for the continuing care of disabled children. Participating states would receive a minimum of $20,000; more funds were available based on the number of disabled children in each state, to a maximum of one-half the cost of a state's program. The original allocation for this part of the act was $2.85 million. Once again, states were encouraged to work with local public and private groups to ensure the treatment and rehabilitation of these children.

In addition to the three specific goals stated above, the Social Security Act contained a yearly appropriation of $1.5 million for the secretary of labor to allocate to the states' public welfare agencies. This money was directed toward improving cooperation between states and the federal government in promoting "the protection and care of homeless, dependent, and neglected children, and children in danger of becoming delinquent." The states were encouraged to develop plans with the Children's Bureau, an agency of the federal government devoted to child welfare. The legislation required states and the bureau to address the problems of children in the areas of highest need and particularly those in rural areas.

Social Security has been amended numerous times since it became law in 1935. Many of these amendments have extended additional benefits to young people. For example, in 1939 Congress passed, and F.D.R. signed into law, an amendment providing coverage to the spouses and dependent children of retired workers or workers who died before reaching retirement. The original Social Security retirement plan covered only the actual employees who had paid into the system; this revolutionary amendment directed retirement benefits to the family, not just the worker.

Later amendments greatly augmented the size and scope of the Social Security Act. For example, in 1954, Congress added a disability insurance program. By 1960 that program, after further amendments, provided benefits not only to disabled workers, but to their dependents as well. In 1971 Congress created the Supplemental Security Income Program (SSI), which provides additional benefits to needy elderly and disabled persons. Two other amendments proved particularly significant to young people. In 1965 Medicaid created basic health insurance benefits for needy children; in 1989 the Children's Health Insurance Program took Medicaid significantly farther, providing much more comprehensive coverage. These additions to the original Social Security Act are discussed later in this book.

Social Security was somewhat controversial at its adoption (like many of F.D.R.'s New Deal programs). No one knew if these programs would work. Some feared that the creation of vast national welfare and employment programs would make the federal government too powerful. Still others feared that Social Security and similar plans signaled the onset of socialism in the United States. Despite these concerns, the original Social Security Act easily passed both houses of Congress. The House approved it by a vote of 288 to 13, the Senate by a vote of 60 to 1. Public officials and citizens alike were willing to try bold new measures to overcome the country's economic crisis.

Today Social Security is considered by many to be an "untouchable" federal entitlement program, both with regard to its social welfare components and to its retirement program. Millions of Americans have paid into and drawn money out of the retirement system. Those approaching retirement expect to receive their life-long contributions back, and those currently paying into the system expect the same payments when they eventually retire. Because so many people have a stake in the current and future health of the program, elected officials find that they must tread carefully where Social Security is concerned. Indeed, both political parties have pledged their loyalty to, and continuing support for, Social Security.

Nevertheless, major changes to the retirement program seem inevitable, as serious problems have emerged with its implementation. For example, at the beginning of the program, there were far more workers contributing to the system than retired workers drawing money from it. Over time the demographic makeup of the nation has changed, as has its labor market. The "Baby Boom" generation born after World War II is now nearing retirement, and its members will be expecting their Social Security checks soon. At the same time, the number of workers paying into the system has significantly declined, meaning that fewer workers are contributing to support more and more retirees. This imbalance threatens to bankrupt the system sometime during the twenty-first century. Indeed, young people paying into the system today may wonder whether it will still be around when they are ready to retire.

An additional problem causing a drain on the money in the system is the fact that Americans are living much longer today than they did when the Social Security program was created. Consequently, retirees are collecting benefits for longer periods of time. In response to these and other problems, Congress continues to make basic changes to the system to ensure its continued viability. For example, the age at which one becomes eligible to receive retirement benefits is gradually being raised from its current level of sixty-five to sixty-seven. Recently some politicians have suggested allowing workers to retain and invest some of their own payroll contributions, believing that individuals can better direct their investments for retirement. Others strongly disagree, arguing the only way to ensure that Social Security funds remain available for everyone's retirement is for workers to continue to direct their contributions to the government for safekeeping.

Experts disagree about whether and when Social Security will go bankrupt. Early predictions suggested that the system would run out of money by the first quarter of the twenty-first century; more recent predictions place the date closer to the middle of the century. In either case, Congress, the president, and indeed all Americans will have to work together to face the problems caused to the system by the upcoming crush of retirees and the decreasing number of contributors to the Social Security program.

To date the major changes proposed for the retirement system have proved highly controversial and difficult to pass into law. Almost everyone agrees that Social Security is flawed but that it is worth saving. Agreeing on how to save it is a different matter—one that will face Americans for years to come. Young people, many of whom begin working and paying into the system in high school, have a direct stake in this debate. They will be affected by any future changes to the system. Given that fact, young working Americans might want to learn more about the current troubles plaguing Social Security. If young people take an active role in fixing the system, they will help to ensure that the money they are currently contributing to it will not be lost, but will be returned to them upon their retirement. Social Security promised a more secure childhood and a more secure retirement for Americans, and with hard work and a little luck, that promise will continue to be fulfilled for future generations.

1. Social Security Act

[The original Social Security Act contained eleven different topic areas, called "Titles." Title IV and Title V deal specifically with aid to young people; key sections from these Titles are excerpted below.]

PREAMBLE

An act to provide for the general welfare by establishing a system of Federal old-age benefits, and by enabling the several States to make more adequate provision for aged persons, blind persons, dependent and crippled children, maternal and child welfare, public health, and the administration of their unemployment compensation laws; to establish a Social Security Board; to raise revenue; and for other purposes.

Be it enacted by the Senate and House of Representatives of the United States of America in Congress assembled . . .

TITLE IV: GRANTS TO STATES FOR AID TO DEPENDENT CHILDREN

Section 401. For the purpose of enabling each State to furnish financial assistance, as far as practicable under the conditions in such State, to needy dependent children, there is hereby authorized to be appropriated for the fiscal year ending June 30, 1936, the sum of $24,750,000, and there is hereby authorized to be appropriated for each fiscal year thereafter a sum sufficient to carry out the purposes of this title. The sums made available under this section shall be used for making payments to States which submitted, and had approved by the Board, State plans for aid to dependent children.

Section 402. A State plan for aid to dependent children must be in effect in all political subdivisions of the State; provide for financial participation by the State; provide for the establishment or designation of a single State agency to administer the plan, or provide for the establishment or designation of a single State agency to supervise the administration of the plan; provide for granting to any individual, whose claim with respect to aid to a dependent child is denied, an opportunity for a fair hearing before such State agency; . . . [and] provide that the State agency will make reports as the Board [may require]. . . .

The Board shall not approve any plan which imposes as a condition of eligibility for aid to dependent children, a residence requirement which denies aid with respect to any child residing in the State . . . for one year immediately preceding the application for such aid or . . . who was born within the State if its mother has resided in the State for one year immediately preceding the birth.

Section 406. When used in this title, the term "dependent child" means a child under the age of sixteen who has been deprived of parental support or care by reason of the death, continued absence from the home, or physical or mental incapacity of a parent, and who is living with his father, mother, grandfather, grandmother, brother, sister, stepfather, stepmother, stepbrother, stepsister, uncle, or aunt, in a place of residence maintained by one or more of such relatives as his or their own home; the term "aid to dependent children" means money payments with respect to a dependent child or dependent children.

TITLE V: GRANTS TO STATES FOR MATERNAL AND CHILD WELFARE

Part 1: Maternal and Child Health Services

Section 501. For the purpose of enabling each State to extend and improve, as far as practicable under the conditions in such State, services for promoting the health of mothers and children, especially in rural areas and in areas suffering from severe economic distress, there is hereby authorized to be appropriated for each fiscal year, beginning with the fiscal year ending June 30, 1936, the sum of $3,800,000. The sums made available under this section shall be used for making payments to States which have submitted, and had approved by the Chief of the Children's Bureau, State plans for such services.

Section 503. A State plan for maternal and child-health services must provide for financial participation by the State; . . . provide that the State health agency will make [required] reports; provide for the extension and improvement of local maternal and child-health services administered by local child health units; provide for cooperation with medical, nursing, and welfare groups and organizations; and provide for the development of demonstration services in needy areas and among groups in special need.

Part 2: Services for Crippled Children

Section 511. For the purpose of enabling each State to extend and improve (especially in rural areas and in areas suffering from severe economic distress), as far as practicable under the conditions in such State, services for locating crippled children and for providing medical, surgical, corrective, and other services and care, and facilities for diagnosis, hospitalization, and aftercare, for children who are crippled or who are suffering from conditions which lead to crippling, there is hereby authorized to be appropriated for each fiscal year beginning with the fiscal year ending June 30, 1936, the sum of $2,850,000. The sums made available under this section shall be used for making payments to States which have submitted, and had approved by the Chief of the Children's Bureau, State plans for such services.

Section 512. Out of the sums appropriated pursuant to section 511 for each fiscal year, the Secretary of Labor shall allot to each State $20,000, and the remainder to the States according to the need of each State as determined by him after taking into consideration the number of crippled children in such State in need of the services referred to in section 511 and the cost of furnishing such service to them. . . .

Section 513. A State plan for services for crippled children must provide for financial participation by the State; . . . provide that the State agency will make [required] reports; provide for carrying out the purposes specified in section 511; and provide for cooperation with medical, health, nursing, and welfare groups and organizations and with any agency in such State charged with administering State laws providing for vocational rehabilitation of physically handicapped children.

Part 3: Child Welfare Services

Section 521. For the purpose of enabling the United States, through the Children's Bureau, to cooperate with State public-welfare agencies establishing, extending, and strengthening, especially in predominantly rural areas, public-welfare for the protection and care of homeless, dependent, and neglected children, and children in danger of becoming delinquent, there is hereby authorized to be appropriated for each fiscal year, beginning with the year ending June 30, 1936, the sum of $1,500,000. [This] amount shall be allotted by the Secretary of Labor for use by cooperating State public-welfare agencies on the basis of plans developed jointly by the State agency and the Children's Bureau. . . . [The allotted funds shall be used] for payment of part of the cost of district, county or other local child-welfare services in areas predominantly rural, and for developing State services for the encouragement and assistance of adequate methods of community child-welfare organization in areas predominantly rural and other areas of special need.

2

Fair Labor Standards Act (FLSA)

1938

America's young people largely expect to work, whether it is to earn spending money, help support their families, or pay college tuition. Today's young workers are protected by a host of federal and state laws regulating child labor. For example, young workers generally can count on a safe workplace, a minimum wage, a work week limited to no more than forty hours, and extra pay for overtime. But this was not always the case. Provisions for a minimum wage, maximum working hours, and the payment of overtime compensation were not guaranteed in this country until 1938, when Congress, after a long and often heated debate, passed the Fair Labor Standards Act.

The Fair Labor Standards Act was the first major piece of federal legislation to survive constitutional scrutiny and establish a basic minimum wage (originally, a whopping twenty-five cents! Today, it's $5.15.) and to set maximum working hours at forty-four hours per week. It was also the first major piece of legislation to survive a constitutional challenge to regulate child labor. Prior to the FLSA children and teenagers were routinely employed in a variety of highly demanding and dangerous occupations. They sweated in textile mills, breathed the coal dust of the nation's mines, baked bread in the earliest hours of the morning, and poured hot steel along with their fathers. The national government did not set the age at which children could start working, nor did it ensure that their working conditions were safe. Some states regulated working conditions, but regulations varied widely from state to state. Industries generally did not set regulations either. Children could work a full week in industry for only a few dollars, money that at the time generally went to support their families. Conditions were very bad, and wages were very low. But for a time inhospitable conditions and inadequate wages were the realities faced by our nation's working youth.

To their credit, Congress and the states had been trying for years to adopt laws that would improve the working conditions for Americans and that would ban, or at least restrict, child labor. The Progressive Movement, which emerged in part to battle the excesses of industrialization, sought better working and living conditions for average Americans. It led to numerous attempts by federal and state reformers to establish, among other things, food and drug safety laws, minimum wage and maximum working hours legislation, and child labor laws. For many years, however, most of these attempts ended in failure. The reason for the failure of this legislation was often, remarkably enough, the United States Supreme Court.

Today we think of the Supreme Court as the champion, or at least the protector, of our civil rights and personal liberties. But that was not always the case. Starting in the late nineteenth century and continuing right through F.D.R.'s New Deal, the Supreme Court lagged behind popular opinion and legislative sentiment by striking down labor laws as unconstitutional. Why would the Court view laws that we take for granted today as unconstitutional? The reasons are complex, but essentially many Americans, including the majority of the Supreme Court at that time, held a completely different view of civil rights than we do today. In the late nineteenth and early twentieth centuries, a person's arguably most important civil right was the "right to contract," which essentially meant the right to use one's own labor.

The idea behind this right was that Americans were free to use their skills and talents—their labor—as they saw fit, without interference from the government. Similarly, employers were allowed to pursue their enterprises largely without government regulation. Employees and employers were considered to be in a contractual relationship in which they negotiated and agreed to the terms of employment, including wages and hours. A person who wanted to work an eighty-hour week, for example, had that right. For government to deny it would amount to a denial of the employee's liberty.

For over forty years the Supreme Court took the right to contract very seriously, believing that it was guaranteed by the Constitution. It took it so seriously, in fact, that it frequently struck down labor reform legislation as unconstitutional. In the famous case of *Lochner v. New York*, decided in 1905, the Court struck down a state law limiting bakers and confectioners to ten-hour days and a sixty-hour work week. In 1916 Congress passed the Child Labor Act prohibiting the transportation in interstate commerce of any product made in a factory that employed children under age fourteen. The act also prohibited the similar transportation of products made in factories where children aged fourteen to sixteen worked more than eight hours a day or six days per week. The Supreme Court responded in 1918, in the equally famous case of *Hammer v. Dagenhart*. The Court struck down the Child Labor Act, thus ensuring that Mr. Dagenhart's children could continue to work in the cotton mills of North Carolina. Similarly, in 1923 the Court, in *Adkins v. Children's Hospital*, struck down a District of Columbia law that had tried to establish a minimum wage for women.

The Court's position did not change, even after the trauma of the stock market crash of 1929 and the widespread suffering of Americans during the Great Depression. For the first five years of the New Deal, the Supreme Court struck down virtually every significant piece of legislation passed by Congress to fix the nation's economic crisis. A key component of the New Deal was the National Industrial Recovery Act, passed by Congress in 1933. It provided incentives for businesses to raise wages (to between $12 to $15 per week) and to limit working hours (to between 35 and 40 hours per week). It also required participating employers to pledge that they would not employ young people under the age of sixteen. But the act was short-lived: the Supreme Court struck it down in 1935 in the controversial case of *A.L.A. Schechter Poultry Corporation v. United States*.

The Supreme Court continued to strike down New Deal legislation until 1937, when it abruptly stopped. F.D.R., frustrated with the Court's behavior, used his landslide re-election victory to propose what has become known as the "Court-packing Plan." Under the plan, which was introduced to Congress, the size of the Supreme Court would be increased from nine justices to fifteen, with President Roosevelt appointing the new justices. Faced with this threat, the Supreme Court backed down from its rigid understanding of the right to contract, finally upholding as constitutional a state minimum wage law in the 1937 case of *West Coast Hotel Company v. Parrish*, which was adopted in furtherance of congressional policy to regulate commerce between the states.

In *West Coast Hotel* the Supreme Court demonstrated that it would now permit the kind of legislation that it had been striking down for decades, and F.D.R. and the Congress immediately took advantage of the Court's new attitude. On May 24, 1937, President Roosevelt sent Congress the Fair Labor Standards Act. In its original form, the act called for a forty-cent-per-hour minimum wage, a maximum work week of forty-four hours, and a requirement that children attain the age of sixteen before being permitted to work in most industries, particularly mining and manufacturing. (Exceptions to all of these requirements were made for the agriculture industry.)

The Senate was not immediately receptive. Some senators, particularly from the South, thought the bill was too sweeping in its regulation of employers and that the minimum wage in particular was too high, given the economic climate of that region. Others thought the bill was too weak. Labor unions, which supported the purposes of the bill in theory, were concerned that a new federal law regulating wages would interfere with their ability to bargain with employers. In short, while many supported the laudable ideas behind the bill, they did not agree on its particulars.

The Senate passed a watered-down version of FLSA in July. But the House did not bring the bill to a vote, and Congress adjourned for the summer without approving it. In response, President Roosevelt called for a rare special session of Congress. Congress reconvened in November to reconsider the legislation. The Democrats eventually gained enough votes to have the bill voted on by the entire House of Representatives, only to have the House reject the bill and send it back to its Labor Committee.

After Christmas Roosevelt submitted a new, much shorter version of the bill to Congress. Additional wrangling led to the minimum wage provision being reduced from forty-cents per hour to twenty-five cents per hour for the first year of the legislation, an action that appeased southern congressmen. Other compromises followed, and the bill finally was approved by both houses of Congress in June. After a year of negotiations and several dozen amendments, President Roosevelt signed the much-weakened bill into law on June 25, 1938. With its many exceptions the original FLSA applied to only about 20 percent of the American labor force, but it was the best that F.D.R. and the badly split Congress could do.

The FLSA has been amended many times since its inception. In its current form, the FLSA now applies to most public and private employers. The child labor provisions of the act set the minimum working age for youths at sixteen. Youths aged fourteen and fifteen can work outside of school, but their hours are limited so as not to interfere with their education. There are some exceptions that allow children of any age to work in certain jobs: most commonly, a young person may babysit, deliver newspapers, perform housekeeping or yard work, or work for their parents. A child of any age can also work on the family's farm. If a job is considered by the government to be "hazardous," the young person must be eighteen before being hired. Hazardous jobs are defined by the Department of Labor and generally include things like working in mines, in manufacturing, or in any job that requires operating heavy machinery or dangerous equipment. An employer who violates these rules is subject to substantial criminal and civil penalties.

Employers are required to keep records of the tasks performed and working hours of any employees under the age of nineteen. Employers are allowed to pay their young workers a reduced "training wage" during the first ninety days of their employment and must pay the minimum wage thereafter. For all employees, the work week has been shortened to forty hours, and the minimum wage has been gradually increased (seemingly always with a congressional fight) to its current rate of $5.15. Proposals to raise the minimum wage continue to be brought regularly before Congress.

The regulation of child labor has come a long way in the past sixty years. The FLSA is but one of many important federal statutes and programs overseeing the employment of children. In addition, all of the states have their own provisions regulating child labor, some of which are even more stringent than the federal laws. Congress has provided that, when federal and state laws conflict, the one most protective of child labor shall govern. Working together, the federal government and the states have greatly improved the working conditions and wages for the nation's youth, and indeed for all Americans.

SCHOOL-TO-WORK OPPORTUNITIES ACT

In 1994 Congress passed the School-to-Work Opportunities Act to encourage high schools and employers to work together more closely to ensure that students who do not plan to attend college are ready for meaningful employment upon graduation. In adopting this law, Congress provided funding for cooperative ventures such as job shadowing, where a student interested in a particular career follows one of its professionals throughout the workday, as well as on-the-job training programs. Collectively, these types of initiatives are known as "work-based learning." They are designed to teach students not only skills particular to certain jobs, but also general job skills such as teamwork and effective communication.

Since passage of the act, confusion has arisen about whether the students participating in school-to-work opportunities are covered by the FLSA. The answer depends on whether the student is actually employed. Students and employers in an employment relationship remain subject to the FLSA, even if the students receive high school credit for the work or are otherwise participating in a high school training program. If an employment relationship exists, the type of work that can be performed, the age of the student, and the number of hours he or she can work are all regulated by the FLSA. The FLSA does not provide any special exceptions or exemptions for students participating in school-to-work activities.

The exception comes for students who are not in an employment relationship, but are rather participating in a qualified school-to-work learning experience. To avoid application of the FLSA, four criteria must be met: first, the student must be continually supervised and instructed at the worksite; second, the presence of the student at the worksite cannot come at the expense of a regular employee (meaning that the student should not take the place of a paid worker); third, the student is not legally entitled to be paid for the work; and, fourth, the employer, school, parents, and student understand that the student is participating in a learning activity and is not entitled to be paid for it. (An employer *may* pay the student, but is not required by law to do so.)

The school-to-work experience, therefore, is akin to a typical college internship, where the student participates in a full- or part-time job for college credit, not pay. In fact, most college students pay tuition to take an internship course. The School-to-Work Opportunities Act provides funds so that high school students can obtain the same type of on-the-job training and experience without cost.

Students participating in activities that are both educational and job based should be aware of the basic differences between an employment relationship and a school-based learning one. The stakes for students are high, for the FLSA, as described above, does not simply regulate child labor, but ensures adequate compensation for all workers. Thus, if an employment relationship exists, the student by law is entitled to all of the protections of the FLSA, including being paid the minimum wage and being paid for overtime.

2. Fair Labor Standards Act (FLSA)

Section 202. Congressional finding and declaration of policy.

(a) The Congress finds that the existence, in industries engaged in commerce or in the production of goods for commerce, of labor conditions detrimental to the maintenance of the minimum standard of living necessary for health, efficiency, and general well-being of workers (1) causes commerce and the channels and instrumentalities of commerce to be used to spread and perpetuate such labor conditions among the workers of the several States; (2) burdens commerce and the free flow of goods in commerce; (3) constitutes an unfair method of competition in commerce; (4) leads to labor disputes burdening and obstructing commerce and the free flow of goods in commerce; and (5) interferes with the orderly and fair marketing of goods in commerce. That Congress further finds that the employment of persons in domestic service in households affects commerce.

(b) It is declared to be the policy of this chapter, through the exercise by Congress of its power to regulate commerce among the several States and with foreign nations, to correct and as rapidly as practicable to eliminate the conditions above referred to in such industries without substantially curtailing employment or earning power.

Section 212. Child labor provisions.

(a) Restrictions on shipment of goods; prosecution; conviction. No producer, manufacturer, or dealer shall ship or deliver for shipment in commerce any goods produced in an establishment situated in the United States in or about which within thirty days prior to the removal of such goods therefrom any oppressive child labor has been employed: Provided, That any such shipment or delivery for shipment of such goods by a purchaser who acquired them in good faith in reliance on written assurance from the producer, manufacturer, or dealer that the goods were produced in compliance with the requirements of this section, and who acquired such goods for value without notice of any such violation, shall not be deemed prohibited by this subsection: And provided further, That a prosecution and conviction of a defendant for the shipment or delivery for shipment of any goods under the conditions herein prohibited shall be a bar to any further prosecution against the same defendant for shipments or deliveries for shipment of any such goods before the beginning of said prosecution.

(b) Investigations and inspections. The Secretary of Labor or any of his authorized representatives, shall make all investigations and inspections under section 211(a) of this title with respect to the employment of minors, and, subject to the direction and control of the Attorney General, shall bring all actions under section 217 of this title to enjoin any act or practice which is unlawful by reason of the existence of oppressive child labor, and shall administer all other provisions of this chapter relating to oppressive child labor.

(c) Oppressive child labor. No employer shall employ any oppressive child labor in commerce or in the production of goods for commerce or in any enterprise engaged in commerce or in the production of goods for commerce.

(d) Proof of age. In order to carry out the objectives of this section, the Secretary may by regulation require employers to obtain from any employee proof of age.

Section 214. Employment under special certificates.

(b) Students.

(1)(A) The Secretary, to the extent necessary in order to prevent curtailment of opportunities for employment, shall by special certificate issued under a regulation or order provide, in accordance with subparagraph (B), for the employment, at a wage rate not less than 85 per centum of the otherwise applicable wage rate in effect under section 206 of this title or not less than $1.60 an hour, whichever is the higher, of full-time students (regardless of age but in compliance with applicable child labor laws) in retail or service establishments.

(2) The Secretary, to the extent necessary in order to prevent curtailment of opportunities for employment, shall by special certificate issued under a regulation or order provide for the employment, at a wage rate not less than 85 per centum of the wage rate in effect under section 206(a)(5) of this title or not less than $1.30 an hour, whichever is the higher, of full-time students (regardless of age but in compliance with applicable child labor laws) in any occupation in agriculture.

(3) The Secretary, to the extent necessary in order to prevent curtailment of opportunities for employment, shall by special certificate issued under a regulation or order provide for the employment by an institution of higher education, at a wage rate not less than 85 per centum of the otherwise applicable wage rate in effect under section 206 of this title or not less than $1.60 an hour, whichever is the higher,

of full-time students (regardless of age but in compliance with applicable child labor laws) who are enrolled in such institution.

(4)(A) A special certificate issued under paragraph (1), (2), or (3) shall provide that the student or students for whom it is issued shall, except during vacation periods, be employed on a part-time basis and not in excess of twenty hours in any work week.

(B) If the issuance of a special certificate under paragraph (1) or (2) for an employer will cause the number of students employed by such employer under special certificates issued under this subsection to exceed six, the Secretary may not issue such a special certificate for the employment of a student by such employer unless the Secretary finds employment of such student will not create a substantial probability of reducing the full-time employment opportunities of persons other than those employed under special certificates issued under this subsection.

(d) Employment by schools. The Secretary may by regulation or order provide that sections 206 and 207 of this title shall not apply with respect to the employment by any elementary or secondary school of its students if such employment constitutes, as determined under regulations prescribed by the Secretary, an integral part of the regular education program provided by such school and such employment is in accordance with applicable child labor laws.

Section 216. Penalties.

(a) Fines and imprisonment. Any person who willfully violates any of the provisions of section 215 of this title shall upon conviction thereof be subject to a fine of not more than $10,000, or to imprisonment for not more than six months, or both. No person shall be imprisoned under this subsection except for an offense committed after the conviction of such person for a prior offense under this subsection.

3

National School Lunch Act

1946

and Child Nutrition Act

1966

In adopting the National School Lunch Act, Congress observed that it was "a measure of national security, to safeguard the health and well-being of the Nation's children and to encourage the domestic consumption of nutritious agricultural commodities and other food. . . ." *National security?* How could school lunches be a matter of national security?

At the time of the act's adoption, America was embroiled in World War II. A draft was in place to enlist soldiers, while many young American men and women also volunteered for the war effort. But in order to serve in the country's military, one has to be physically able to do so. And draft boards were increasingly finding that thousands of young men were malnourished, and this malnourishment was leading to their disqualification from military service. A shortage of eligible draftees, among other reasons, led to the adoption of the National School Lunch Act.

America learned a lot about itself during World War II. One of the things it discovered rather accidentally was the fact that millions of Americans were not getting enough to eat. Now we are taught that a person should have "three square meals per day." Back then, many Americans had only one. The school lunch program, therefore, was designed to ensure that needy schoolchildren received a nutritious meal at a minimal cost. For the poorest children the meals were and still are provided free of charge.

Today the Department of Agriculture, which is responsible for administering the program, maintains an Internet website dedicated to child nutrition. It contains a comprehensive history of the school lunch program, eligibility requirements, and the current amounts charged to students for their lunches. The website is a good reference for children and parents because the rules regarding eligibility and fees for this and other federal meal programs are tied to the economy (specifically, to the determination of the federal poverty level) and change on July 1st of each year.

In general, however, in order to be eligible for a free school lunch, a child must come from a family with an income at or below 130 percent of the federal poverty level. To qualify for a reduced priced lunch, the child's family income must be at or below 185 percent of the federal poverty level. The "federal poverty level" refers to guidelines set by the federal government each year as an indicator of when, in the government's view, an individual or family is considered impoverished. The poverty level changes each year as the economy fluctuates, and it is adjusted for family size. (For example, the 2002 federal poverty level for a family of four residing in the forty-eight contiguous states is $18,100.) The poverty level is an important measure of the health of the nation, and many federal and state social welfare programs use it to determine eligibility for benefits.

Most schools today simply offer lunches to the entire student body; students can choose to eat the school's lunch or bring their own lunch from home. The Congress has made it clear, however, that students who receive free or reduced-price lunches should not be singled out, identified, or discriminated against in any way. The schools keep track of the number of these lunches served, and the federal government reimburses them a set amount of money for each lunch. The reimbursement amount also changes regularly, as food prices and the costs of program implementation increase or decrease. Each state that participates in the school lunch program is required under the act to contribute to its costs.

In addition to providing funds to the states and schools, the federal government also purchases large amounts of commodities every year that it offers to schools as part of the program. These commodities include food items that the school can serve directly, such as canned, frozen, or fresh fruits and vegetables and meats, or items that the schools can use in preparing meals, such as flour and vegetable oil. Some schools choose to receive only commodities from the federal government and are not reimbursed for the cost of the meals they serve.

Over time the school lunch program has expanded significantly.

In its first year the program served just over seven million students. Today it serves nearly twenty-seven million students. The Department of Agriculture, which keeps track of statistics related to the program, estimates that over 170 billion lunches have been served to the nation's children since the program's inception.

The program has expanded in other ways as well. In 1966 Congress passed the Child Nutrition Act to complement the School Lunch Act. The Child Nutrition Act, as its name implies, aims to ensure that nutritional standards are set and met for federal meal programs. The act reflects the fact that, since the adoption of the original School Lunch Act in 1946, the nation had learned a lot about childhood nutrition and development. One of the most important discoveries was the importance of breakfast for children (and, indeed, for everyone). Children need a healthy breakfast to get them off to a good start for the day and to enhance their ability to learn. Consequently, as part of the Child Nutrition Act, Johnson's Great Society Congress created the School Breakfast Program. This program has the same eligibility requirements and is administered in the same manner as the school lunch program.

The Child Nutrition Act also includes a national program to provide milk to schools and other nonprofit organizations that care for children, such as nursery schools, child care centers, and summer camps. The act also creates a supplemental nutrition program for disadvantaged pregnant women, infants, and young children to ensure that they have a healthy start to life.

The School Lunch Act, too, has been amended over the years to reflect changes in American society. Congress has taken note of the increased number of women in the work force, and, as a result, the increased number of children in after school programs. Given that many children now remain on school grounds until the end of the work day, Congress amended the act to provide for afternoon snacks (officially called "meal supplements") for children and has extended the lunch and snack programs to include summers. In addition, the Congress has given the Secretary of Agriculture authority to devise programs that will extend federal meal programs to pre-schools and day care centers as well.

Federal nutrition programs have a long history of broad and bipartisan support from Congress. During the Reagan and Bush (Sr.) presidential administrations, however, some members of Congress supported efforts to move certain federal welfare programs to the states for administration. This process, known as "devolution," was intended to return authority to the states to implement and oversee welfare programs as they saw fit, giving local authorities greater ability to tailor programs to local conditions and concerns. At the same time, devolution would cut back on the size and scope of the federal government and help to even out the distribution of power between the federal government and the states.

Despite the persisting popularity of devolution, Congress has chosen not to transfer the school lunch program and other federal meal programs to the states. Instead, they remain a cooperative effort between the federal and state governments, with the federal government ultimately responsible for them. The programs themselves are probably secure for the foreseeable future, given their widespread acceptance by the American people, which makes them easy for legislators to support. But the exact nature and extent of the programs, including how much funding they will receive and who should administer them, will remain a national political issue.

3a. National School Lunch Act

Section 1751. Congressional declaration of policy.

It is declared to be the policy of Congress, as a measure of national security, to safeguard the health and well-being of the Nation's children and to encourage the domestic consumption of nutritious agricultural commodities and other food, by assisting the States, through grants-in-aid and other means, in providing an adequate supply of foods and other facilities for the establishment, maintenance, operation, and expansion of nonprofit school lunch programs.

Section 1752. Authorization of appropriations; "Secretary" defined.

For each fiscal year, there is authorized to be appropriated, out of money in the Treasury not otherwise appropriated, such sums as may be necessary to enable the Secretary of Agriculture to carry out the provisions of this chapter. . . .

Section 1753. Apportionments to States.

(a) The sums appropriated for any fiscal year shall be available to the Secretary for supplying agricultural commodities and other food for the program in accordance with the provisions of this chapter.

(b)(1) The Secretary shall make food assistance payments to each State educational agency each fiscal year. [The total amount of payments to a state is] equal to the product obtained by multiplying: the number of lunches served during such fiscal year in schools in such State by the national average lunch payment.

Section 1755. Direct expenditures for agricultural commodities and other foods.

[The Secretary is authorized to use some of the appropriated funds to purchase commodities such as fruits and vegetables and deliver them directly to participating schools.]

Section 1756. Payments to States.

(a) State revenue matching requirements.

(1) The Secretary and such State educational agencies [shall enter into agreements] for the purpose of assisting schools within the States in obtaining agricultural commodities and other foods for consumption by children [to carry out] the school lunch program authorized under this chapter. For any school year, such payments shall be made to a State only if, during such school year, the amount of the State revenues appropriated or used specifically for program purposes is not less than 30 percent of the funds made available to such State. [Author's Restatement: States need to contribute to this program, allocating at least 30 percent of the amount of money that Congress has given it for the program.]

Section 1757. State disbursement to schools.

(a) Disbursement by State educational agency. Funds paid to any State [by the federal government] during any fiscal year shall be disbursed by the State educational agency, in accordance with [this law], [to schools] eligible to participate in the school lunch program.

(d) Use of funds. Use of funds paid to States may include, in addition to the purchase price of agricultural commodities and other foods, the cost of processing, distributing, transporting, storing or handling thereof.

(e) Limitation. In no event shall such disbursement for food to any school for any fiscal year exceed an amount determined by multiplying the number of lunches served in the school in the school lunch program under this chapter during such year by the maximum per meal reimbursement rate for the State, for the type of lunch served, as prescribed by the Secretary.

Section 1758. Program requirements.

(a) Nutritional standards; medical and special dietary needs of individual students; compliance assistance; fluid milk; acceptance of offered foods.

(1)(A) Lunches served by schools participating in the school lunch program under this chapter shall meet minimum nutritional requirements prescribed by the Secretary on the basis of tested nutritional research. . . .

(B) The Secretary shall provide technical assistance and training, including technical assistance and training in the preparation of lower-fat versions of foods commonly used in the school lunch program under this chapter, to schools participating in the school lunch program to assist the schools in complying with the nutritional requirements [outlined by the government] and in providing appropriate meals to children with medically certified special dietary needs. The Secretary shall provide additional technical assistance to schools that are having difficulty maintaining compliance with the requirements.

(2) Lunches served by schools participating in the school lunch program under this chapter shall offer students fluid milk.

(b) Income eligibility guidelines. . . .

(1)(A) Not later than June 1 of each fiscal year, the Secretary shall prescribe income guidelines for determining eligibility for free and reduced price lunches during the 12-month period beginning July 1 of such fiscal year and ending June 30 of the following fiscal year. The income guidelines for determining eligibility for free lunches shall be 130 percent of the applicable family size income levels contained in the nonfarm income poverty guidelines prescribed by the Office of Management and Budget [also known as the "federal poverty level"].

(B) The income guidelines for determining eligibility for reduced price lunches for any school year shall be 185 percent of the applicable family size income levels contained in the [same] nonfarm income poverty guidelines.

(2)(A) Following the determination by the Secretary under paragraph (1) of this subsection of the income eligibility guidelines for each school year, each State educational agency shall announce the income eligibility guidelines, by family size, to be used by schools in the State in making determinations of eligibility for free and reduced price lunches. Local school authorities shall, each year, publicly announce the income eligibility guidelines for free and reduced price lunches on or before the opening of school.

(B) Applications for free and reduced price lunches, in such form as the Secretary may prescribe or approve, and any descriptive material, shall be distributed to the parents or guardians of children in attendance at the school, and shall contain only the family size income levels for reduced price meal eligibility with the explanation that households with incomes less than or equal to these values would be eligible for free or reduced price lunches. Such forms and descriptive material may not contain the income eligibility guidelines for free lunches.

(C) [Some students will be presumptively eligible for free or reduced price breakfasts and lunches, including children from households that are receiving food stamps, are receiving federal funds under certain provisions of the Social Security Act, or are enrolled in Head Start.]

(3) Any child who is a member of a household whose income [meets the eligibility guidelines for a free lunch] shall be served a free lunch. Any child who is a member of a household whose income [meets the eligibility guidelines for a reduced price lunch] shall be served a reduced price lunch.

(4) No physical segregation of or other discrimination against any child eligible for a free lunch or a reduced price lunch under this subsection shall be made by the school nor shall there be any overt identification of any child by special tokens or tickets, announced or published lists of names, or by other means. [Author's Restatement: Students receiving free or reduced price lunches shall not be identified, made to sit at a separate lunch table, or otherwise discriminated against.]

(f) Nutritional requirements.

(1) Nutritional requirements. Schools that are participating in the school lunch or school breakfast program shall serve lunches and breakfasts under the program that are consistent with the goals of the most recent Dietary Guidelines for Americans [and that] provide, on the average over each week, at least: (i) with respect to school lunches, 1/3 of the daily recommended dietary allowance established by the Food and Nutrition Board of the National Research Council of the National Academy of Sciences; and (ii) with respect to school breakfasts, 1/4 of the daily recommended dietary allowance established by the Food and Nutrition Board of the National Research Council of the National Academy of Sciences.

Section 1760. Miscellaneous provisions.

(d) Definitions. For the purposes of this chapter:

(2) "Commodity only schools" means schools that do not participate in the school lunch program under this chapter, but which receive commodities made available by the Secretary for use by such schools in nonprofit lunch programs.

(3) "School" means any public or nonprofit private school of high school grade or under, and any public or licensed nonprofit private

residential child care institution (including, but not limited to, orphanages and homes for the mentally retarded).

Section 1761. Summer food service programs for children in service institutions.

(a) Assistance to States. . . .

(1) The Secretary is authorized to carry out a program to assist States, through grants-in-aid and other means, to initiate and maintain nonprofit [summer] food service programs for children . . . participating in the National Youth Sports Program and residential public or private nonprofit summer camps that develop special summer or school vacation programs [and that provide] food service similar to that made available to children during the school year under the school lunch program. . . .

Section 1766. Child and adult care food program.

(a) Grants-in-aid; "institution" defined; guidelines for institutions providing care to children outside of school. The Secretary may carry out a program to assist States through grants-in-aid and other [funding methods] to initiate and maintain nonprofit food service programs for children in institutions providing child care. . . . [These institutions include], but [are] not limited to, child care centers, settlement houses, recreational centers, Head Start centers, and institutions providing child care facilities for children with disabilities; and such term shall also mean any other private organization providing nonresidential day care services for which it receives compensation [under] the Social Security Act. In addition, the term "institution" shall include programs developed to provide day care outside school hours for schoolchildren, public or nonprofit private organizations that sponsor family or group day care homes, and emergency shelters.

Section 1766a. Meal supplements for children in after school care.

(a) (1) Grants to States. The Secretary shall carry out a program to assist States through grants-in-aid and other means to provide meal supplements under a program organized primarily to provide care for children in after school care in eligible elementary and secondary schools.

(2) Eligible schools. For the purposes of this section, the term "eligible elementary and secondary schools" means schools that operate school lunch programs under this chapter, sponsor after school care programs, and operate after school programs with an educational or enrichment purpose. . . .

Section 1769c. Compliance and accountability.

(a) Unified accountability system. There shall be a unified system [of rules written] and administered by the Secretary for ensuring that local food service authorities that participate in the school lunch program under this chapter comply with [this law]. Such system shall be established through the publication of regulations and the provision of an opportunity for public comment.

Section 1769h. Accommodation of the special dietary needs of individuals with disabilities.

(b) Activities. The Secretary may carry out activities to help accommodate the special dietary needs of individuals with disabilities who are participating in a covered program.

3b. Child Nutrition Act

Section 1771. Congressional declaration of purpose.

In recognition of the demonstrated relationship between food and good nutrition and the capacity of children to develop and learn, based on the years of cumulative successful experience under the national school lunch program with its significant contributions in the field of applied nutrition research, it is hereby declared to be the policy of Congress that these efforts shall be extended, expanded, and strengthened under the authority of the Secretary of Agriculture as a measure to safeguard the health and well-being of the Nation's children, and to encourage the domestic consumption of agricultural and other foods, by assisting States, through grants-in-aid and other means, to meet more effectively the nutritional needs of our children.

Section 1772. Special program to encourage the consumption of fluid milk by children. . . .

(a)(1) [Congress authorizes the funds] necessary to enable the Secretary of Agriculture to encourage consumption of fluid milk by children in the United States in nonprofit schools of high school grade and under which do not participate in a meal service program authorized under this chapter or the National School Lunch Act and nonprofit nursery schools, child care centers, settlement houses, summer camps, and similar nonprofit institutions devoted to the care and training of children, which [also] do not participate in a meal service program authorized under this chapter or the National School Lunch Act.

(5) Any school or nonprofit child care institution which does not participate in a meal service program authorized under this chapter or the National School Lunch Act shall receive the special milk program upon its request.

(6) Children who qualify for free lunches under guidelines set forth

by the Secretary shall, at the option of the school involved (or of the local educational agency involved in the case of a public school) be eligible for free milk upon their request.

(b) Commodity only schools shall not be eligible to participate in the special milk program under this section.

Section 1773. School breakfast program.

(a) Establishment; authorization of appropriations. There is hereby authorized to be appropriated such sums as are necessary to enable the Secretary to carry out a program to assist the States and the Department of Defense through grants-in-aid and other means to initiate, maintain, or expand nonprofit breakfast programs in all schools which make application for assistance and agree to carry out a nonprofit breakfast program in accordance with this chapter. Appropriations and expenditures for this chapter shall be considered Health and Human Services functions for budget purposes rather than functions of Agriculture.

(b) Breakfast assistance payments to State educational agencies. . . .

(1)(A)(i) The Secretary shall make breakfast assistance payments to each State educational agency each fiscal year, at such times as the Secretary may determine, from the sums appropriated for such purpose, in an amount equal to the product obtained by multiplying the number of breakfasts served during such fiscal year to children in schools in such States which participate in the school breakfast program by the national average breakfast payment for free breakfasts, for reduced price breakfasts, or for breakfasts served to children not eligible for free or reduced price meals. . . .

(D) No breakfast assistance payment may be made under this subsection for any breakfast served by a school unless such breakfast consists of a combination of foods which meet the minimum nutritional requirements prescribed by the Secretary.

(2)(A) The Secretary shall make additional payments for breakfasts served to children qualifying for a free or reduced price meal at schools that are in severe need. . . .

(c) Disbursement of apportioned funds by State. . . .

. . . In selecting schools for participation [in the school breakfast program], the State educational agency shall give first consideration to those schools drawing attendance from areas in which poor economic conditions exist, to those schools in which a substantial proportion of the children enrolled must travel long distances daily, and to those schools in which there is a special need for improving the nutrition and dietary practices of children of working mothers and children from low-income families.

(e) Nutritional requirements; service free or at reduced price. . . .

(1) (A) Breakfasts served by schools participating in the school breakfast program under this section shall consist of a combination of foods and shall meet the minimum nutritional requirements prescribed by the Secretary on the basis of tested nutritional research. Such breakfasts shall be served free or at a reduced price to children in school under the same terms and conditions as are set forth with respect to the service of lunches free or at a reduced price.

(B) The Secretary shall provide [to the states] technical assistance and training, including technical assistance and training [in nutrition and food preparation, and especially] in the preparation of foods high in complex carbohydrates and lower-fat versions of foods commonly used in the school breakfast program . . . to assist the schools in complying with the nutritional requirements prescribed by the Secretary and in providing appropriate meals to children with medically certified special dietary needs.

Section 1781. Preschool programs.

The Secretary may extend the benefits of all school feeding programs conducted and supervised by the Department of Agriculture to include preschool programs operated as part of the school system.

Section 1782. Centralization in Department of Agriculture of administration of food service programs for children.

Authority for the conduct and supervision of Federal programs to assist schools in providing food service programs for children is assigned to the Department of Agriculture. To the extent practicable, other Federal agencies administering programs under which funds are to be provided to schools for such assistance shall transfer such funds to the Department of Agriculture for distribution through the administrative channels and in accordance with the standards established under this chapter and the National School Lunch Act.

Section 1786. Special supplemental nutrition program for women, infants, and children.

(a) Congressional findings and declaration of purpose.

Congress finds that substantial numbers of pregnant, postpartum, and breastfeeding women, infants, and young children from families with inadequate income are at special risk [of] physical and mental health [problems because of] inadequate nutrition or health care, or both. It is, therefore, the purpose of the program authorized by this section to provide supplemental foods and nutrition education [to these persons] through any eligible local agency that applies for participation in the program. The program shall serve as an adjunct to good health care, during critical times of growth and development, to prevent the occurrence of health problems, including drug abuse, and improve the health status of these persons.

(c) Grants-in-aid; cash grants. . . .

(1) The Secretary may carry out [this] special supplemental nutrition program . . . at no cost. . . . The program shall be supplementary to the food stamp program; any program under which foods are distributed to needy families in lieu of food stamps; and receipt of food or meals from soup kitchens, or shelters, or other forms of emergency food assistance.

(d) Eligible participants. Participation in the program under this section shall be limited to pregnant, postpartum, and breastfeeding women, infants, and children from low-income families who are determined by a competent professional authority to be at nutritional risk.

Section 1790. Breastfeeding promotion program.

(a) In general. The Secretary shall establish a breastfeeding promotion program to promote breastfeeding as the best method of infant nutrition, foster wider public acceptance of breastfeeding in the United States, and assist in the distribution of breastfeeding equipment to breastfeeding women.

4

Medicaid

1965

and Early and Periodic Screening, Diagnosis, and Treatment for Children (EPSDT)

1967 and 1989

Although the Social Security Act provided some safeguards for children, by the mid-1960s it became clear that millions of our nation's poor, including millions of children, were not receiving basic medical care. Congress responded by amending and expanding Social Security to achieve what remains to this day the two most comprehensive pieces of medical care legislation in American history: Medicare and Medicaid. These two programs became law in 1965, after decades of on and off debate over whether the government should adopt universal health care. Ultimately, Congress stopped short of universal coverage: Medicare ensures health insurance for the elderly and disabled, while Medicaid provides insurance for low income Americans of all ages, including children.

The Medicaid program (formally named "Grants to States for Medical Assistance Programs") formed an integral part of what President Lyndon B. Johnson called "The Great Society," a series of federal programs designed to assist underprivileged Americans. During his administration, Congress passed and President Johnson approved a number of programs aimed at providing enhanced assistance and opportunities to needy adults and children. The programs provided federal assistance for housing, education, and, in the case of Medicaid, much needed basic health care.

Medicaid was designed to be a joint venture between the states and the federal government. Congress required each state to set up a Medicaid agency to administer and oversee the provision of health care services to the poor. The agency was responsible for selecting medical providers and offering medical care in accordance with federal laws and regulations. Each state was instructed to set up a "state health plan." States had a large degree of flexibility in how they went about creating and structuring their plans, and also in the kind of medical services they chose to offer. Within certain limits, each state could determine who was eligible for medical care, what type of care it would sponsor, and whether the patient would be required to contribute to his or her care in the form of a premium or co-payment.

Congress, for its part, provided the basic guidelines for creating the Medicaid program. More importantly, it provided the lion's share of the money to fund it. Originally Congress intended to contribute approximately 60 percent of the cost of the program, with the states picking up the other 40 percent. Today the actual rate varies by state, with the federal government reimbursing the states between 50 and 80 percent of the costs for medical services. (Poorer states are reimbursed at a higher rate, wealthier states at a lower rate.) The federal government also contributes to the administrative costs of implementing the states' plans, usually with matching funds. Given this substantial contribution, Medicaid quickly became and remains one of the largest social welfare programs in the federal budget.

Congress gave federal administration and oversight of Medicaid to the Department of Health and Human Services, a cabinet-level department in the executive branch that is headed by a secretary. Like all cabinet secretaries, the Secretary of Health and Human Services is appointed by the president with the approval of the Senate. The Secretary answers directly to the president and reports to Congress on all matters originating from his or her department, including the progress made through Medicaid in providing health care coverage to needy Americans.

The department monitors each state's health care plan. Once each year the state is required to file with the department an extensive report explaining how it has complied with the provisions of the Medicaid program. Among other things, the report must detail how many persons the state health plan has served and what the state intends to do in the future to increase the provision of health care within its plan.

From the beginning Medicaid has included some type of health care coverage for needy children. In 1967 Congress gave the states the *option* to extend coverage for children's treatment beyond what they provided to adults. This children's benefit package became commonly referred to as EPSDT, which stands for "Early and Periodic Screening, Diagnosis, and Treatment." For the first two decades of the program, this coverage was fairly basic, including benefits like examinations; treatment of covered illnesses; and limited vision, hearing, and dental care. If children had illnesses that were not covered by the state's health care plan, they had to seek treatment elsewhere. In addition, if the state did not provide coverage for prescription drugs or durable medical goods (such as eyeglasses and hearing aids), children whose families could not afford these things often did without them.

While the Medicaid program had been a landmark and was certainly benefiting America's poor, over the years it became apparent that millions of children were still not receiving essential medical care, either because they were not enrolled in the program, or because the states were not providing sufficient benefits. Thus, in 1989 a bipartisan Congress passed a major expansion of Medicaid directed specifically at improving medical coverage for children. (The proposal was eventually included as part of the Omnibus Budget Reconciliation Act of 1989, which contained numerous reforms to both Medicare and Medicaid.) In brief, the expanded law now *required* states to treat children for medical problems even if the state did not provide the same treatment to adults. States must provide treatment whenever "medically necessary" to correct physical or mental illnesses or defects discovered during an EPSDT screening. "Medically necessary" treatments that children are now entitled to receive include prescription drugs, eyeglasses and hearing aids, speech therapy, physical therapy, and enhanced dental services. A state that does not provide these services to adults *must* provide them to its children. Moreover, if a state limits certain services (such as the number of days a Medicaid patient can stay in a hospital), it must suspend those limits if a child's treatment requires it.

Determining eligibility for EPSDT services can be somewhat complicated. Family income remains the most important factor. For example, children born after September 30, 1983, in families with incomes at or below the federal poverty level are eligible for the enhanced EPSDT services. (For the year 2002 the federal poverty level, formally called the "federal poverty guideline," is $18,100 for a family of four living in the forty-eight contiguous United States.) A child can also qualify under certain other standards; for example, an infant under one year of age qualifies if its family earns income at a rate of 133 percent of the federal poverty level. In general, most children who are eligible for Medicaid are automatically eligible to receive EPSDT services. States are required to inform children and their families of these services; in fact, states are required to perform outreach by seeking out children within their borders who are eligible and enrolling them in the state's health plan. The state must identify and provide essential health services to all of its eligible children until they reach age twenty-one.

The 1989 expansion of health coverage for children was a practical solution to the loopholes that had developed in Medicaid coverage. Congress recognized that treating children and adults as if they had the same medical needs did not make sense. An adult may be able to go without eyeglasses and still function in society; a child without eyeglasses cannot learn to read and cannot develop and thrive. By providing enhanced services to children (and particularly to children under the age of five), Medicaid EPSDT seeks to ensure a better, healthier start to their lives.

The following two excerpts summarize the most essential components of Medicaid as it applies to children. The first, from the U.S. Code, shows how Congress set up the Medicaid program, what the states' responsibilities are in creating their health plans, and how the law provides certain extra protections for pregnant women and children. These extra protections, including a presumption of coverage for pregnant women and children and an extension of Medicaid benefits for up to one year after eligibility runs out, were adopted in 1997 as part of the Balanced Budget Act. As explained in the next section, these 1997 changes to Medicaid were but a small part of Congress' increased efforts to provide health care to all low-income children.

The second excerpt, concerning EPSDT, comes from the Code of Federal Regulations. After the passage of any law, Congress leaves it up to the appropriate department of the executive branch (in this case, the Department of Health and Human Services) to adopt the regulations necessary to further implement and explain that law. Once adopted, these regulations are printed in the Code of Federal Regulations and are legally binding. The excerpt included here spells out in detail what the states must do to provide "early and periodic screening, diagnosis, and treatment" to Medicaid-eligible children.

4a. Medicaid

Section 1396. Appropriations.

For the purpose of enabling each State, as far as practicable under the conditions in such State, to furnish (1) medical assistance on behalf of families with dependent children and of aged, blind, or disabled individuals, whose income and resources are insufficient to meet the costs of necessary medical services, and (2) rehabilitation and other services to help such families and individuals attain or retain capability for independence or self-care, there is hereby authorized to be appropriated for each fiscal year a sum sufficient to carry out [these] purposes.

Section 1396a. State plans for medical assistance.

A State plan for medical assistance must . . . be in effect [throughout] the State. [The State shall contribute 40 percent of the cost of the plan; the federal government shall contribute 60 percent of the cost of the plan.]

[The State shall create] a single State agency to administer or supervise the administration of [its health] plan. [This agency will make reports to the federal government] and comply with [the] provisions [of this law].

[A State] shall be responsible for establishing and maintaining health standards for private and public institutions [that provide] medical assistance under [its] plan.

[A State is responsible] for making medical assistance available, including at least the [following] care and services: inpatient hospital services, outpatient hospital services, laboratory and x-ray services, early periodic screening, diagnostic, and treatment services . . . for individuals who are eligible under the plan and are under the age of 21, family planning services and supplies furnished (directly or under arrangements with others) to [eligible] individuals of child-bearing age (including minors who can be considered sexually active), physicians' services . . . whether furnished in the office, the patient's home, a hospital, or a nursing facility, or elsewhere, medical and surgical [dental] services, [and] services by a [certified] nurse-midwife, a certified nurse practitioner, or [a] certified family nurse practitioner.

[Among others, a State must make the above services available to] qualified women or children [who meet the income eligibility standards. In addition, the State must provide] ambulatory services [to children] . . . and prenatal care and delivery services [to pregnant women.]

[The State must provide] safeguards . . . to assure that eligibility for care and services under the plan will be determined, and such care and services will be provided, . . . with simplicity of administration and the best interests of the recipients [in mind].

[The State must inform] all persons in the State who are under the age of 21 and who have been determined to be eligible for medical assistance . . . of the availability of early and periodic screening, diagnostic, and treatment services, [as well as] age-appropriate immunizations. [The State must also provide] screening services [and arrange for] corrective treatment. [Each year, the State must report to the federal government about] the number of children provided child health screening services, the number of children referred for corrective treatment, the number of children receiving dental services, [and] the State's results in attaining the participation goals set [under this act.]

Section 1396r-1. Presumptive eligibility for pregnant women.

[When a State] determines, on the basis of preliminary information, that the family income of [a pregnant] woman does not exceed the [eligibility limits for Medicaid, it] shall inform [her] that she is required to [apply] for medical assistance, [and that this application may be used to receive the benefits of this program, including] ambulatory medical care.

Section 1396r-1a. Presumptive eligibility for children.

[When a State] determines, on the basis of preliminary information, that the family income of the child does not exceed the [eligibility limits for Medicaid, it] . . . shall inform the parent or custodian of the child . . . that [he or she] is required to [apply] for medical assistance, [and that this application may be used to receive all of the benefits of this program.]

Section 1396r-6. Extension of eligibility for medical assistance.

[Each state] must provide that, [when a] family becomes ineligible for . . . aid, [the family,] without any reapplication for benefits under [the State's] plan [will] remain eligible for assistance [for an additional] 6-month period. . . . [Moreover,] the State shall offer to each family . . . the option of extending coverage for [another] 6-month period, [so long as certain conditions are met.]

Section 1396s. Program for distribution of pediatric vaccines.

[E]ach State shall establish a pediatric vaccine distribution program . . . under which . . . each vaccine-eligible child . . . is entitled to receive [his or her] immunization[s] without charge.

Section 1396u-2. Provisions relating to managed care.

[A State] . . . may require an individual who is eligible for medical assistance . . . to enroll with a managed care entity [such as an HMO] as a condition of receiving such assistance.

4b. Early and Periodic Screening, Diagnosis, and Treatment for Children (EPSDT)

A State . . . Medicaid agency . . . [must] inform effectively all EPSDT eligible individuals (or their families) about the EPSDT program. . . . Using clear and nontechnical language, [it must] provide information about: [t]he benefits of preventive health care, the services available under the EPSDT program, and where and how to obtain those services. [It must also tell recipients that] the services provided under the EPSDT program are [free] to eligible individuals under 18 years of age, and if the agency chooses, to those 18 or older, up to age 21, except for any enrollment fee, premium, or similar charge that may be imposed on medically needy recipients, . . . and that . . . necessary transportation and scheduling assistance . . . is available to the EPSDT [recipient] upon request.

The agency must provide to eligible EPSDT recipients who request it, screening (periodic comprehensive child health assessments); that is, regularly scheduled examinations and evaluations of general physical and mental health, growth, development, and nutritional status of infants, children, and youth. . . . As a minimum, these screenings must include, but are not limited to: comprehensive health and developmental history, comprehensive unclothed physical examination, vision testing, hearing testing, laboratory tests, [and] dental screening services.

The agency must provide to eligible EPSDT recipients, the following services [as indicated by screening], even if the services are not [provided to adults]: [d]iagnosis of and treatment for defects in vision and hearing, including eyeglasses and hearing aids; [d]ental care, at as early an age as necessary, needed for the relief of pain and infections, restoration of teeth and maintenance of dental health; and, appropriate immunizations.

Under the EPSDT program, the agency may provide [additional] medical or remedial care . . . even if the agency does not provide [this same care to adults.]

The agency must provide referral assistance for treatment not covered by the plan. This referral assistance must include giving the family or recipient the names, addresses, and telephone numbers of providers who have expressed a willingness to furnish uncovered services at little or no expense to the family.

The agency must make available a variety of individual and group providers qualified and willing to provide EPSDT services. . . . [It must also] make appropriate use of State health agencies, State vocational rehabilitation agencies, . . . and other public health, mental health, and education programs . . . such as Head Start, Title XX (Social Services) programs, and the Special Supplemental Food Program for Women, Infants and Children (WIC), to ensure an effective child health program.

5

National Childhood Vaccine Injury Act

1986

Today's young people, and even their parents, do not remember what it was like in the first half of the twentieth century when infectious diseases like influenza and polio ravaged America. These and other diseases caused hundreds of thousands of deaths and disabilities, particularly among children. The main reason we no longer fear common childhood diseases is because of the development of antibiotic medicines and vaccines. Indeed, the development of the polio vaccine was considered such an important achievement that its inventors were deemed national heroes.

When the polio vaccine was developed in the early 1950s, Congress responded by appropriating funds to help state and local governments purchase the vaccine in an effort to immunize children quickly. This 1955 legislation marked the government's first involvement in nationwide vaccination efforts; it was followed in 1962 by the Vaccination Assistance Act. As new vaccines were developed, the federal government expanded its role to ensure that they remained available and affordable for American families.

Almost all American children with access to medical care are now vaccinated against a host of childhood diseases. (Schools and even colleges and universities routinely require proof of vaccinations before admitting students.) For low-income or uninsured children, the federal government sponsors free vaccinations with the aim of having every child vaccinated. The current program, adopted in 1993, is called the Vaccines for Children Program (VFC). Under the VFC Program, the federal government allocates funds to the Centers for Disease Control and dozens of other agencies for the purchase of vaccines. The vaccines are distributed to public and private health care providers, often through existing federal children's health programs, including Medicaid and CHIP, both of which are discussed elsewhere in this book. The vaccines are available free of charge to any child through age eighteen who does not have health insurance, who is enrolled in Medicaid, or who is a Native American or Alaskan Native. Currently all fifty states and the U.S. commonwealths and territories participate in this program.

As a result of these widespread vaccination efforts, many childhood diseases have been all but eliminated. They certainly do not pose the serious health threats that they did just a few generations ago. But while vaccinations protect the health of almost all children, no vaccine is foolproof. On occasion, a child might experience a reaction to a vaccine. Although rare, adverse reactions can be very serious, resulting in permanent injury or even death. In the past when such a tragedy occurred, bereaved parents commonly sought answers about and compensation for their child's injury by turning to the courts. The parents would file a lawsuit, typically against the doctor who administered the vaccine and the drug manufacturer that produced it.

In America, which does not have a system of universal health insurance, it is quite common for victims of accidents or injuries to use the courts to obtain reimbursement for their unpaid medical expenses. In legal language personal injuries are called "torts," and the lawsuits that are filed seeking compensation for these injuries are called "tort lawsuits" or "tort litigation." America relies heavily on tort litigation to redistribute resources from alleged wrongdoers to their victims. If the injured person (the plaintiff) can prove in court that the accused person (the defendant) harmed him or her in violation of some legal duty, the plaintiff can collect money (compensatory damages) for unpaid medical bills, lost wages, and pain and suffering. Sometimes a judge or jury will even seek to punish the wrongdoer by imposing "punitive damages" as well. Because punitive damages basically aim to teach the wrongdoer a lesson, they can often be quite substantial. It is not unusual for punitive damage awards to run into the millions of dollars.

While the American system of tort litigation is helpful for those who have been injured and want their day in court, it has serious drawbacks. Suing someone is a lengthy, emotional, and often draining process. The plaintiff cannot simply assert that someone wronged him or her, but must prove it. The jury might not believe the plaintiff or might award only a small amount of money after years of litigation.

There are serious drawbacks for defendants too. One common fear for a corporate defendant is that, if its product causes an injury, a lawsuit might cost the company a significant sum of money. Many lawsuits could potentially bankrupt the company. Pharmaceutical companies that produced vaccines feared this result. While they tried to make vaccines that were safe and effective, the simple fact remained that no vaccine was or is completely safe for all children. If sued by the families of children who had developed complications from their vaccines, the vaccine manufacturers potentially could be put out of business.

The Congress addressed these problems in the National Childhood Vaccine Injury Act of 1986. Congress recognized the need to encourage the continued research, development, and production of childhood vaccines and the need to protect vaccine manufacturers from lawsuits. At the same time, Congress recognized that injuries to children would continue to occur and that the victims of vaccine complications deserved compensation. To meet both of these important goals, Congress decided to take vaccine injury lawsuits out of the tort system and redirect them to the federal government. The government would pay the claims arising out of proven vaccine injuries.

Although the act was passed in 1986, it did not take effect until 1988. Originally the act covered seven common childhood vaccines: measles, mumps, rubella (also called German measles), polio, tetanus, diphtheria, and pertussis (whooping cough). In 1997 Congress added hepatitis B, varicella (chicken pox), and hemophilus influenzae type b (Hib). A year later Congress also added the rotavirus vaccine. For the purposes of providing compensation, Congress divided the injured into two groups: those injured before the program went into effect (October 1, 1988) and those injured afterward. Those injured prior to the start of the program were allowed to pursue a lawsuit or to file a claim under the act. Those injured after the program's effective date were required to file a claim under the act first and could pursue a lawsuit only if they were refused compensation or were not satisfied with the compensation offered to them. The act set up the Vaccine Trust Fund to pay victims' claims. Money for the trust fund comes from annual appropriations by Congress and, more importantly, from a tax placed on every dose of vaccine sold in the nation. Today the trust fund is worth more than a billion dollars.

A person injured by a vaccine who seeks compensation must file a claim in the U.S. Court of Federal Claims against the Department of Health and Human Services. The Department of Justice serves as the government's lawyer, helping to ensure that the claims are indeed vaccine-related and that the damages suffered by the claimants are real. If claimants can establish these facts, the Court of Claims will award them compensation out of the trust fund. Claimants can recover for their past and future medical expenses, for future lost income, and even for pain and suffering. Punitive damages are not allowed. The act provides that a claimant's attorneys' fees and costs are paid regardless of whether the claimant wins or loses, so long as the claim was made in good faith. A claimant who loses, or who feels that the damage award is too low, can refuse it and file a regular tort lawsuit in court.

Like the tort system, the federal Vaccine Injury Compensation Program has certain drawbacks. Claims must be filed relatively quickly, within two years of a death or three years of an injury. While some injuries are common and easy to establish, others require that the claimant prove that the injury was vaccine-related. It can commonly take two or more years to prove a claim and receive compensation. Even if the claim is meritorious, damage awards are limited. The act sets an award of $250,000 when a person dies as a result of a vaccine. Pain and suffering damages, if awarded at all, are also limited to a maximum of $250,000.

On the other hand, the program has accomplished its goal of resolving cases without resort to the legal system. Very few vaccine injury cases now end up in court. The trust fund has paid out nearly one billion dollars in claims since its inception. Vaccine manufacturers are protected from lawsuits, and vaccine victims are assured compensation. Congress is currently working with the Court of Claims and Department of Health and Human Services to improve the procedures for reviewing claims. They hope to resolve claims more efficiently in order to ensure that the victims of vaccine injuries receive their compensation more quickly.

5. National Childhood Vaccine Injury Act

Section 300aa-1. Establishment [of the current Vaccines for Children Program].

The Secretary shall establish in the Department of Health and Human Services a National Vaccine Program to achieve optimal prevention of human infectious diseases through immunization and to achieve optimal prevention against adverse reactions to vaccines. The Program shall be administered by a Director selected by the Secretary.

Section 300aa-10. Establishment of [the National Vaccine Injury Compensation Program].

(a) Program established. There is established the National Vaccine Injury Compensation Program to be administered by the Secretary under which compensation may be paid for a vaccine-related injury or death.

(b) Attorney's obligation. It shall be the ethical obligation of any attorney who is consulted by an individual with respect to a vaccine-related injury or death to advise such individual that compensation may be available under the Program for such injury or death.

(c) Publicity. The Secretary shall undertake reasonable efforts to inform the public of the availability of the Program.

Section 300aa-11. Petitions for compensation.

(a) General rule. (1) A proceeding for compensation under the Program for a vaccine-related injury or death shall be initiated by service upon the Secretary and the filing of a petition containing the matter prescribed by . . . this section with the United States Court of Federal Claims. (2)(A) No person may bring a civil action for damages in an amount greater than $1,000 or in an unspecified amount against a vaccine administrator or manufacturer in a State or Federal court for damages arising from a vaccine-related injury or death associated with the administration of a vaccine after October 1, 1988. . . . (3) No vaccine administrator or manufacturer may be made a party to a civil action (other than a civil action which may be brought under paragraph (2)) for damages for a vaccine-related injury or death associated with the administration of a vaccine after October 1, 1988.

Section 300aa-12. Court jurisdiction.

(a) General rule. The United States Court of Federal Claims and the United States Court of Federal Claims special masters shall, in accordance with this section, have jurisdiction over proceedings to determine if a petitioner under section 300aa-11 of this title is entitled to compensation under the Program and the amount of such compensation. The United States Court of Federal Claims may issue and enforce such orders as the court deems necessary to assure the prompt payment of any compensation awarded. [Author's Note: The Court of Claims was established by Congress to handle certain lawsuits brought against the federal government. The court is located in Washington, D.C.]

Section 300aa-13. Determination of eligibility and compensation.

(a) General rule. (1) Compensation shall be awarded under the Program to a petitioner [the alleged victim of the vaccine] if the special master or court finds on the record as a whole: (A) that the petitioner has demonstrated by a preponderance of the evidence the matters required in the petition . . . and (B) that there is not a preponderance of the evidence that the illness, disability, injury, condition, or death described in the petition is due to factors unrelated to the administration of the vaccine described in the petition. The special master or court may not make such a finding based on the claims of a petitioner alone, unsubstantiated by medical records or by medical opinion. [Author's Notes: A "special master" is an expert in a particular field that is appointed, usually by the judge, to advise and assist the court. Sometimes a special master is used in place of a judge to make certain legal decisions, particularly in administrative matters. A "preponderance of the evidence" is a common standard of proof in civil lawsuits. "Preponderance" essentially means "more likely than not." If the jury, or in this case the court, finds that the victim has proven his case by a preponderance of the evidence, that person will receive compensation in accordance with this statute.]

(b) Matters to be considered. (1) In determining whether to award compensation to a petitioner under the Program, the special master or court shall consider, in addition to all other relevant medical and scientific evidence contained in the record: (A) any diagnosis, conclusion, medical judgment, or autopsy or coroner's report which is contained in the record regarding the nature, causation, and aggravation of the petitioner's illness, disability, injury, condition, or death, and (B) the results of any diagnostic or evaluative test which are contained in the record and the summaries and conclusions.

Section 300aa-15. Compensation.

(a) General rule. Compensation awarded under the Program to a petitioner under section 300aa-11 of this title for a vaccine-related injury or death associated with the administration of a vaccine after October 1, 1988, shall include the following:

(1)(A) Actual and reasonable projected unreimbursable expenses [such as, for example, an expense not covered by a person's health insurance] which: (i) result from the vaccine-related injury for which the petitioner seeks compensation, (ii) have been or will be incurred by or on behalf of the person who suffered such injury, and (iii) (I) have been or will be for diagnosis and medical or other remedial care determined to be reasonably necessary, or (II) have been or will be for rehabilitation, developmental evaluation, special education, vocational training and placement, case management services, counseling, emotional or behavioral therapy, residential and custodial care and service expenses, special equipment, related travel expenses, and facilities determined to be reasonably necessary.

(2) In the event of a vaccine-related death, an award of $250,000 for the estate of the deceased.

(3) (A) In the case of any person who has sustained a vaccine-related injury after attaining the age of 18 and whose earning capacity is or has been impaired by reason of such person's vaccine-related injury for which compensation is to be awarded, compensation for actual and anticipated loss of earnings determined in accordance with generally recognized actuarial principles and projections. (B) [The victim is entitled to lost wages. The amount of lost wages will be determined by the court based on factors such as the nature and extent of the disability, income potential, and life expectancy.] In the case of any person who has sustained a vaccine-related injury before attaining the age of 18 and whose earning capacity is or has been impaired by reason of such person's vaccine-related injury for which compensation is to be awarded and whose vaccine-related injury is of sufficient severity to permit reasonable anticipation that such person is likely to suffer impaired earning capacity at age 18 and beyond, compensation after attaining the age of 18 for loss of earnings determined on the basis of the average gross weekly earnings of workers in the private, non-farm sector, less appropriate taxes and the average cost of a health insurance policy, as determined by the Secretary.

(4) For actual and projected pain and suffering and emotional distress from the vaccine-related injury, an award not to exceed $250,000.

Section 300aa-21. Authority to bring actions.

(a) Election. After judgment has been entered by the United States Court of Federal Claims or, if an appeal is taken under section 300aa-12(f) of this title, after the appellate court's mandate is issued, the petitioner who filed the petition under section 300aa-11 of this title shall file with the clerk of the United States Court of Federal Claims: (1) if the judgment awarded compensation, an election in writing to receive the compensation or to file a civil action for damages for such injury or death, or (2) if the judgment did not award compensation, an election in writing to accept the judgment or to file a civil action for damages for such injury or death. . . . [Once the Court of Claims decides the case, the victim may accept its decision, appeal it, or file his or her own lawsuit in federal court.] If a person elects to receive compensation under a judgment of the court in an action for a vaccine-related injury or death associated with the administration of a vaccine before October 1, 1988, or is deemed to have accepted the judgment of the court in such an action, such person may not bring or maintain a civil action for damages against a vaccine administrator or manufacturer for the vaccine-related injury or death for which the judgment was entered.

6

Residential Lead-Based Paint Hazard Reduction Act

1992

and Clean Air Act Amendments

1990

Today everyone agrees that lead poisoning poses a serious health risk to children. For decades, however, the government, medical experts, and the private sector greatly underestimated the nature and extent of this risk. As our understanding of the dangers of lead increased, Congress responded by passing a number of measures designed to address this major public health problem. Most of the legislation aims to prevent lead exposure in children and to screen for and treat children with lead poisoning.

In the early part of the twentieth century, many European countries began restricting the use of lead-based paint after observing health problems in people, and particularly children, who had been exposed to lead. The United States, to the contrary, did not act to limit the use of lead in paint until nearly fifty years later. In fact, as late as 1970 the government considered lead levels of 60 ig/dl (micrograms per deciliter) in a person's blood to be acceptable. This level has been repeatedly lowered; today, the government admits that a blood level as low as 10 ig/dl can be toxic in some people.

Lead poisoning is a particularly insidious threat because it usually has no symptoms. The absence of symptoms makes lead poisoning difficult to diagnose, so many children with this condition go untreated. Children are much more susceptible to poisoning than adults because their bodies are not fully developed and because they are more likely to ingest lead. Children under age six are the most at risk. Minority children are at higher risk because of environmental factors—specifically, they tend to live and play in places where the presence of lead remains a problem (urban areas, industrial areas, older homes, and the like).

The effects of lead poisoning are varied, as it can target almost every system in the body. Common health problems for children caused by exposure to lead include reduced birth weight, impaired hearing, slower cognitive development, and decreased motor skills. Lead poisoning can also lead to reading problems and learning disabilities. Lead poisoning has been linked to lower IQs, hyperactivity, and attention span problems. In significant concentrations lead can cause convulsions or even death.

Lead poisoning occurs when lead is ingested, whether it's eaten, breathed in, or otherwise absorbed by the body. Small children can unknowingly ingest lead when they eat flakes of lead-based paint or, more surreptitiously, when they take in dust with traces of such paint, either by eating or breathing that dust. A child's world is potentially full of lead: it can exist in the paint in the child's house or on playground equipment, in the soil in which the child plays, in the air, or even in the water the child drinks.

Given the fact that lead can appear almost anywhere, Congress over the years has systematically restricted or banned the use of lead in numerous products, including food packaging, cans, plumbing pipes, and ceramics. Two products in particular posed significant threats: lead-based paint and leaded gasoline. Congress' first major effort in preventing lead poisoning was the Lead-Based Paint Poisoning Prevention Act of 1971. This legislation, which was amended and augmented in 1973 and again in 1977, allocated funds for the mass screening of children for lead poisoning. It ordered the removal of lead-based paint in federally sponsored or subsidized housing and provided funds to the states to establish lead abatement programs. It also provided funds for the treatment of lead poisoning.

Congress followed this act with the Lead Contamination and Control Act in 1988. The act called for the federal Centers for Disease Control to work with states and localities to prevent lead poisoning. In 1992 Congress acted again, this time shifting its emphasis to combating lead hazards. It passed the Residential Lead-Based Paint Hazard Reduction Act. This law called for the removal of lead-based paint in all federally owned or federally subsidized housing when it posed a hazard—for example, when the paint was found to be chipping, peeling, or otherwise deteriorating. In enacting this legislation, Congress targeted the homes that posed the highest contamination risks.

The act also targeted private homes. Although Congress did not ban lead-based paint outright, it created significant disincentives for using it. For example, the act requires residential property owners (and their real estate agents and other representatives) to disclose known lead hazards when they sell or rent any property built before 1978. They must also provide to a prospective purchaser or tenant a federally issued brochure describing the risks of lead exposure to children. Builders or contractors who renovate or remodel these properties must distribute a similar brochure to their clients. Finally, the act appropriated several million dollars in grant money for the states to use to abate lead in privately held residential properties rented by low-income families. The provisions of the act were and are implemented by several federal agencies, including the Environmental Protection Agency, the Department of Housing and Urban Development, and the Department of Health and Human Services. As the use of these agencies reveals, the federal government today attacks the problem of lead poisoning on many fronts.

The other major source of lead in the environment was leaded gasoline. Today our automobiles run on unleaded gasoline. But it took over two decades to get to this point, and the legislative path to this result was somewhat convoluted.

In 1970 Congress passed the Clean Air Act, an unprecedented, sweeping law designed to improve air quality throughout the nation. A year earlier Congress had created the Environmental Protection Agency (EPA) and granted it broad authority to clean up the air by, among other things, regulating automobile emissions. Pursuant to its grant of power from Congress, the EPA in 1973 announced the first restrictions on leaded gasoline. In addition, it began implementation of the "Lead Phasedown Program," which would reduce the levels of lead in gasoline over a period of years. In adopting these regulations, the EPA noted that lead posed significant risks of harm to people, and especially to children, in urban areas where smog from auto emissions was most prevalent.

As a result of the new restrictions on lead and the requirement that new automobiles have catalytic converters to reduce toxic emissions, the oil industry began to develop unleaded gasoline. By the late 1970s unleaded gasoline was commonly used in new vehicles. The phasedown effort was a success: by 1988, the EPA estimated that the total lead used in gasoline had been reduced to less than 1 percent of the 1970 total.

Congress took action again against the hazards of lead in 1990 when it passed major changes to the original Clean Air Act. The Clean Air Act Amendments of 1990 called for a ban on lead in gasoline for motor vehicles. Congress gave auto manufacturers until January 1, 1996, to complete phasing out the use of leaded gasoline. Today leaded gasoline is no longer used in passenger cars or buses. In fact, automobile manufacturers, in partnership with the government, are working to develop vehicles that do not run on gasoline at all, but on cleaner and healthier alternative energy sources.

As a result of years of efforts by the Congress and numerous federal agencies acting pursuant to Congress' charge, the incidence of lead poisoning in America's children has dropped dramatically. Today all children receiving health care under Medicaid are automatically tested for lead contamination. The use of lead has been reduced and restricted, and cleanup efforts to remove old sources of lead continue. Although the health risks remain wherever lead exists, today's children are safer and healthier than ever before.

6a. Residential Lead-Based Paint Hazard Reduction Act

Section 4851. Findings. The Congress finds that:

(1) low-level lead poisoning is widespread among American children, afflicting as many as 3,000,000 children under age 6, with minority and low-income communities disproportionately affected;

(2) at low levels, lead poisoning in children causes intelligence quotient deficiencies, reading and learning disabilities, impaired hearing, reduced attention span, hyperactivity, and behavior problems;

(3) pre-1980 American housing stock contains more than 3,000,000 tons of lead in the form of lead-based paint, with the vast majority of homes built before 1950 containing substantial amounts of lead-based paint;

(4) the ingestion of household dust containing lead from deteriorating or abraded lead-based paint is the most common cause of lead poisoning in children;

(5) the health and development of children living in as many as 3,800,000 American homes is endangered by chipping or peeling lead paint, or excessive amounts of lead-contaminated dust in their homes;

(6) the danger posed by lead-based paint hazards can be reduced by abating lead-based paint or by taking interim measures to prevent paint deterioration and limit children's exposure to lead dust and chips;

(7) despite the enactment of laws in the early 1970's requiring the Federal Government to eliminate as far as practicable lead-based paint hazards in federally owned, assisted, and insured housing, the Federal response to this national crisis remains severely limited; and

(8) the Federal Government must take a leadership role in building the infrastructure—including an informed public, State and local delivery systems, certified inspectors, contractors, and laboratories, trained workers, and available financing and insurance—necessary to ensure that the national goal of eliminating lead-based paint hazards in housing can be achieved as expeditiously as possible.

Section 4851a. Purposes. The purposes of this chapter are:

(1) to develop a national strategy to build the infrastructure necessary to eliminate lead-based paint hazards in all housing as expeditiously as possible;

(2) to reorient the national approach to the presence of lead-based paint in housing to implement, on a priority basis, a broad program to evaluate and reduce lead-based paint hazards in the Nation's housing stock;

(3) to encourage effective action to prevent childhood lead poisoning by establishing a workable framework for lead-based paint hazard evaluation and reduction and by ending the current confusion over reasonable standards of care;

(4) to ensure that the existence of lead-based paint hazards is taken into account in the development of Government housing policies and in the sale, rental, and renovation of homes and apartments;

(5) to mobilize national resources expeditiously, through a partnership among all levels of government and the private sector, to develop the most promising, cost-effective methods for evaluating and reducing lead-based paint hazards;

(6) to reduce the threat of childhood lead poisoning in housing owned, assisted, or transferred by the Federal Government; and

(7) to educate the public concerning the hazards and sources of lead-based paint poisoning and steps to reduce and eliminate such hazards.

Section 4852. Grants for Lead-Based Paint Hazard Reduction In Target Housing.

(a) General Authority. The Secretary [of Housing and Urban Development] is authorized to provide grants to eligible applicants to evaluate and reduce lead-based paint hazards in priority housing that is not federally assisted housing, federally owned housing, or public housing, in accordance with the provisions of this section.

(e) Eligible Activities. A grant under this section may be used to:

(1) perform risk assessments and inspections in priority housing;

(2) provide for the interim control of lead-based paint hazards in priority housing;

(5) ensure that risk assessments, inspections, and abatements are carried out by certified contractors in accordance with [the Toxic Substances Control Act];

(7) assist in the temporary relocation of families forced to vacate priority housing while lead hazard reduction measures are being conducted;

(8) educate the public on the nature and causes of lead poisoning and measures to reduce the exposure to lead, including exposure due to residential lead-based paint hazards;

(9) test soil, interior surface dust, and the blood-lead levels of children under the age of 6 residing in priority housing after lead-based paint hazard reduction activity has been conducted, to assure that such activity does not cause excessive exposures to lead; and

(10) carry out such activities that the Secretary determines appropriate to promote the purposes of this Act.

Section 4852a. Task force on lead-based paint hazard reduction and financing.

(a) In General. The Secretary, in consultation with the Administrator of the Environmental Protection Agency [shall] establish a task force to make recommendations on expanding resources and efforts to evaluate and reduce lead-based paint hazards in private housing.

Section 4852d. Disclosure of information concerning lead upon transfer of residential property.

(a) Lead Disclosure in Purchase and Sale or Lease of Target Housing.

(1) Lead-based paint hazards. The Secretary and the Administrator of the Environmental Protection Agency shall [create] regulations under this section for the disclosure of lead-based paint hazards in target housing which is offered for sale or lease. The regulations shall require that, before the purchaser or lessee is obligated under any contract to purchase or lease the housing, the seller or lessor shall: (A) provide the purchaser or lessee with a lead hazard information pamphlet; (B) disclose to the purchaser or lessee the presence of any known lead-based paint, or any known lead-based paint hazards, in such housing and provide to the purchaser or lessee any lead hazard evaluation re-

port available to the seller or lessor; and (C) permit the purchaser a 10-day period (unless the parties mutually agree upon a different period of time) to conduct a risk assessment or inspection for the presence of lead-based paint hazards. [Before you rent or buy a home, you must be informed of any existing lead-based paint; in fact, you must be informed of the mere possibility of lead-based paint and given a pamphlet describing its dangers. You can inspect the property and potentially cancel your lease or purchase agreement if you believe you are at risk from lead-based paint hazards.]

(2) Contract for purchase and sale. Regulations [created] under this section shall provide that every contract or the purchase and sale of any interest in target housing shall contain a Lead Warning Statement and a statement signed by the purchaser. . . .

Section 4854a. Testing technologies.

The Secretary [of Housing and Urban Development], in cooperation with other Federal agencies, shall conduct research [among other things] to: develop improved methods for evaluating lead-based paint hazards in housing; develop improved methods for reducing lead-based paint hazards in housing; develop improved methods for measuring lead in paint films, dust, and soil samples; establish appropriate cleanup standards; evaluate the relative performance [and cost effectiveness of interim control and] various abatement techniques. . . .

[Author's Note: This act also amended the Toxic Substances Control Act, 15 U.S.C. § 2501 et seq., by adding a new title to it. The new title includes the following excerpts. Citation for these amendments is to the Public Law version of the Residential Lead-Based Paint Hazard Reduction Act, Pub. L. 102–550 & 1001 et seq.].

Section 1021. [The Toxic Substances Control Act is amended to include the following new title.]

TITLE IV: LEAD EXPOSURE REDUCTION

Section 402. Lead-based paint activities training and certification.
(a) Regulations.

(1) In general. The Administrator [of the EPA] shall, in consultation with the Secretary of Labor, the Secretary of Housing and Urban Development, and the Secretary of Health and Human Services (acting through the Director of the National Institute for Occupational Safety and Health), [create] final regulations governing lead-based paint activities [such as removing lead-based paint from structures] to ensure that individuals engaged in such activities are properly trained; that training programs are accredited; and that contractors engaged in such

activities are certified. Such regulations shall contain standards for performing lead-based paint activities, taking into account reliability, effectiveness, and safety. Such regulations shall require that all risk assessment, inspection, and abatement activities performed in target housing shall be performed by certified contractors. . . . [Author's Note: Lead-based paint, like asbestos, is considered very dangerous and should be removed only by trained professionals.]

(c) Renovation and Remodeling.

(1) Guidelines. In order to reduce the risk of exposure to lead in connection with renovation and remodeling of target housing, public buildings constructed before 1978, and commercial buildings, the Administrator shall, within 18 months after the enactment of this section, [create] guidelines for the conduct of such renovation and remodeling activities which may create a risk of exposure to dangerous levels of lead. The Administrator shall disseminate such guidelines to persons engaged in such renovation and remodeling through hardware and paint stores, employee organizations, trade groups, State and local agencies, and through other appropriate means.

Section 405. Lead abatement and measurement.

(a) Program To Promote Lead Exposure Abatement. The Administrator, in cooperation with other appropriate Federal departments and agencies, shall conduct a comprehensive program to promote safe, effective, and affordable monitoring, detection, and abatement of lead-based paint and other lead exposure hazards.

6b. Clean Air Act Amendments

Section 220. Lead phasedown.

Section 211 of the Clean Air Act is amended by adding the following new subsection at the end thereof:

(n) Prohibition on Leaded Gasoline for Highway Use. After December 31, 1995, it shall be unlawful for any person to sell, offer for sale, supply, offer for supply, dispense, transport, or introduce into commerce, for use as fuel in any motor vehicle . . . any gasoline which contains lead or lead additives.

Section 226. Prohibition on production of engines requiring leaded gasoline.

Part A of title II of the Clean Air Act is amended by adding the following new section after section 217: *Section 218.* Prohibition on production of engines requiring leaded gasoline. The [EPA] Administrator shall [create] regulations applicable to motor vehicle engines and non-road engines manufactured after model year 1992 that prohibit the manufacture, sale, or introduction into commerce of any engine that requires leaded gasoline.

Section 227. Urban buses.

Part A of title II of the Clean Air Act is amended by adding the following new section after section 218: *Section 219.* Urban bus standards. (a) Standards for Model Years After 1993. Not later than January 1, 1992, the Administrator shall [create] regulations . . . applicable to urban buses for the model year 1994 and thereafter. Such standards shall be based on the best technology that can reasonably be anticipated to be available at the time such measures are to be implemented, taking costs, safety, energy, lead time, and other relevant factors into account. Such regulations shall require that such urban buses [significantly reduce emissions as described in these amendments].

7

Safe Drinking Water Act Amendments

1996

and Food Quality Protection Act

1996

In the early 1970s, in response to a growing environmental movement and citizens' demands for a cleaner and safer environment, Congress passed several pieces of sweeping legislation in a flurry of activity reminiscent of the New Deal. The first piece of legislation was the National Environmental Policy Act, adopted in 1969, which created the Environmental Protection Agency. That law was quickly followed by the Clean Air Act (1970), the Federal Insecticide, Fungicide and Rodenticide Act (FIFRA) (1972), the Endangered Species Act (1973), the Safe Drinking Water Act (1974), the Resource Conservation and Recovery Act (RCRA) (1976), the Toxic Substances Control Act (TSCA) (1976), and the Clean Water Act (1977). These laws and many others required the federal government to become directly involved in and responsible for protecting the health of our nation's citizens and our natural environment and resources.

Since the passage of Congress' original environmental protection and health regulation measures, medical research has given us a much better understanding of the impact of environmental hazards on children. (We understand much more about the toxic effects of lead, for example, as explained earlier in this book.) In general, we now know that children cannot be treated simply as "little adults," the common phrase used to describe our past thinking when considering children in our environmental and health regulations. Children are very different from adults both physiologically and behaviorally, and both kinds of differences put them at higher risk for complications from environmental contaminants.

Why are children so different? Physiologically, they are not yet fully developed. Their bodies are therefore more susceptible to the adverse effects of environmental hazards. Because children's immune systems are still developing, moreover, they have less ability to fight off any toxicity or illness to which they might be exposed. Behaviorally, children engage in more activities that can lead to exposure to unsafe substances: they eat and drink proportionately more than adults, they play outside more, and they have much more hand to skin contact and hand to mouth contact than adults. And, obviously, young children do not know how to take adequate precautions against poisoning or other exposure to dangerous substances. In short, children are more prone to suffer the bad consequences of a polluted environment.

Armed with this new information, Congress has acted repeatedly in the past decade to revise existing environmental protection legislation to make it more attentive to the special needs of children. The EPA has also responded by adopting a seven-point plan entitled the "National Agenda to Protect Children's Health from Environmental Threats." In addition, in 1997 President Clinton signed an executive order instructing the EPA and all federal agencies to make children's health an important consideration in the adoption of federal policies and regulations. In response to this order, the EPA created the Office of Children's Health Protection to oversee its efforts at protecting children. The decade of the 1990s demonstrated that both legislative and executive efforts could be simultaneously directed toward making childhood healthier and safer.

Although any one of Congress' original environmental laws could be analyzed in regard to its impact on children's health, two laws bear special mention because of their recent children-focused amendments. In 1996 Congress amended the Safe Drinking Water Act. Also in 1996 Congress amended FIFRA and the Food, Drug, and Cosmetic Act by adopting a new law, the Food Quality Protection Act. Both of these laws made significant improvements to existing legislation and dramatically increased the protection of children from water- and food-borne health risks.

In passing the original Safe Drinking Water Act, Congress gave the EPA the ability to set national standards for what constituted safe drinking water. The EPA was directed to identify possible contaminants in drinking water and reduce their current levels to safe levels. The "safe level" for any substance found in drinking water is to be set by the agency. In 1986 Congress amended the act to give the EPA even more authority and to ban the use of lead (in pipes and soder, for example) in the public's drinking water.

In 1996 Congress once again amended the act and, in doing so, significantly reformed it. The 1996 amendments set forth several new requirements. They instruct the EPA to assess the risks posed by various substances in drinking water, thus allowing the agency to target the most dangerous substances for regulation; they require a cost-benefit analysis so that the EPA can use its resources in a cost-efficient way; they emphasize the use of solid, widely accepted scientific techniques and findings in determining, among other things, safe levels for substances in water; they create a multi-billion-dollar fund to assist states in developing better and safer water systems; they provide for greater protection of existing important aquifers and other water sources; and they adopt extensive consumer information provisions, so that citizens have a greater "right to know" about the conditions of their drinking water and the efforts being made to improve it.

The Safe Drinking Water Act amendments passed the House of Representatives by a vote of 392 to 30 and the Senate by a vote of 98 to 0. Since then occasional controversies have emerged over the EPA's activities under the act. Perhaps the most well known recent concern was voiced by groups opposed to the use of fluoride in community drinking water systems. Although the choice to add fluoride to drinking water is determined locally by each water system (often after a vote by the community), opponents to fluoride argue that the EPA, which regulates the acceptable amount of flouride in drinking water, has not sufficiently justified its decision about what constitutes a "safe level" of flouride. The opponents have asked Congress to investigate the EPA, and to require it to reexamine the issue of flouride's safety. The majority of health professionals and medical associations, however, including the American Dental Association, continue to maintain that the dental health benefits to children from the inclusion of flouride in their drinking water far outweigh the risks associated with its use.

Just a week before signing the Safe Drinking Water Act amendments into law, President Clinton signed into law the Food Quality Protection Act. This act instructs the EPA to take a new, more children-sensitive approach to its regulation of pesticides. As indicated above, recent research shows that children are more exposed to pesticides in their diets and play environments and are much more susceptible than adults to their toxic effects. Recognizing these facts, the act requires that children's health be the benchmark by which toxic tolerances are set. ("Toxic tolerances" are the amounts of toxins that can safely and legally remain on food). The EPA must find that the tolerances it sets do not pose a health risk to children. The act threw out the old, nonuniform standards for determining safe levels of pesticides and adopted a single new standard called "a reasonable certainty of no harm." In cases where it is unclear what the safe level for a substance actually is, the act instructs the EPA to use a "10-fold safety factor"—meaning that the safe level for that particular substance must be set at ten times greater than what is generally considered to be safe.

Among other things, the Food Quality Protection Act also provides that grocery stores distribute brochures describing the adverse health effects of pesticides, with information about how to avoid these risks. It also gives the EPA more power to punish violators of the act and related laws. In addition, it approves of the states' use, at their discretion, of pesticide warning labels on food.

The Food Quality Protection Act was heralded as a dramatic improvement in the way this nation regulates pesticides. At its passage the act enjoyed widespread support from many constituencies: consumers, farmers, environmentalists, medical organizations, and children's watchdog groups, not to mention the Congress and the president. In fact, Congress passed the act unanimously. In adopting the Food Quality Protection Act and the Safe Drinking Water Act amendments by such overwhelming margins, Congress demonstrated its commitment to updating environmental laws to reflect our new awareness of the dangers of environmental hazards. In doing so, it has dedicated significant federal resources to protect all Americans from these dangers, including especially its children.

7a. Safe Drinking Water Act Amendments

An Act [t]o reauthorize and amend title XIV of the Public Health Service Act (commonly known as the "Safe Drinking Water Act"), and for other purposes.

Section 3. Findings. The Congress finds that:

(1) [S]afe drinking water is essential to the protection of public health;

(2) because the requirements of the Safe Drinking Water Act now exceed the financial and technical capacity of some public water systems, especially many small public water systems, the Federal Government needs to provide assistance to communities to help the communities meet Federal drinking water requirements;

(3) the Federal Government commits to maintaining and improving its partnership with the States in the administration and implementation of the Safe Drinking Water Act;

(4) States play a central role in the implementation of safe drinking water programs, and States need increased financial resources and appropriate flexibility to ensure the prompt and effective development and implementation of drinking water programs;

(5) the existing process for the assessment and selection of additional drinking water contaminants needs to be revised and improved to ensure that there is a sound scientific basis for setting priorities in establishing drinking water regulations;

(6) procedures for assessing the health effects of contaminants and establishing drinking water standards should be revised to provide greater opportunity for public education and participation;

(7) in considering the appropriate level of regulation for contaminants in drinking water, risk assessment, based on sound and objective science, and benefit-cost analysis are important analytical tools for improving the efficiency and effectiveness of drinking water regulations to protect human health;

(8) more effective protection of public health requires: (A) a Federal commitment to set priorities that will allow scarce Federal, State, and local resources to be targeted toward the drinking water problems of greatest public health concern; (B) maximizing the value of the different and complementary strengths and responsibilities of the Federal and State governments in those States that have primary enforcement responsibility for the Safe Drinking Water Act; and (C) prevention of drinking water contamination through well-trained system operators, water systems with adequate managerial, technical, and financial capacity, and enhanced protection of source waters of public water systems;

(9) compliance with the requirements of the Safe Drinking Water Act continues to be a concern at public water systems experiencing technical and financial limitations, and Federal, State, and local governments need more resources and more effective authority to attain the objectives of the Safe Drinking Water Act; and

(10) consumers served by public water systems should be provided

with information on the source of the water they are drinking and its quality and safety, as well as prompt notification of any violation of drinking water regulations.

Section 102. General Authority.

[Congress makes the following amendment.]

Section 1412 (b). Standards. (1) Identification of contaminants for listing.

(A) General authority. The Administrator shall, in accordance with the procedures established by this subsection, publish a maximum contaminant level goal and [create] a national primary drinking water regulation for a contaminant . . . if the Administrator determines that: (i) the contaminant may have an adverse effect on the health of persons; (ii) the contaminant is known to occur or there is a substantial likelihood that the contaminant will occur in public water systems with a frequency and at levels of public health concern; and (iii) in the sole judgment of the Administrator, regulation of such contaminant presents a meaningful opportunity for health risk reduction for persons served by public water systems.

(B) Regulation of unregulated contaminants.

(i) Listing of contaminants for consideration. (I) Not later than 18 months after the date of enactment of the Safe Drinking Water Act Amendments of 1996 and every 5 years thereafter, the Administrator, after consultation with the scientific community, including the Science Advisory Board, after notice and opportunity for public comment, and after considering the occurrence data base [for incidents of contamination], shall publish a list of contaminants which, at the time of publication, are not subject to any proposed or [actual] national primary drinking water regulation, which are known or anticipated to occur in public water systems, and which may require regulation under this title. [Author's Note: Congress has given the EPA the responsibility to identify contaminants in drinking water. The EPA cannot act alone in developing this list. It must consult with scientists and consider comments from the public. Congress has also told the EPA to consider how prevalent the potential contaminants are in the nation's water systems, so that the common ones can be targeted. The EPA must balance the prevalence of the contaminants and the dangers they pose. For example, a prevalent but not very dangerous contaminant might not make the list.] . . .

(III) The Administrator's decision whether or not to select an unregulated contaminant for a list under this clause shall not be subject to judicial review. [Author's Note: If the EPA follows the above requirements, it may not be sued by others who disagree with its selections.]

(ii) Determination to regulate. (I) Not later than 5 years after the date of enactment of the Safe Drinking Water Act Amendments of 1996, and every 5 years thereafter, the Administrator shall, after notice of the preliminary determination and opportunity for public comment, for not fewer than 5 contaminants included on the list published under clause (i), make determinations of whether or not to regulate such contaminants. (II) A determination to regulate a contaminant . . . shall be based on the best available public health information. . . . [Author's Note: Once the EPA develops a list of contaminants, it must carefully determine which ones to regulate. It must regulate at least five new contaminants every five years. Regulation of these contaminants (which are usually chemicals) might include restricting their use in agriculture or manufacturing, or even banning them.]

(C) Priorities. In selecting unregulated contaminants for consideration under subparagraph (B), the Administrator shall select contaminants that present the greatest public health concern. The Administrator, in making such selection, shall take into consideration, among other factors of public health concern, the effect of such contaminants upon subgroups that comprise a meaningful portion of the general population (such as infants, children, pregnant women, the elderly, individuals with a history of serious illness, or other subpopulations) that are identifiable as being at greater risk of adverse health effects due to exposure to contaminants in drinking water than the general population. [Author's Note: Congress has instructed the EPA to regulate the contaminants that pose the greatest public health risk. In making this determination, the EPA is legally required to consider the health risks posed to certain groups in the population, including the ones noted above.]

Section 103. Risk Assessment, Management, and Communication.

[Congress continues with the following new criteria for EPA decisionmaking.]

Section 1412 (b) (3) Risk assessment, management, and communication.

(A) Use of science in decisionmaking. In carrying out this section . . . the Administrator shall use . . . the best available, peer-reviewed science and supporting studies conducted in accordance with sound and objective scientific practices. . . .

(B) Public information. In carrying out this section, the Administrator shall ensure that the presentation of information on public health effects is comprehensive, informative, and understandable. The Administrator shall, in a document made available to the public in support of a regulation [created] under this section, specify, to the extent practicable . . . each population addressed by any estimate of public health effects [and] the expected risk or central estimate of risk for the specific populations [including children]. . . .

Section 130. State Revolving Loan Funds.

[Congress adds the following new program]:

Section 1452. (a) General Authority.

(1) Grants to states to establish state loan funds. (A) In general: The Administrator shall offer to enter into agreements with eligible States to make capitalization grants [grants for building water filtration systems or other structures aimed at cleaning the water], including letters of credit [money loaned as credit, not unlike credit cards], to the States under this subsection to further the health protection objectives of this title, promote the efficient use of fund resources, and for other purposes as are specified in this title.

Section 137. Drinking water studies.

[Congress adds the following amendment]:

Section 1458. (a) Subpopulations at Greater Risk.

(1) In general. The Administrator shall conduct a continuing program of studies to identify groups within the general population that may be at greater risk than the general population of adverse health effects from exposure to contaminants in drinking water. The study shall examine whether and to what degree infants, children, pregnant women, the elderly, individuals with a history of serious illness, or other subpopulations that can be identified and characterized are likely to experience elevated health risks, including risks of cancer, from contaminants in drinking water.

(2) Report. Not later than 4 years after the date of enactment of this subsection and periodically thereafter as new and significant information becomes available, the Administrator shall report to the Congress on the results of the studies.

7b. Food Quality Protection Act

An Ac[t] to amend the Federal Insecticide, Fungicide, and Rodenticide Act [FIFRA] and the Federal Food, Drug, and Cosmetic Act, and for other purposes.

Subtitle C: Public Health Pesticides

Section 230. Definitions.

(a) Adverse effects. [FIFRA] is amended by adding at the end the following: The [EPA] Administrator shall consider the risks and benefits of public health pesticides separate from the risks and benefits of other pesticides. In weighing any regulatory action concerning a public health pesticide under this Act, the Administrator shall weigh any risks of the pesticide against the health risks [posed by the organism] to be controlled by the pesticide.

(b) New definitions. (nn) Public health pesticide: The term 'public health pesticide' means any minor use pesticide product registered for use and used predominantly in public health programs for vector control or for other recognized health protection uses, including the prevention or mitigation of viruses, bacteria, or other microorganisms (other than viruses, bacteria, or other microorganisms on or in living man or other living animals) that pose a threat to public health. . . . (oo) Vector: The term 'vector' means any organism capable of transmitting the causative agent of human disease or capable of producing human discomfort or injury, including mosquitoes, flies, fleas, cockroaches, or other insects and ticks, mites, or rats.

TITLE III: DATA COLLECTION ACTIVITIES TO ASSURE THE HEALTH OF INFANTS AND CHILDREN AND OTHER MEASURES

Section 301. Data collection activities to assure the health of infants and children.

(a) In general. The Secretary of Agriculture, in consultation with the Administrator of the Environmental Protection Agency and the Secretary of Health and Human Services, shall coordinate the development and implementation of survey procedures to ensure that adequate data on food consumption patterns of infants and children are collected.

(b) Procedures. To the extent practicable, the procedures referred to [above] shall include the collection of data on food consumption patterns of a statistically valid sample of infants and children.

(c) Residue data collection. The Secretary of Agriculture shall ensure that the residue data collection activities conducted by the Department of Agriculture in cooperation with the Environmental Protection Agency and the Department of Health and Human Services, provide for the improved data collection of pesticide residues, including guidelines for the use of comparable analytical and standardized reporting methods, and the increased sampling of foods most likely consumed by infants and children. [Author's Restatement: These three entities must cooperate closely when measuring pesticide residues in food. They must use the same testing approach and make certain that they take samples from foods that are favored by infants and children.]

Section 302. Collection of pesticide use information.

(a) In general. The Secretary of Agriculture shall collect data of state-wide or regional significance on the use of pesticides to control pests and diseases of major crops and crops of dietary significance, including fruits and vegetables.

(b) Collection. The data shall be collected by surveys of farmers or from other sources offering statistically reliable data.

Section 303. Integrated pest management.

The Secretary of Agriculture, in cooperation with the [EPA] Administrator, shall implement research, demonstration, and education programs to support adoption of Integrated Pest Management. Integrated Pest Management is a sustainable approach to managing pests by combining biological, cultural, physical, and chemical tools in a way that minimizes economic, health, and environmental risks. The Secretary of Agriculture and the Administrator shall make information on Integrated Pest Management widely available to pesticide users, including Federal agencies. Federal agencies shall use Integrated Pest Management techniques in carrying out pest management activities and shall promote Integrated Pest Management through procurement and regulatory policies, and other activities. [Author's Restatement: In order to reduce the amount of pesticides in food, farmers, ranchers, and other involved in food production must decrease reliance on pesticides and try new approaches to pest management. The Agriculture Department and the EPA must help to develop and promote alternative methods for reducing pests and must train people to use them.]

Section 305. Pesticide use information study.

(a) The Secretary of Agriculture shall, in consultation with the Administrator of the Environmental Protection Agency, prepare a report to Congress evaluating the current status and potential improvements in Federal pesticide use information gathering activities. . . .

TITLE IV: AMENDMENTS TO THE FEDERAL FOOD, DRUG, AND COSMETIC ACT

Section 405. Tolerances and Exemptions for Pesticide Chemical Residues

Section 408 [of the Food, Drug, and Cosmetic Act] is amended to read as follows:

(a) Requirement for Tolerance or Exemption.

(1) General rule. Except as provided . . . , any pesticide chemical res-

idue in or on a food shall be deemed unsafe . . . unless a tolerance for such pesticide chemical residue in or on such food is in effect under this section and the quantity of the residue is within the limits of the tolerance or an exemption from the requirement of a tolerance is in effect under this section for the pesticide chemical residue. For the purposes of this section, the term 'food', when used as a noun without modification, shall mean a raw agricultural commodity or processed food. [Author's Note: A "tolerance" as used in this law essentially means the acceptable level of something in the human body. For example, many states regulate the amount of alcohol a person can consume if that person is going to drive an automobile. A "blood alcohol level" (often called a "blood alcohol tolerance") is a type of tolerance. State legislatures set acceptable blood alcohol levels for drivers within the state; the EPA sets national tolerance levels for pesticides.]

(b) Authority and Standard for Tolerance.

    (2) Standard.

        (A) General rule.

            (i) Standard. The Administrator may establish or leave in effect a tolerance for a pesticide chemical residue in or on a food only if the Administrator determines that the tolerance is safe. The Administrator shall modify or revoke a tolerance if the Administrator determines it is not safe. [Author's Note: The amount of a pesticide that is acceptable to the EPA is the amount it considers safe to consume. It is practically impossible to remove all pesticides from food; therefore, tiny concentrations of certain pesticides are allowed.]

            (ii) Determination of safety. As used in this section, the term 'safe', with respect to a tolerance for a pesticide chemical residue, means that the Administrator has determined that there is a reasonable certainty that no harm will result from aggregate exposure to the pesticide chemical residue, including all anticipated dietary exposures and all other exposures for which there is reliable information. [Author's Note: But even tiny concentrations of pesticides are carefully considered; if a pesticide is present in too great an amount (concentration), it will be regulated. The goal is to protect consumers from the health risks associated with ingestion of dangerously high amounts of pesticides.]

        (B) Tolerence for eligible pesticide chemical residues.

            (i) Definition. As used in this subparagraph, the term 'eligible pesticide chemical residue' means a pesticide chemical residue as to which the Administrator is not able to identify a level of exposure to the residue at which the residue will not cause or contribute to a known or anticipated harm to human health (referred to in this section as a 'nonthreshold effect'); the lifetime risk of experiencing the nonthreshold effect is appropriately assessed by quantitative risk assessment; and with regard to any known or anticipated harm to human health for which the Administrator is able to identify a level at which the residue will not cause such harm (referred to in this section as a 'threshold effect'), the Administrator determines that the level of aggregate exposure is safe. [Author's Note: Sometimes it is impossible to know what amount (concentration) of a pesticide is safe. In that case, the EPA must use scientific, professional risk assessment methods to determine, to the best of its ability, what is to be considered safe.]

(vi) Infants and children. Any tolerance under this subparagraph shall meet the requirements of subparagraph (C) [below].

(C) Exposure of infants and children. [Author's Note: Although the EPA is a highly specialized agency with extensive powers, it still must follow Congress' guidelines. In the next sections, Congress tells the EPA some of the factors to consider in setting or changing the acceptable levels (tolerances) for pesticides in food.] In establishing, modifying, leaving in effect, or revoking a tolerance or exemption for a pesticide chemical residue, the Administrator:

(i) shall assess the risk of the pesticide chemical residue based on available information about consumption patterns among infants and children that are likely to result in disproportionately high consumption of foods containing or bearing such residue among infants and children in comparison to the general population; available information concerning the special susceptibility of infants and children to the pesticide chemical residues, including neurological differences between infants and children and adults, and effects of in utero exposure to pesticide chemicals; and available information concerning the cumulative effects on infants and children of such residues and other substances that have a common mechanism of toxicity; and

(ii) shall ensure that there is a reasonable certainty that no harm will result to infants and children from aggregate exposure to the pesticide chemical residue; and publish a specific determination regarding the safety of the pesticide chemical residue for infants and children. The Secretary of Health and Human Services and the Secretary of Agriculture, in consultation with the Administrator, shall conduct surveys to document dietary exposure to pesticides among infants and children. In the case of threshold effects, . . . an additional tenfold margin of safety for the pesticide chemical residue and other sources of exposure shall be applied for infants and children to take into account potential pre- and post-natal toxicity and completeness of the data with respect to exposure and toxicity to infants and children. Notwithstanding such requirement for an additional margin of safety, the Administrator may use a different margin of safety for the pesticide chemical residue only if, on the basis of reliable data, such margin will be safe for infants and children. . . . [Author's Note: Congress requires that the EPA give special consideration to the effects on children of pesticides in food. Because children's bodies are still developing, they are at increased risk of adverse health effects from pesticides. Congress and the EPA need to ensure that pesticide levels are reduced enough to protect infants and children. If it is impossible to know the level at which a pesticide becomes dangerous, the EPA must build in a significant cushion or margin of safety to protect young people.]

8

State Children's Health Insurance Program (CHIP)

1997

The adoption of enhanced Early and Periodic Screening, Diagnosis, and Treatment benefits for children marked a major step in providing comprehensive health care to our nation's low-income young people. But the problem of affordable health care did not go away, for children or for adults. As we approached the end of the twentieth century, affordable health insurance became an issue for all Americans.

Unlike most European democracies and Canada, where medical coverage is provided to all citizens by their government and paid for by tax revenues, the United States has relied largely on a system of private health insurance, whereby individual citizens either purchase their own medical insurance coverage or, more typically, receive coverage through their employers. The idea of making health insurance coverage government mandated and funded has always been controversial in this country, which has a long history of independence, self-reliance, and suspicion of governmental authority. Still, Americans have come to embrace certain universal entitlement programs: Social Security, as previously discussed, was controversial upon its adoption but now enjoys enviable political popularity among federal programs. As the century closed, it remained to be seen whether a system of universal health insurance, though controversial, could be similarly adopted and accepted in the United States.

The last decades of the twentieth century were marked by significant advances in diagnosis and treatment for major diseases, as well as by the development of many promising new prescription drugs.

But along with these developments came a sharp rise in medical costs. It grew increasingly more expensive to perform medical research and development, to administer both public and private health insurance programs, and to pay for elaborate but effective new treatments. As medical costs continued to rise, many employers began to pass the increases on to their employees. Other employers simply chose not to offer medical insurance or offered reduced medical benefits. Within a few years middle-class Americans began to feel the effects of these steadily rising medical costs. More middle-income working people became uninsured, but they found that they were not poor enough to qualify for Medicaid or other government programs aimed at our nation's most needy. As the number of uninsured Americans rose, our nation found itself faced with what became known as its "health care crisis."

With health care costs spiraling out of control, Americans in large numbers called for reform. In 1993 First Lady Hillary Rodham Clinton chaired a nationwide task force of experts and citizens dedicated to health care reform. The task force sought to identify solutions to the health care crisis. At the same time numerous other public and private organizations also pursued this goal. A range of possible solutions emerged, from adopting universal health care for all Americans to fixing certain, specific problems with private health insurance (such as the common refusal of insurance companies to cover people with pre-existing medical conditions). Doing nothing seemed less and less of an option.

Over time both the states and Congress passed significant laws to alleviate some of the problems of the health care crisis, and it continues to consider others. Although Congress has not adopted universal health care coverage for Americans, the issue remains hotly debated. However, while Congress did not fix the problem of providing health care coverage for all, it did take another very significant step in ensuring health care coverage for children. In 1997 it adopted the State Children's Health Insurance Program, commonly referred to as "CHIP" or sometimes "SCHIP."

The legislation that became CHIP was introduced by Senators Edward Kennedy (D-MA) and Orrin Hatch (R-UT). As senior members of the Senate and leaders in their respective political parties, their sponsorship invited wide-spread bipartisan support; indeed, numerous co-sponsors immediately joined on from both parties. In a press release describing the bill, Senator Kennedy remarked that, "This is not a Republican plan. It's not a Democratic plan. It's an

American plan—and we're optimistic that we'll have broad support from all parts of the political spectrum." They did. Ultimately, the bill became part of the Balanced Budget Act of 1997, as an addition to the Social Security Act. President Clinton signed the act on August 5, 1997, and this major bipartisan children's health insurance legislation became law.

CHIP's primary purpose is to expand coverage for and provide treatment to low-income, uninsured children whose families earn too much income to qualify them for Medicaid. The federal government estimated that ten million additional children could be covered by CHIP. Once again, the program was to be administered by the states, with the states and the federal government sharing the costs. Each state had the option of expanding its existing Medicaid program to include CHIP, to create a separate CHIP program, or to do both.

The CHIP program, like Medicaid, requires participating states to actively seek out and enroll eligible children. It calls for the provision of a basic health insurance package, including inpatient and outpatient care, x-rays and laboratory services, surgical services, and the like. Once again, the states are given flexibility in structuring their programs, including the determination of who is eligible to receive care and the nature and extent of care to be provided. To date, approximately half the states have simply chosen to follow Medicaid guidelines and provide the same Early and Periodic Screening, Diagnosis, and Treatment (EPSDT) package of benefits to greater numbers of children. While Medicaid is available to children at or below 100 percent of the federal poverty level, many states provide CHIP coverage to children at or below 200 percent of the poverty level. (In 2002, that's $36,200 for a family of four.) Almost all states have chosen to provide coverage to eligible children until they reach the age of eighteen.

Children enrolled in CHIP receive a health insurance card, much like they would if they received private health insurance. Families that can afford it are often asked to make a small contribution to their child's care typically in the form of a yearly enrollment fee or premium. Asking parents to contribute helps to ensure their involvement in their children's health care, and makes them responsible along with the government in meeting the costs of that care.

Since CHIP is relatively recent legislation, many states are still in the process of creating and refining their programs. As of August 1, 2000, all fifty states had received approval for their initial or amended CHIP plan. Since the legislation stressed that health insurance had to be provided efficiently and effectively to children, the states are required to coordinate CHIP with other federal and state children's programs. Indeed, many states are taking a practical approach by combining all available services into a package and offering them to children in one location, such as their school or place of worship. This approach, known as "program linkages," better enables state governments to locate and enroll as many eligible children as possible in child health and welfare programs.

Approximately two million children were enrolled into CHIP in 1999, leaving more than seven million to go. Given this number, the federal government, in cooperation with the states, has recently launched the national "Covering Kids" campaign to inform families about the availability of CHIP and to encourage them to enroll. In addition, Congress continues to modify the legislation to make it more responsive to the needs of the states and to ensure that as many uninsured children as possible receive coverage under the program.

The excerpt of the law provided here outlines the basic structure and coverage requirements of CHIP. Because the administration of CHIP varies from state to state, readers are encouraged to investigate how their states have responded to Congress' call to provide health care coverage to all of our nation's low-income children.

8. State Children's Health Insurance Program (CHIP)

Section 1397aa. Purpose; State child health plans.

The purpose of this title is to provide funds to States to enable them to initiate and expand the provision of child health assistance to uninsured, low-income children in an effective and efficient manner that is coordinated with other sources of health benefits coverage for children. Such assistance shall be provided [by either] obtaining coverage [for the children] that meets the criteria of this act, [by] providing benefits under the State's [M]edicaid plan, [or by] a combination of both.

A state is not eligible for payment under [this act] unless [it submits a plan that explains] how [the State] will use the [federal] funds . . . to provide health assistance to needy children . . . and [receives approval from the federal government for its plan.]

Section 1397bb. General contents of state child health plan; eligibility; outreach.

A State child health plan shall include [how the State targets and selects low-income children, a description of the State's current efforts to provide health insurance coverage for these children, an explanation of how any existing plan will be coordinated with this act, a description of the health care provided to the children, and an explanation of the State's methods of quality control.] [The State can set eligibility standards, but it] may not discriminate on the basis of diagnosis . . . [and] may not deny eligibility based on a child having a preexisting medical condition.

A State health plan shall [describe] the procedures to be used by the State to [identify the] families of children likely to be eligible for child health assistance [or other] public or private health coverage programs, to inform these families of [these programs, and] to assist them in enrolling their children in [these programs.]

Section 1397cc. Coverage requirements for children's health insurance.

The child health assistance provided to a targeted, low-income child under the [State's] plan . . . shall consist of benchmark coverage or benchmark equivalent coverage, including: inpatient and outpatient hospital services, physicians' surgical and medical services, laboratory and x-ray services, [and] well-baby and well-child care, including age-appropriate immunizations. [The State can choose to provide additional services, including, for example,] coverage of prescription drugs, mental health services, vision services, [and] hearing services.

A State child health plan shall include a [published] description . . . of the amount (if any) of premiums, deductibles, coinsurance, and other cost sharing imposed [upon families.]

[The State may require "cost-sharing" by families, that is, it may require families to pay] premiums, deductibles, coinsurance, [and other medical costs, but it may] not favor children from families with higher income over children from families with lower income. [And, it] may not impose deductibles, coinsurance, or other cost sharing [for preventive services.]

[Moreover, if a child comes from a family whose income is] at or below 150 percent of the poverty line, the State child health plan may not impose [an excessive] enrollment fee or premium [or anything but a nominal] deductible, cost sharing, or similar charge.

[For other low-income children,] any premiums, deductibles, cost sharing or similar charges imposed [upon a family] under the State child health plan may be imposed on a sliding scale related to income, [but only up to a total of] 5 percent of [a] family's income [per] year.

Section 1397dd. Allotments.

[To fund this act, Congress will give the states between 3 to 5 billion dollars for each of the next 10 years. Allotments to each state shall be based on numerous factors, including] the number of low-income children in the State with no health insurance coverage, the [total] number of low-income children in the State, [and] geographic variations [in health care costs.] [The minimum allotment] for one of the 50 States or the District of Columbia [shall not be] less than $2,000,000 [per year]. [United States commonwealths and territories, including] Puerto Rico, Guam, the Virgin Islands, American Samoa, [and] the Northern Mariana Islands [are also eligible for funds if they have approved child health plans.]

Section 1397ee. Payment to States.

[The federal government] shall pay to each State with [an approved child health plan an allotment for] child health assistance, for outreach activities, and for other reasonable costs incurred by the State to administer the plan. [However, the federal government will not reimburse a State for abortion coverage unless the abortion was] necessary to save the life of the mother or if the pregnancy [was] the result of an act of rape or incest. [In addition, the State shall not be reimbursed if payment can be obtained] under any other federally operated or financed health care insurance program. [The amount of payment will be reduced to the extent that funds are received from other sources, such as family cost sharing.] [Author's note: Abortion continues to be a controversial issue in Congress. While Congress is willing to fund a state's health care plan, and even to pay for the state's promoting and advertising of that plan, it will not reimburse the state for abortions, except in the unusual situations described above.]

Section 1397hh. Annual reports; evaluations.

[As part of its responsibilities under this act, the State must] assess the operation of [its health] plan . . . each . . . year, including the progress made in reducing the number of uncovered low-income children, [and] report [its findings to the federal government.] [This annual report must include] an assessment of the effectiveness of the State plan in increasing the number of children with creditable health coverage, a description and analysis of the effectiveness of the . . . State plan, an assessment of the effectiveness of other public and private programs in the State in increasing the availability of affordable quality individual and family health insurance for children, an assessment of State activities [to coordinate the provision of child health care services], [a]n analysis of changes and trends in the State that affect the provision of accessible, affordable, quality health insurance and health care to children, [a] description of any plans the State has for improving the availability of health insurance and health care to children, [and] . . . any recommendations for improving [this federal program.] [Author's Note: The state must prepare a yearly report detailing the successes and failures of its children's health insurance program. Congress wishes to use federal funds effectively and efficiently, and often insists that states report on how federal funds were spent. The supervising federal agency will usually require changes in a state's program or give it advice or assistance in using the funds in a more skillful manner.]

PART II

CITIZENSHIP AND DEMOCRATIC PARTICIPATION LAWS

9

Fourteenth Amendment

1868

Child Citizenship Act

2000

and Intercountry Adoption Act

2000

The Fourteenth Amendment is perhaps the Constitution's most important amendment. Passed by Congress and ratified by the states in the wake of the Civil War, it outlined significant new principles regarding citizenship and the rights associated with it. The impact of the amendment was not immediately realized, however. It would take another century for its force to be fully felt.

Volumes have been written on the meaning of and the benefits bestowed by the Fourteenth Amendment. For the purposes of this book, the focus will be on citizenship rights for children that have been guaranteed by the amendment and subsequent immigration laws. But young people should understand that the importance of the amendment goes far beyond issues of citizenship. Arguably, the Fourteenth Amendment affects their lives in a more regular and meaningful way than any other constitutional provision or right.

Why is this the case? Over time the Supreme Court has interpreted the amendment very broadly and has created new rights and protections for individuals from its language. In addition, the Congress has used its authority under the amendment to pass sweeping legislation, particularly in the area of civil rights and voting rights. Basically, the contributions of the Fourteenth Amendment have come in three areas: incorporation, equal protection, and due process.

First, the Fourteenth Amendment provides that the Bill of Rights restricts the behavior of the states. When the Bill of Rights was adopted, it governed only the relationship between the people and the federal government. The states were not bound by the Bill of Rights and did not have to adhere to it. After adoption of the Fourteenth Amendment, however, the Supreme Court determined in a series of cases that the amendment was intended to change the relationship between the states and their citizens. The most important provisions of the Bill of Rights were applied to the states (incorporated) through the language of the Fourteenth Amendment. For example, in a series of cases decided in the 1960s, the Supreme Court determined that the states should afford criminal defendants the same protections guaranteed in the Bill of Rights, including protection from unreasonable search and seizure. This process of incorporation essentially meant that the provisions of the Bill of Rights, channeled through the language of the Fourteenth Amendment, would restrict the behavior of both the federal and state governments. Today, almost all of the provisions of the Bill of Rights have been "incorporated" in this way.

The second contribution of the Fourteenth Amendment is its equal protection clause. "Equal protection" essentially means that similar groups of persons must be treated alike. In recent decades the Supreme Court and the Congress have used the equal protection clause to outlaw various forms of discrimination. These forms of discrimination are often based on class or group status, such as race, ethnicity, gender, religious preference, and so forth. For example, if the federal government wishes to give aid to children, it should not discriminate against some children based on their race, on their legitimacy, or some other immutable factor; generally, the equal protection clause requires the government to give the aid without consideration of such factors. Thus, the Fourteenth Amendment is a powerful tool for fighting discrimination and for making sure that federal and state expenditures are made fairly and consistently.

The third contribution of the Fourteenth Amendment is its due process clause. Again, the Supreme Court has interpreted this clause rather broadly and, among other things, has extended new protections to persons accused of crimes or who try to challenge governmental decisions regarding their rights or entitlements. For instance, the due process clause provided the basis for the right to counsel, the Miranda warnings ("you have the right to remain silent . . ."), the exclusionary rule (illegally seized evidence cannot be used at trial), and numerous other protections for criminal defendants that we take for granted today.

Children and young adults enjoy the benefits of all of these Fourteenth Amendment protections. But another part of the amendment, often overlooked, is equally important and perhaps even more fundamental: its guarantee of citizenship to all persons born in the United States.

Prior to the Civil War there was significant disagreement over both who could be considered a citizen and whether that person was a citizen of the United States, a particular state, or both. In the infamous *Dred Scott v. Sanford* decision rendered just before the Civil War, the Supreme Court held that the Constitution did not bestow citizenship on slaves, even after they had escaped to free territories within the United States. Rather, the slaves remained the property of their owners. This decision outraged many, and after the war the Congress (dominated by the victorious Northern states) vowed to overturn *Dred Scott.* It did so by proposing, approving and encouraging (some would say forcing, as the Southern states had little choice) the ratification of the Fourteenth Amendment.

The language of the Fourteenth Amendment that ensured citizenship for the freed slaves and indeed for anyone born in America, was succinct: "All persons born or naturalized in the United States and subject to the jurisdiction thereof, are citizens of the United States and of the State wherein they reside." In adopting this provision, Congress cleared up much of the confusion regarding citizenship. After ratification of the amendment, any person born in this country became a citizen both of the country and of his or her state of residence. Thus, a child born in the United States today is a citizen even if his or her parents are not citizens or are not eligible for citizenship. If, for example, a child's parents are illegal aliens, the child born on U.S. soil is a citizen nonetheless.

For foreigners the process of becoming a citizen is set forth in the lengthy provisions of the Immigration and Nationality Act, often referred to as the "INA." The modern INA was adopted by Congress in 1952. Also called the "McCarran-Walter Bill" after its congressional sponsors, this act focused U.S. immigration policy on country quotas and removed race and gender prohibitions on immigration. Since then, the act has undergone several significant amendments, most notably perhaps in 1965, when Congress abandoned the country quota approach. In its place Congress adopted an immigration policy based primarily on reuniting separated families, granting asylum to political refugees, and filling needs in the American workforce.

Two INA amendments recently passed by Congress directly concern children. The first grants citizenship automatically to foreign children adopted by American parents. Called the Child Citizenship Act of 2000, it provides that, as of February 27, 2001, parents who adopt foreign-born children do not need to apply to the Immigration and Naturalization Service (INS) to establish a child's citizenship, a complicated and costly procedure. On that date approximately 75,000 adopted children automatically became U.S. citizens. There are some conditions, of course: for example, the child must be under age eighteen; at least one parent must be a U.S. citizen; the child must reside with the parent in the United States; and the child, if old enough, must take an oath of loyalty to the United States. Still, the process of becoming a citizen could not be more streamlined. Today's foreign-born adopted children enjoy all of the rights and privileges of American-born children as soon as their adoption is final.

At the same time it approved the Child Citizenship Act, Congress also passed important legislation guaranteeing that overseas adoptions would be handled in an appropriate, nonexploitative manner. The Intercountry Adoption Act of 2000 amended the INA and ratified the Hague Convention's treaty provisions regarding international adoptions.

In passing this act, the United States joined approximately forty other countries in committing to the protection of adopted children. These countries (called "Hague countries") have promised to cooperate to ensure that intercountry adoptions are handled properly. The countries have agreed to protect against the kidnapping and selling of children and to ensure that proper consents have been received before adoptions are completed. The treaty also oversees the adopted children's transport to their new countries and establishes their new citizenship or legal status.

In addition, the act also expands the current INA definition of "orphans," to make it easier for American parents to adopt children from overseas.

Taken together, the Fourteenth Amendment and the Immigration and Nationality Act demonstrate the nation's commitment to expanding the definition of U.S. citizenship, protecting children from international exploitation, facilitating foreign adoptions, and providing virtually instantaneous citizenship to newly adopted children.

9a. Fourteenth Amendment

Section 1. All persons born or naturalized in the United States and subject to the jurisdiction thereof, are citizens of the United States and of the State wherein they reside. No State shall make or enforce any law which shall abridge the privileges or immunities of citizens of the United States; nor shall any State deprive any person of life, liberty, or property, without due process of law; nor deny to any person within its jurisdiction the equal protection of the laws.

Section 5. The Congress shall have power to enforce, by appropriate legislation, the provisions of this article.

9b. Child Citizenship Act

An Act [t]o amend the Immigration and Nationality Act to modify the provisions governing acquisition of citizenship by children born outside of the United States, and for other purposes.

Section 1. Short Title. This Act may be cited as the "Child Citizenship Act of 2000."

TITLE I: CITIZENSHIP FOR CERTAIN CHILDREN BORN OUTSIDE THE UNITED STATES

Section 101. [Section 320 of the Immigration and Nationality Act is amended to read as follows:]

Section 320. (a) A child born outside of the United States automatically becomes a citizen of the United States when all of the following conditions have been fulfilled: (1) At least one parent of the child is a citizen of the United States, whether by birth or naturalization. (2) The child is under the age of eighteen years. (3) The child is residing in the United States in the legal and physical custody of the citizen parent pursuant to a lawful admission for permanent residence.

(b) Subsection (a) shall apply to a child adopted by a United States citizen parent if the child satisfies the requirements applicable to adopted children under [the act].

Section 102. Acquisition of certificate of citizenship for certain children born outside the United States.

[Section 322 of the Immigration and Nationality Act is amended to read as follows:]

Section 322. (a) A parent who is a citizen of the United States may apply for naturalization on behalf of a child born outside of the United States who has not acquired citizenship automatically under section 320. The Attorney General shall issue a certificate of citizenship to such parent upon proof, to the satisfaction of the Attorney General, that the following conditions have been fulfilled: (1) At least one parent is a citizen of the United States, whether by birth or naturalization. (2) The United States citizen parent: (A) has been physically present in the United States or its outlying possessions for a period or periods totaling not less than five years, at least two of which were after attaining the age of fourteen years; or (B) has a citizen parent who has been physically present in the United States or its outlying possessions for a period or periods totaling not less than five years, at least two of which were after attaining the age of fourteen years. (3) The child is under the age of eighteen years. (4) The child is residing outside of the United States in the legal and physical custody of the citizen parent, is temporarily present in the United States pursuant to a lawful admission, and is maintaining such lawful status.

(b) Upon approval of the application (which may be filed from abroad), and . . . upon taking . . . the oath of allegiance required by this Act of an applicant for naturalization, the child shall become a citizen of the United States and shall be furnished by the Attorney General with a certificate of citizenship.

(c) Subsections (a) and (b) [above] shall apply to a child adopted by a United States citizen parent if the child satisfies the requirements applicable to adopted children. . . .

Section 104. Effective date. The amendments made by this title shall take effect 120 days after the date of the enactment of this Act and shall apply to individuals who satisfy the requirements of section 320 or 322 of the Immigration and Nationality Act, as in effect on such effective date.

9c. Intercountry Adoption Act

An Act to provide for implementation by the United States of the Hague Convention on Protection of Children and Co-operation in Respect of Intercountry Adoption, and for other purposes. . . .

[Author's Note: Many international treaties are written and adopted at

The Hague, Netherlands. These treaties, which cover a variety of subjects, are commonly referred to as "Hague Conventions." Generally, the president and the executive branch are responsible for negotiating treaties with other nations. Under the Constitution, however, each treaty negotiated by the United States must be approved by the Senate. This act, therefore, accomplishes two goals: it gives official Senate approval to the Hague Convention on Intercountry Adoptions, and it provides guidelines and powers to the Executive Branch (and particularly to the Secretary of State) for implementing the terms of that convention.]

Section 2. Findings and purposes.

(a) Findings. Congress recognizes [that] (1) the international character of the Convention on Protection of Children and Co-operation in Respect of Intercountry Adoption (done at The Hague on May 29, 1993); and (2) the need for uniform interpretation and implementation of the Convention in the United States and abroad, and therefore finds that enactment of a Federal law governing adoptions and prospective adoptions subject to the Convention involving United States residents is essential.

(b) Purposes. The purposes of this Act are: (1) to provide for implementation by the United States of the Convention; (2) to protect the rights of, and prevent abuses against, children, birth families, and adoptive parents involved in adoptions (or prospective adoptions) subject to the Convention, and to ensure that such adoptions are in the children's best interests; and (3) to improve the ability of the Federal Government to assist United States citizens seeking to adopt children from abroad and residents of other countries party to the Convention seeking to adopt children from the United States.

TITLE I: UNITED STATES CENTRAL AUTHORITY

Section 102. Responsibilities of the Secretary of State.

(a) Liaison responsibilities. The Secretary [of State] shall have responsibility for: (1) liaison with the central authorities of other [Hague] Convention countries; and (2) the coordination of activities under the Convention by persons subject to the jurisdiction of the United States.

(c) Accreditation and approval responsibilities. The Secretary shall carry out the functions prescribed by the Convention with respect to the accreditation of agencies and the approval of persons to provide adoption services in the United States in cases subject to the Convention as provided in title II. Such functions may not be delegated to any other Federal agency. [Author's Note: The Secretary of State is charged with appointing agencies and persons who are familiar with the requirements of the Hague Convention, and who will cooperate with similar representatives from other nations to ensure that intercountry adoptions are properly handled.]

(d) Additional responsibilities. The Secretary (1) shall monitor individual Convention adoption cases involving United States citizens; and (2) may facilitate interactions between such citizens and officials of other Convention countries on matters relating to the Convention in any case in which an accredited agency or approved person is unwilling or unable to provide such facilitation. [Author's Restatement: If the designated agencies or persons cannot help adoptive parents resolve their difficulties with other nations, the Secretary of State may step in to help.]

(e) Establishment of registry. The Secretary and the Attorney General shall jointly establish a case registry of all adoptions involving immigration of children into the United States and emigration of children from the United States, regardless of whether the adoption occurs under the Convention. Such registry shall permit tracking of pending cases and retrieval of information on both pending and closed cases.

TITLE III: RECOGNITION OF CONVENTION ADOPTIONS IN THE UNITED STATES

Section 301. Adoptions of children immigrating to the United States.
(a) Legal effect of certificates issued by the Secretary of State.

(1) Issuance of certificates by the Secretary of State. The Secretary of State shall, with respect to each Convention adoption, issue a certificate to the adoptive citizen parent domiciled [living] in the United States that the adoption has been granted or, in the case of a prospective adoptive citizen parent, that legal custody of the child has been granted to the citizen parent for purposes of emigration and adoption, pursuant to the Convention and this Act, if the Secretary of State: (A) receives appropriate notification from the central authority of such child's country of origin; and (B) has verified that the requirements of the Convention and this Act have been met with respect to the adoption. [Author's Note: The certificate is essentially the proof of a legal adoption. As noted in the next section, any adopted child who receives such a certificate automatically becomes a citizen of the United States.]

(2) Legal effect of certificates. If appended to an original adoption decree, the certificate described in paragraph (1) shall be treated by Federal and State agencies, courts, and other public and private persons and entities as conclusive evidence of the facts certified therein and shall constitute the certification required by . . . the Immigration and Nationality Act, as amended by this Act.

(b) Legal effect of convention adoption finalized in another convention country. A final adoption in another Convention country, certified by the Secretary of State . . . shall be recognized as a final valid adoption for purposes of all Federal, State, and local laws of the United States.

(c) Condition on finalization of convention adoption by state court. In the case of a child who has entered the United States from another Convention country for the purpose of adoption, an order declaring the adoption final shall not be entered unless the Secretary of State has issued the certificate provided for in subsection (a) with respect to the adoption.

Section 302. Immigration and nationality act amendments relating to children adopted from convention countries.

(a) Definition of child. The Immigration and Nationality Act is amended [to reflect the provisions of this act, including the requirement that a child eligible for adoption under this act must come from] a foreign state that is a party to the Convention on Protection of Children and Cooperation in Respect of Intercountry Adoption done at The Hague on May 29, 1993, or who is emigrating from such a foreign state to be adopted in the United States, by a United States citizen and spouse jointly, or by an unmarried United States citizen at least 25 years of age. . . .

[In reviewing applications for these Intercountry adoptions and granting citizenship certification, the Attorney General must determine that:]

(I) care will be furnished the child if admitted to the United States;

(II) the child's natural parents (or parent, in the case of a child who has one sole or surviving parent because of the death or disappearance of, abandonment or desertion by, the other parent), or other persons or institutions that retain legal custody of the child, have freely given their written irrevocable consent to the termination of their legal relationship with the child, and to the child's emigration and adoption; [Author's Restatement: A child cannot be adopted unless the parents or guardians clearly and freely give up their relationship with the child.]

(III) in the case of a child having two living natural parents, the natural parents are incapable of providing proper care for the child;

(IV) the purpose of the adoption is to form a bona fide parent-child relationship, and the parent-child relationship of the child and the natural parents has been terminated . . . ; and

(V) in the case of a child who has not [yet] been adopted, [that:] (aa) the competent authority of the foreign state has approved the child's emigration to the United States for the purpose of adoption by the prospective adoptive parent or parents; and (bb) the prospective adoptive parent or parents has or have complied with any pre-adoption requirements of the child's proposed residence.

[N]o natural parent or prior adoptive parent of any such child shall thereafter, by virtue of such parentage, be accorded any right, privilege, or status under this Act.

TITLE V: GENERAL PROVISIONS

Section 501. Recognition of convention adoptions.

Subject to Article 24 of the Convention, adoptions concluded between two other Convention countries that meet the requirements of Article 23 of the Convention and that became final before the date of entry into force of the Convention for the United States shall be recognized thereafter in the United States and given full effect. Such recognition shall include the specific effects described in Article 26 of the Convention.

Section 502. Special rules for certain cases.

(a) Authority to establish alternative procedures for adoption of children by relatives. To the extent consistent with the Convention, the Secretary may establish by regulation alternative procedures for the adoption of children by individuals related to them by blood, marriage, or adoption, in cases subject to the Convention.

(b) Waiver authority. Notwithstanding any other provision of this Act, to the extent consistent with the Convention, the Secretary may, on a case-by-case basis, waive applicable requirements of this Act or regulations issued under this Act, in the interests of justice or to prevent grave physical harm to the child.

10

Twenty-sixth Amendment

1971

Since the Civil War Congress and the states have taken numerous steps to expand voting opportunities for the American people. The primary changes have come in the form of amendments to the Constitution. Amendments are introduced in Congress and must receive approval of two-thirds of both houses; once approved, they proceed to the state legislatures. When three-fourths of the states approve an amendment, it is certified and becomes official. From 1865 to 1870 the states ratified what became known as the "Civil War Amendments." The Thirteenth, Fourteenth, and Fifteenth Amendments were aimed at securing citizenship rights for newly emancipated African-Americans. The Fifteenth Amendment specifically granted them the right to vote (a right that was routinely denied until the 1960s, when the Supreme Court declared unconstitutional several practices commonly used to disenfranchise voters, and Congress passed the first Voting Rights Act.) In 1913 the Seventeenth Amendment allowed citizens of the states to vote directly for their senators. (Previously, state legislatures had selected senators.) In 1920 the states ratified the Nineteenth Amendment, giving women the right to vote.

During World War II (1941–1945), citizens began calling for the right of younger Americans to vote. The common voting age at that time was twenty-one for federal and state elections. The fact that American men and women were serving their country in its war effort but could not vote for its leaders led some states to lower their voting age to eighteen. During the Vietnam War a national effort to lower the voting age emerged with more force. The controversial nature of the war, plus the fact that thousands of young people were drafted and were dying in combat, led great numbers of college students and other young people to protest. One of their demands was a lowered voting age. The students argued persuasively that anyone who is old enough to fight and die for the nation should be considered old enough to vote. They argued that, since the draft age was eighteen, the voting age should be lowered to eighteen.

In 1970, bowing to increasing political pressure, Congress reauthorized its landmark Voting Rights Act of 1965. In doing so, it proposed and passed an amendment to the act that lowered the voting age to eighteen for both federal and state elections. President Richard Nixon signed the revised act into law.

But the constitutionality of the voting age amendment was challenged immediately. Some states believed that Congress did not have the right to dictate the voting age for state elections. In a federal system, they argued, the states are supreme within their own boundaries and are free to set their own rules for governing themselves. For Congress to impose a uniform voting age on the states would infringe upon the states' independence and sovereignty, which were guaranteed by the Constitution.

The Supreme Court decided this issue very quickly in the 1970 case of *Oregon v. Mitchell.* It held that Congress did indeed have the power to lower the voting age for federal elections, but that it could not interfere with the states' authority to set the voting age for state and local elections. To do so would violate the principle of federalism and give Congress authority that it did not have.

With the voting age law stricken, many states faced the rather ugly possibility of having to administer separate elections, one for federal offices with a voting age of eighteen, and another for state offices with a voting age set by the state. Given the Supreme Court's ruling in *Mitchell,* an amendment would be the only way to obtain a universal voting age for the nation.

Congress responded by proposing the Twenty-sixth Amendment to the Constitution. The Amendment was passed resoundingly by the Senate on March 10, 1971, and by the House on March 23, 1971. Ratification began immediately: in fact, five states ratified the amendment the same day it was passed by the House. The Twenty-sixth Amendment enjoyed one of the quickest ratifications in history. By July 1 thirty-eight states had ratified the amendment, giving it the three-fourths majority of states necessary for passage. President Richard Nixon certified the amendment at a White House ceremony on July 5, 1971, less than four months after it had been approved by Congress.

Since the passage of the Twenty-sixth Amendment, some human rights groups have called for the voting age to be lowered again, this time to age sixteen. There are even groups dedicated to removing all age restrictions on voting. Neither of these proposals seems destined to succeed, at least not in the near future.

Although the Twenty-sixth Amendment opened the electoral system to millions of young Americans, studies show that only a small percentage of them actually exercise the right to vote. The reasons for low voter turnout among young Americans are numerous. Some young voters are apathetic. But more of them simply do not know how to vote, and therefore have not registered to vote. Voting is not a very "user-friendly" process in America. All states require voters to be registered, a process where one essentially signs up in advance to vote by giving proof of age, identity, and residence before an election. (A few states allow same-day registration, which entitles a person both to register and vote on election day.) The failure to register remains a significant reason why young people do not vote.

Now, however, steps are being taken to make voter registration easier. In 1993, for example, the Congress passed and President Bill Clinton signed the "Motor Voter Law," which allows citizens to register to vote at a state's Department of Motor Vehicles. Since it took effect in 1995, millions of Americans have used Motor Voter either to register for the first time or to update their registration. Young people aged eighteen who seek to obtain or renew their driver's license or to title their first car can take advantage of this easy way to register to vote. In addition, certain Internet websites have been devised to allow people to register on-line. Many young Americans are familiar with the MTV "Rock the Vote" campaign, which encourages them to participate in politics. The "Rock the Vote" website is just one of many offering voter registration over the Internet. Hopefully, these and other improvements to voter registration will encourage more young people to become registered and to make their voices heard on issues of importance to them—including perhaps the Uniform Drinking Age Act discussed later in this part.

10. Twenty-sixth Amendment

Section 1. The right of citizens of the United States, who are eighteen years of age or older, to vote shall not be denied or abridged by the United States or by any State on account of age.

Section 2. The Congress shall have power to enforce this article by appropriate legislation.

11

Military Selective Service Act

1980

In one form or another, the United States has relied on the draft for over a century. The first federal draft (called "conscription" at that time) occurred during the Civil War. Both the North and the South required their young men to serve in their respective armies. However, a man could avoid military service by providing a substitute to perform for him or by buying his way out of service with a payment of a few hundred dollars.

The second major draft occurred during World War I, under the Selective Service Act of 1917. All men age twenty-one to thirty were required to register, but again many could take advantage of exemptions based on, among other things, disability, a role as sole family provider, or conscientious objector status. A "conscientious objector" is a person who can establish a legitimate, fundamental moral opposition to combat or to military service in general. Conscientious objectors are usually required to perform an alternative service, such as working for a social service or charitable organization.

Just prior to World War II the Congress passed the "Selective Training and Service Act," which was technically the nation's first peace-time draft, but given conditions in Europe and the impending catastrophe of Pearl Harbor, one might argue that it was a draft in anticipation of war. In any event, after war was officially declared, Congress passed an additional Selective Service Act that required men age eighteen to sixty-five to register and serve in the military. Exemptions were given again based on certain disabilities and family circumstances.

After World War II Congress passed the Selective Service Act of 1948 requiring all men age eighteen to twenty-six to register. During the Korean War Congress passed another version of the act. Finally, during the Vietnam War Congress passed the Selective Service Act of 1967. This act required men age eighteen to twenty-six to register for the draft, but again registration could be avoided by seeking exemptions. For example, a young man enrolled full-time in college was eligible for an educational deferment that postponed his registration until after graduation.

The Vietnam War draft proved particularly unpopular for a number of reasons. The first, detailed in the discussion of the Twenty-sixth Amendment earlier in this part, was the sheer unpopularity of the war itself. In cities and towns and on college campuses throughout America, young people by the thousands took to the streets to protest what they believed to be an unjust war and the government's refusal to withdraw its troops from Vietnam.

The illegal burning of draft cards became a favorite symbol of the protesters, who opposed the draft as well as the war. Among young people the draft was widely viewed as unfair, because middle-class and upper-middle-class men could avoid it by enrolling in college, by having useful "connections," or by leaving the country. (Escaping to Canada became a choice of some young men of this generation.) That left poor or less-educated persons to serve in the war, as they were not able to avail themselves of the various legal and illegal methods to avoid the draft. Consequently, lower-class males, including minorities, were conscripted in large numbers.

This double standard made the draft extremely unpopular, not just among those who were eligible to be drafted, but eventually among policymakers as well. Thus, in 1973, acting on the recommendation of military and political leaders, the United States abolished the draft. It chose instead to create a volunteer-based armed services, which it still has today.

Given the move to a volunteer military, draft registration was abolished in 1975. However, the president retained the power to reinstate registration if he thought it necessary and to ask Congress for an appropriation to do so. In 1980, after the Soviet Union's invasion of Afghanistan, President Carter asked Congress to bring back registration (but not the draft). It complied. Government officials were quick to explain that registration was different from a draft. Registration is simply a list of names of persons eligible to be drafted, should the need arise. Keeping a list is prudent, government and military officials argued, because it might be needed in the event of a military conflict or war. If the need arose young men would be drafted at random from the names on the registration list.

Thus, since 1980 all men born after December 31, 1959 who are age eighteen to twenty-five must register their names with the Selective Service System. Typically, a man must register either before or within thirty days after his eighteenth birthday. "All men," as the phrase implies, means just that: any male citizen or immigrant— including illegal aliens—must register within thirty days of becoming eighteen. A man aged eighteen to twenty-five who enters this country with an intention to stay must register upon arrival; in fact, registration is a prerequisite for young men who seek U.S. citizenship.

Failure to register can have serious consequences. Technically, the federal government can prosecute someone who fails to register, and upon conviction that person faces a maximum five-year prison term and a $10,000 fine. As a practical matter, however, the government to date has not proven aggressive in criminally prosecuting nonregistrants. Its civil penalties usually provide sufficient reason for young men to register: a person who fails or refuses to register cannot obtain a federal job, cannot participate in federal job training, and cannot receive federal student financial aid. Indeed, the most popular student aid programs are closed to nonregistrants, including the federal student loan, Pell grant, and Work-Study programs.

In addition, many states prohibit nonregistrants from obtaining state jobs or state education aid. Some states will not even allow a nonregistrant to obtain a driver's license. To date, twenty-eight states have placed some form of job, student funding, or license restriction on nonregistrants. Moreover, if a young man never registers and passes his twenty-sixth birthday, he is permanently barred from receiving the federal aid described above unless he can provide a compelling reason for his failure to register.

But what about our nation's young women? Shouldn't they be required to register, too? President Jimmy Carter thought so, and when he asked Congress to reactivate the Selective Service Act, he also requested that it amend the law to include the registration of women. After significant debate Congress refused to amend the act, and registration remained limited to young men. Congress based its decision in large part on the fact that, under existing military rules, women could not serve in combat roles. And since the purpose of registration was to create a list of possible combat forces, it was unnecessary to include women in the registration process.

Of course, many perceived this distinction between men and women to be unfair, and ultimately the question of female registration made its way to the Supreme Court in the famous 1981 case of *Rostker v. Goldberg*. In a six to three decision, the Supreme Court upheld as constitutional Congress' decision to exclude females from registration. The Court majority reasoned that the distinction between men and women was not based on generalizations or stereotypes, but rather on a carefully researched and reasoned decision by both houses of Congress that registration of women was not needed given the restrictions on women in combat. The Court noted that Congress had broad authority under the Constitution to "raise and support armies," and that traditionally the Court granted Congress and the Armed Services great deference in making decisions about military affairs. The Court explained that the government did not have to undergo the extra expense and administrative burden associated with registering women who could not serve the combat functions anticipated for those on the registration list.

The dissent, on the other hand, argued that the registration list was not necessarily limited to combat roles, and for that reason both men and women could be eligible for inclusion on it. At least one dissenter voiced skepticism about the military's restrictions on women in combat, believing the majority's ruling sanctioned gender discrimination.

Since the Supreme Court's decision, the rule has not changed: only males are required to register with the Selective Service System. But the arguments over the inclusion of women on the list and the role of women in the military generally continue to be heated ones. Should the United States find that it can no longer rely solely on a volunteer army and that it needs to use the registration list, chances are very high that the males-only rule will be challenged again both in Congress and before the Supreme Court.

The need for peacetime registration continues to be a subject of debate. In 1999 the House of Representatives voted to repeal the Selective Service Act by a vote of 232 to 187. The Senate did not act on the bill proposed by Representative Ron Paul (R-Tex.), who is philosophically opposed to the draft. Others in Congress, even if not philosophically opposed, question the need for continuing the registration program during peacetime. In April 2001 Representative Paul reintroduced his bill to repeal the Selective Service Act. After the events of September 11th, however, the law is unlikely to be repealed any time soon; nevertheless, young persons, both men and women, would be wise to make their voices heard if they wish to influence Congress' future decisionmaking on this very important policy issue.

11. Military Selective Service Act

Section 453. Registration.

(a) Except as otherwise provided in this title, it shall be the duty of every male citizen of the United States, and every other male person residing in the United States, who, on the day or days fixed for the first or any subsequent registration, is between the ages of eighteen and twenty-six, to present himself for and submit to registration at such time or times and place or places, and in such manner, as shall be determined by proclamation of the President and by rules and regulations prescribed hereunder. The provisions of this section shall not be applicable to any alien lawfully admitted to the United States as a nonimmigrant, for so long as he continues to maintain a lawful nonimmigrant status in the United States.

(b) Regulations prescribed pursuant to subsection (a) may require that persons presenting themselves for and submitting to registration under this section provide, as part of such registration, such identifying information (including date of birth, address, and social security account number) as such regulations may prescribe. [Author's Restatement: A person who registers with Selective Service must provide identification, including an address where he can be reached. If a registrant moves, he must always inform Selective Service of his change of address.]

Section 462. Offenses and penalties.

(a) Any member of the Selective Service System, or any other person charged with the duty of carrying out any of the provisions of this title, who knowingly fail[s] or neglect[s] to perform such duty [by falsifying registrations, counseling someone to evade registration, or interfering in any way with the implementation and enforcement of this act] shall, upon conviction in any district court of the United States of competent jurisdiction, be punished by imprisonment for not more than five years or a fine of not more than $10,000, or both. [If the person is] subject to military or naval law, [he or she] may be tried by court martial, and, on conviction, shall suffer such punishment as a court martial may direct. No person shall be tried by court martial unless [he or she] has been actually inducted [into the military].

(b) Any person who knowingly [prepares, possesses,] transfers or delivers to another, for the purpose of aiding or abetting the making of any false identification or representation, any registration certificate, alien's certificate of nonresidence, or any other certificate issued pursuant to or prescribed by the provisions of this title . . . [or] who knowingly violates or evades any of the provisions of this title or rules and regulations [created] pursuant thereto relating to the issuance, transfer, or possession of such certificate, shall, upon conviction, be fined not to exceed $10,000, or be imprisoned for not more than five years, or both. . . . Possession of a [false identification or certificate] shall be deemed sufficient evidence to establish an intent to use it for the purposes of false identification or representation, unless the defendant explains such possession to the satisfaction of the jury. [Author's Note: Under this act, it is illegal both to evade or lie about your selective service registration or to help someone else evade or lie about his registration.]

(c) The Department of Justice shall proceed as expeditiously as possible with a prosecution under this section, or with an appeal, upon the request of the Director of Selective Service System or shall advise the House of Representatives and the Senate in writing the reasons for its failure to do so.

(d) No person shall be prosecuted, tried, or punished for evading, neglecting, or refusing to perform the duty of registering unless the indictment is found within five years next after the last day before such person attains the age of twenty-six, or within five years next after the last day before such person does perform his duty to register, whichever shall first occur.

12

Uniform Drinking Age Act

1984

and Federal Zero Tolerance Law

1995

The passage of the Twenty-sixth Amendment in 1971 was in large part an effort to remove a double standard in this nation's treatment of its young people: young adults old enough to go to war were not eligible to vote. The unfairness of this double standard was only heightened by the fact that thousands of American soldiers had lost their lives in Vietnam. The political and social climate of the time demanded that this double standard be addressed, and it was.

In the wake of the Twenty-sixth Amendment, a number of states sought to remove additional double standards present in their laws. They argued that a person old enough to die in Vietnam and to vote for president should be considered old enough to consume alcohol. Thus, in the mid-1970s over half of the states lowered the drinking age, at least for wine and beer, from twenty-one to eighteen, nineteen, or twenty. (They also lowered the "age of adulthood" in other areas, such as criminal justice.) States that kept age twenty-one as the legal drinking age increasingly saw their young adults crossing state lines to purchase and consume alcohol in bordering states where it was legal to do so at a younger age.

As the decade of the 1970s gave way to the 1980s, sentiment about the lowered drinking age began to change, and new interest groups emerged to challenge teenage drinking. Chief among these groups was Mothers Against Drunk Driving (MADD), founded in 1980 by Candy Lightner, whose thirteen-year-old daughter had been killed by a drunk driver. MADD started in California, but grew quickly. In only two years MADD had one hundred chapters across the country. It organized local and then national campaigns aimed at moving the drinking age back up to twenty-one. In pursuit of this goal, MADD was helped by a number of studies showing that the recent lowering of the drinking age had increased the number of alcohol-related driving accidents and fatalities among young people.

The students of the 1960s who had protested for lowering the voting age were now in or near their thirties. Many had their own children; age and parenthood tended to make them less sympathetic to the causes of eighteen-year-olds that they once rallied behind. Indeed, by the mid-1980s the protests and calls for social action were emanating from very different sources, ones that believed the states' lowering of the drinking age had been a terrible mistake.

Congress addressed the issue in 1984, when it considered legislation to set a national drinking age. Given the constraints of federalism, Congress could not have simply demanded that the states follow a uniform, mandatory drinking age. The states, after all, had autonomy over their own laws, so long as those laws did not conflict with the U.S. Constitution. But Congress did have carrots to dangle in front of the states, and the particular carrot it chose in this instance was federal highway funds.

The Uniform Drinking Age Act proposed that all states set their minimum legal drinking age for alcohol (including wine, beer, and liquor) at twenty-one. States that did not comply faced losing 5 to 10 percent of their federal highway funds—monies the states used to build and repair roadways. These funds amounted to several million dollars per year per state. Through this act Congress sought to impose a new condition on the states for receipt of these funds: If the states wanted to continue receiving federal highway funds, they would have to comply with this new drinking age.

Congress held heated debates about the proposal. At first many senators and representatives felt that this kind of arm-twisting was a form of blackmail, a way to get around the constraints of federalism and to tell the states what to do. Others pointed out that the drinking age had been lowered precisely because the states were trying to remove a double standard and arrive at a consistent age for measuring adulthood. But, led by the untiring lobbying of MADD and faced with statistics that demonstrated the dangers associated with young adults' drinking and driving, Congress eventually passed the act with bipartisan support. President Ronald

Reagan, who had convened a presidential commission on drunk driving several months earlier, signed the bill into law on July 17, 1984.

South Dakota did not take the new law lightly. In fact, it sued the federal government because it believed the Uniform Drinking Age Act to be an unconstitutional infringement on the state's authority. The Supreme Court disagreed. In the case of *South Dakota v. Dole*, decided in 1987, the justices held by a vote of seven to two that Congress had properly exercised its constitutional spending power in linking federal highway funds to the raising of the drinking age. It determined that Congress had enacted a specific, lawful condition on this aid, and had justified this condition as necessary for the "general welfare," in that it sought to promote safe travel and reduce the dangers of alcohol-impaired driving. The Court observed that South Dakota was not forced to comply with the law; it could choose not to follow it, and the penalty for that choice would be the loss of a small percentage of its highway funds. Faced with the Supreme Court's decision, South Dakota eventually raised its drinking age to twenty-one. Today all fifty states observe this drinking age.

Some American young people continue to be offended by the fact that they can be forced to register for the draft, can serve in combat, can vote for president, and can be tried and sentenced as adults for certain crimes—but are still forbidden to drink alcohol. They have a point. Federal and state lawmakers have proven rather inconsistent in setting and maintaining the age of adulthood. As a result, young people in some states are tried, convicted, and sentenced as adults at age thirteen or fourteen; persons under age eighteen generally cannot make a binding contract; and persons under twenty-one can vote but cannot drink. The standards for adulthood simply are not uniform and likely never will be.

Nonetheless, student groups and youth advocacy organizations continue to fight to lower the drinking age. They try to organize young people to speak out and vote for legislation allowing alcohol consumption at age eighteen. At the same time, however, MADD, SADD (Students Against Destructive Decisions), RID (Remove Intoxicated Drivers) and similar organizations continue to push for limits on drunk driving and underage alcohol consumption and for stricter penalties for alcohol-related criminal offenses. In 1995, for example, these groups helped assure the passage of the Federal Zero Tolerance Law. The law, similar to the Uniform Drinking Age

Act, ties federal highway funds to the states' adoption of zero tolerance (that is, no measurable alcohol in the bloodstream) for drivers under age twenty-one. In its current campaign MADD is lobbying the states to lower their legal standard for intoxication from a blood alcohol level of .1 milligrams percent to a blood alcohol level of .08 milligrams percent.

MADD currently boasts a membership of over two million people in six hundred chapters. It also has a number of major corporate sponsors and partners. Until student and youth groups can organize, participate, and vote like MADD, the drinking age will almost certainly remain twenty-one, and the punishments for the abuse of this standard will continue to increase.

12.a Uniform Drinking Age Act

Section 158. National Minimum Drinking Age.

(a) Withholding of Funds for Noncompliance.

(1) In general. The Secretary shall withhold 10 per centum of the amount required to be apportioned to any State under this title on the first day of each fiscal year after the second fiscal year beginning after September 30, 1985, in which the purchase or public possession in such State of any alcoholic beverage by a person who is less than twenty-one years of age is lawful.

(b) Effect of Withholding of Funds. No funds withheld under this section from apportionment to any State after September 30, 1988, shall be available for apportionment to that State.

(c) Alcoholic Beverage Defined. As used in this section, the term "alcoholic beverage" means:

(1) beer as defined in section 5052(a) of the Internal Revenue Code of 1986, (2) wine of not less than one-half of 1 per centum of alcohol by volume, or (3) distilled spirits as defined in section 5002(a)(8) of such Code.

[Author's Note: The Department of Transportation has issued regulations precisely defining alcoholic beverages. The pertinent part from the Code of Federal Regulations provides:]

TITLE 23

Section 1208.3. Definitions.

As used in this part:

"Alcoholic beverage" means beer, distilled spirits and wine containing one-half of one percent or more of alcohol by volume. Beer includes, but is not limited to, ale, lager, porter, stout, sake, and other similar fermented beverages brewed or produced from malt, wholly or in part or from any substitute therefore. "Distilled spirits" include alcohol, ethanol or spirits or wine in any form, including all dilutions and mixtures thereof from whatever process produced. "Public possession" means the possession of any alcoholic beverage for any reason, including consumption on any street or highway or in any public place or in any place open to the public (including a club which is de facto open to the public). The term does not apply to the possession of alcohol for an established religious purpose; when accompanied by a parent, spouse or legal guardian age 21 or older; for medical purposes when prescribed or administered by a licensed physician, pharmacist, dentist, nurse, hospital or medical institution; in private clubs or establishments; or to the sale, handling, transport, or service in dispensing of any alcoholic beverage pursuant to lawful employment of a person under the age of twenty-one years by a duly licensed manufacturer, wholesaler, or retailer of alcoholic beverages. "Purchase" means to acquire by the payment of money or other consideration.

12b. Federal Zero Tolerance Law

Section 161. Operation of Motor Vehicles by Intoxicated Minors.
(a) Withholding of Apportionments for Noncompliance.

(1) Fiscal year 1999. The Secretary shall withhold 5 percent of the amount required to be apportioned to any State ... on October 1, 1998, if the State does not meet the [zero tolerance] requirement[s] [by] that date.

(2) Thereafter. The Secretary shall withhold 10 percent of the amount required to be apportioned to any State [if it does not comply by] on October 1, 1999, and on October 1 of each fiscal year thereafter, if the State does not meet the requirement of paragraph (3) on that date.

(3) Requirement. A State meets the requirement of this paragraph if the State has enacted and is enforcing a law that considers an individual under the age of 21 who has a blood alcohol concentration of 0.02 percent or greater while operating a motor vehicle in the State to be driving while intoxicated or driving under the influence of alcohol.
(b) Period of Availability; Effect of Compliance and Noncompliance.

(1) Period of availability of withheld funds.

(A) Funds withheld on or before September 30, 2000. Any funds withheld under subsection (a) from apportionment to any State on or before September 30, 2000, shall remain available until the end of the third fiscal year following the fiscal year for which the funds are authorized to be appropriated.

(B) Funds withheld after September 30, 2000. No funds withheld under this section from apportionment to any State after September 30, 2000, shall be available for apportionment to the State.

(2) Apportionment of withheld funds after compliance. If, before the last day of the period for which funds [are] withheld, the State meets [its] requirement[s], the Secretary shall, on the first day on which the State meets the requirement, apportion to the State the funds withheld under subsection (a) that remain available for apportionment to the State. [Author's Restatement: If a state has been denied funds, but promptly changes its law to comply with this act, the funds will be reinstated.]

(3) Period of availability of subsequently apportioned funds. Any funds apportioned pursuant to paragraph (2) shall remain available for expenditure until the end of the third fiscal year following the fiscal year in which the funds are so apportioned. Sums not obligated at the end of that period shall lapse. [Author's Note: But if the state does not act in a timely manner, it risks losing these funds.]

(4) Effect of noncompliance. If, at the end of the period for which funds are available for apportionment, the State does not meet [its] requirements, the funds shall lapse.

13

Fair Housing Act Amendments

1988

Imagine a time when a landlord could advertise an apartment for rent to "Christians Only." Or when a real estate agent would refuse to show homes in a white neighborhood to African-American clients. Or even when an entire apartment complex was off limits to families with children. These discriminatory practices, once commonplace in America, have been significantly reduced by the passage of the Fair Housing Act and particularly by the Fair Housing Act Amendments of 1988. All of the above practices are now illegal, and persons who undertake them face severe penalties.

The mid- to late-1960s was the heyday of new federal civil rights legislation. In 1965 Congress passed the Voting Rights Act, affording additional federal protections to disfranchised Americans. In 1964 it passed the Civil Rights Act, making many forms of discrimination illegal. The Civil Rights Act, perhaps the most significant piece of civil rights legislation ever passed by Congress, has been amended and reenacted over the years. As part of the 1968 Civil Rights Act, Congress included Title VIII, the Fair Housing Act.

The original Fair Housing Act was passed with great difficulty. Many citizens, and legislators as well, perceived the act as excessive interference in their personal lives and business decisions. Members of real estate industry, including landowners, landlords, and real estate brokers and agents, were certainly not used to the federal government telling them to whom they must sell or rent properties. Often, however, their practices were based on racial and cultural stereotypes that were becoming increasingly unacceptable and that had, in fact, been made illegal in other contexts by earlier federal and state civil rights legislation.

Nevertheless, it was a tough battle to pass the act. Proponents of individual autonomy, privacy, and the right to private property opposed the measure. Sympathetic members of Congress sought to defeat or delay the act, using tactics such as the filibuster, where a senator begins speaking to the chamber and refuses to relinquish the microphone for hours or perhaps even days. In order to ensure passage of some bill outlawing housing discrimination, the Congress finally decided upon a compromise measure. The original Fair Housing Act prohibited discrimination in the sale or rental of housing on the grounds of a person's race, color, religion, or national origin.

But a law is often only as good as its enforcement mechanism, and in this case the Fair Housing Act's enforcement provisions proved very weak. Although strong federal enforcement provisions had been proposed, they were removed from the bill to ensure its passage. In the end the Department of Housing and Urban Development (HUD) was empowered to investigate violations of the act and to seek settlement of disputes. If a settlement could not be reached, HUD action ended, and the person discriminated against was left to file his or her own lawsuit. Of course, most people who had been improperly denied housing were in no position to pursue legal action, which is both costly and time-consuming. Eventually, buyers and renters realized that, although the law protected them, they were pretty much on their own against its violators.

The act had other important compromises as well. For example, it exempted certain classes of property owners. Exemptions were granted to persons selling their own homes, persons renting to someone who would share their home, and landlords with buildings of four units or fewer who lived in one of those units. These exemptions were made largely because of the belief that an individual should retain the right to determine with whom he or she lives. Additional exemptions were granted to religious institutions; they similarly were not forced to make their religious housing available to nonmembers.

The Fair Housing Act, in its original form, proved a good but largely unenforceable idea. Over the next twenty years property owners and rental management companies continued blatantly and routinely to discriminate against persons of various classes. In fact, the discrimination expanded to include two groups that had not been covered by the act, children and the disabled. Families with children were finding it increasingly difficult to obtain suitable rental housing, as many apartment and condominium complexes were run as "adult only" establishments. The disabled, too, found it difficult to pursue their hopes for independent living, because of inaccessible housing and the skepticism of property owners.

By 1988 it was clear that something needed to be done to bolster the Fair Housing Act. This time, however, there was widespread bipartisan support in Congress for amending the law to make it tougher. The amendments passed both houses of Congress by a landslide, with a vote of 367 to 23 in the House and 94 to 3 in the Senate. President Reagan signed what was effectively a brand new Fair Housing Act into law on September 13, 1988.

The previous version of the law prohibited housing discrimination on the basis of race, color, religion, national origin, and gender (which had been added to the list through an earlier amendment). Two new categories were added to these: familial status and disability. "Familial status" includes parents or legal guardians with children eighteen or younger, people seeking custody of children eighteen or younger, and pregnant women. Under the act it is illegal for a person to refuse to rent or sell housing to anyone on the basis of the above characteristics; lie about the availability or suitability of housing; hold any person to different standards, or impose different conditions on anyone in the sale or rental of housing; refuse to make a mortgage loan or impose new or different terms for such a loan; or segregate someone by directing them to a particular building in an apartment complex or to a particular neighborhood of single-family homes.

In addition, Congress made it illegal to advertise housing in a discriminatory manner (no more "adults only" classified ads) and to threaten or intimidate individuals seeking their fair housing rights or pursuing a violation of those rights.

The original exemptions remained in place, and one important one was added. Congress created an exemption for senior citizen housing, by providing that children could be excluded from any federal or state housing program for the elderly, from housing explicitly designated for persons age sixty-two and older, and from facilities such as "retirement communities" that are at least 80 percent occupied by persons age fifty-five or older. Such communities must allow federal inspection and cooperate with federal authorities to ensure that they maintain their character as senior communities.

The amendments clearly signaled that the federal government was going to get tough on those who practiced housing discrimination. The amendments include powerful new enforcement mechanisms for HUD, the Attorney General's Office, and for private litigants. The Act encourages persons who have been discriminated against to file a complaint with HUD, which is required by the act to investigate it quickly. If discrimination is found HUD will seek to settle the matter among the parties in a process called "conciliation." If the matter does not settle, the complaint will be adjudicated by either a HUD administrative law judge (ALJ) or litigated in court by the Attorney General's Office. Whether an ALJ or a court is used is up to the parties; either the complainant or the respondent can choose to move the complaint to court. In addition, if the complainant wishes to file a private lawsuit, he or she may do so within two years of the alleged violation. (Often, matters that involve state programs or violations of state housing laws will be referred to state housing agencies and state courts for resolution.)

Both the ALJ and the court can award substantial damages if a violation is proved. The person who was discriminated against can receive compensatory damages (out-of-pocket expenses), pain and suffering damages, and reasonable attorneys' fees. The court can award punitive damages as well. In addition, a violator is subject to civil penalties by the government ranging from $10,000 for a first offense to $50,000 for a repeat offender. And, if someone threatens or coerces a person seeking fair housing rights, recent new amendments to the act subject the offender to penalties up to $100,000 and even to criminal prosecution.

In short, the Fair Housing Act is now very tough, and those who ignore it do so at their peril. Nevertheless, housing discrimination continues to exist, although it now takes subtler forms. For example, some landlords try to prohibit children by claiming that the family is too large for a particular rental unit. Others might try to charge parents a larger security deposit because they have children or might make certain facilities of an apartment complex "off limits" to children. Still others require that children be continually supervised on the premises. Another common tactic is to limit families with children to particular buildings in a complex or, for example, to basement apartments only. All of these practices are discriminatory or at least, depending on circumstances, strongly suggest a violation of the Fair Housing Act. (Incidentally, the federal courts have held that a rule of two persons per bedroom is the presumptive minimum; therefore, for example, if a single mother with three children is told that a two bedroom apartment is too small for her family, the landlord may very well be in violation of the Fair Housing Act.)

The Fair Housing Act offers powerful protection for families with children and for young adults as well who have or who are about to have their own children. If you suspect that either you or your family has been discriminated against under the act, Congress has provided many tools to investigate, negotiate, and if necessary, adjudicate your claim. The message from Congress could not be more clear: fair housing is a right, and Americans should insist upon it.

13. Fair Housing Act Amendments

Section 3601. Declaration of policy.

It is the policy of the United States to provide, within constitutional limitations, for fair housing throughout the United States.

Section 3602. Definitions.

As used in this subchapter:

(b) "Dwelling" means any building, structure, or portion thereof which is occupied as, or designed or intended for occupancy as, a residence by one or more families, and any vacant land which is offered for sale or lease for the construction or location thereon of any such building, structure, or portion thereof.

(c) "Family" includes a single individual.

(e) "To rent" includes to lease, to sublease, to let and otherwise to grant for a consideration the right to occupy premises not owned by the occupant.

(f) "Discriminatory housing practice" means an act that is unlawful under section 3604, 3605, 3606, or 3617 of this title [described below].

(k) "Familial status" means one or more individuals (who have not attained the age of 18 years) being domiciled [living] with (1) a parent or another person having legal custody of such individual or individuals; or (2) the designee of such parent or other person having such custody, with the written permission of such parent or other person. The protections afforded against discrimination on the basis of familial status shall apply to any person who is pregnant or is in the process of securing legal custody of any individual who has not attained the age of 18 years.

Section 3603. Effective dates of certain prohibitions.

(a) Application to certain described dwellings. The prohibitions against discrimination in the sale or rental of housing [now apply to all types of housing, except the following:]

(b) Exemptions. [The following types of housing are exempt from this title]:

(1) any single-family house sold or rented by an owner, provided that such private individual owner does not own more than three such single-family houses at any one time. [The owner's houses are exempt] only if such [houses are] sold or rented without the use in any manner [of real estate brokers, agents, or other such professionals].

(2) rooms or units in dwellings containing living quarters occupied or intended to be occupied by no more than four families living independently of each other, if the owner actually maintains and occupies one of such living quarters as his residence.

Section 3604. Discrimination in the sale or rental of housing and other prohibited practices.

[Unless otherwise noted in this law,] it shall be unlawful:

(a) To refuse to sell or rent after the making of a bona fide offer, or to refuse to negotiate for the sale or rental of, or otherwise make unavailable or deny, a dwelling to any person because of race, color, religion, sex, familial status, or national origin.

(b) To discriminate against any person in the terms, conditions, or privileges of sale or rental of a dwelling, or in the provision of services or facilities in connection therewith, because of race, color, religion, sex, familial status, or national origin.

(c) To make, print, or publish, or cause to be made, printed, or published any notice, statement, or advertisement, with respect to the sale or rental of a dwelling that indicates any preference, limitation, or discrimination based on race, color, religion, sex, handicap, familial status, or national origin, or an intention to make any such preference, limitation, or discrimination.

(d) To represent to any person because of race, color, religion, sex, handicap, familial status, or national origin that any dwelling is not available for inspection, sale, or rental when such dwelling is in fact so available.

(e) For profit, to induce or attempt to induce any person to sell or rent any dwelling by representations regarding the entry or prospective entry into the neighborhood of a person or persons of a particular race, color, religion, sex, handicap, familial status, or national origin. [Author's Note: For example, an apartment rental agent who charges a fee for that service cannot suggest that a landlord rent to a prospective tenant because of that tenant's race.]

(f)(1) To discriminate in the sale or rental, or to otherwise make unavailable or deny, a dwelling to any buyer or renter because of a handicap. . . .

(3) For purposes of this subsection, discrimination includes:

(A) a refusal to permit, at the expense of the handicapped person, reasonable modifications of existing premises occupied or to be occupied by such person if such modifications may be necessary to afford such person full enjoyment of the premises. . . .

(B) a refusal to make reasonable accommodations in rules, policies, practices, or services, when such accommodations may be necessary to afford such person equal opportunity to use and enjoy a dwelling; or

(C) in connection with the design and construction of covered multifamily dwellings [such as apartment complexes] for first occupancy after [March 13, 1991], a failure to design and construct those dwellings in such a manner that [is accessible to the disabled].

Section 3605. Discrimination in residential real estate-related transactions.

(a) In general. It shall be unlawful for any person or other entity whose business includes engaging in residential real estate-related transactions to discriminate against any person in making available such a transaction, or in the terms or conditions of such a transaction, because of race, color, religion, sex, handicap, familial status, or national origin.

(b) "Residential real estate-related transaction" [includes the] . . . making or purchasing of loans or providing other financial assistance . . . for purchasing, constructing, improving, repairing, or maintaining a dwelling; or . . . the selling, brokering, or appraising of residential real property.

Section 3607. Religious organization or private club exemption.

(a) Nothing in this subchapter shall prohibit a religious organization, association, or society, or any nonprofit institution or organization operated, supervised or controlled by or in conjunction with a religious organization, association, or society, from limiting the sale, rental or occupancy of dwellings which it owns or operates for other than a commercial purpose to persons of the same religion, or from giving preference to such persons, unless membership in such religion is restricted on account of race, color, or national origin. [Author's Restatement: Religious organizations are exempt from the provisions of this act so long as they are not engaged in commercial real estate activities and do not discriminate on the basis of race, color, or national origin.] Nor shall anything in this subchapter prohibit a private club not in fact open to the public, which as an incident to its primary purpose or purposes provides lodgings which it owns or operates for other than a commercial purpose, from limiting the rental or occupancy of such lodgings to its members or from giving preference to its members. [Author's Note: Similarly, a private club, such as a members-only golf club, is also exempt. Congress created these exceptions to the Fair Housing Act because of the widespread belief that religious and private groups should be able to determine their membership and limit use of their facilities to members. The Constitution can be read to support these exemptions, in that it provides for the free exercise of religion and for the right to privacy.]

(b)(1) Nothing in this subchapter limits the applicability of any reasonable local, State, or Federal restrictions regarding the maximum number of occupants permitted to occupy a dwelling. Nor does any provision in this subchapter regarding familial status apply with respect to housing for older persons.

(2) As used in this section, "housing for older persons" means housing:

(A) provided under any State or Federal program that the Secretary [of Housing and Urban Development] determines is specifically designed and operated to assist elderly persons (as defined in the State or Federal program); or (B) intended for, and solely occupied by, persons 62 years of age or older; or (C) intended and operated for occupancy by persons 55 years of age or older, and (i) at least 80 percent of the occupied units are occupied by at least one person who is 55 years of age or older; (ii) the housing facility or community publishes and adheres to policies and procedures that demonstrate the intent required under this subparagraph; and (iii) the housing facility or community complies with rules issued by the Secretary for verification of occupancy [by older persons]. . . . [Author's Note: Again, Congress created an exemption for housing complexes for the elderly. Congress was politically motivated to create this exception—senior citizens, and particularly the members of the American Association of Retired Persons (AARP) are dependable voters and a powerful political force.]

Section 3610. Administrative enforcement; preliminary matters.

(a) Complaints and answers.

(1)(A)(i) An aggrieved person may, not later than one year after an alleged discriminatory housing practice has occurred or terminated, file a complaint with the Secretary alleging such discriminatory housing practice. The Secretary, on the Secretary's own initiative, may also file such a complaint.

   (iv) the Secretary shall make an investigation of the alleged discriminatory housing practice and complete such investigation within 100 days after the filing of the complaint, unless it is impracticable to do so.

(b) Investigative report and conciliation.

   (1) During the period beginning with the filing of such complaint and ending with the filing of a charge or a dismissal by the Secretary, the Secretary shall, to the extent feasible, engage in conciliation [settlement pursuant to written agreement] with respect to such complaint.

   (5) (A) At the end of each investigation under this section, the Secretary shall prepare a final investigative report. . . .

(c) Failure to comply with conciliation agreement. Whenever the Secretary has reasonable cause to believe that a respondent has breached a conciliation agreement, the Secretary shall refer the matter to the Attorney General with a recommendation that a civil action be filed . . . for the enforcement of such agreement.

Section 3612. Enforcement by Secretary.

(a) Election of judicial determination. When a charge [of housing discrimination] is filed, a complainant, a respondent, or an aggrieved person on whose behalf the complaint was filed, may [choose] to have the claims asserted in that charge decided in a civil [lawsuit] [or by an administrative law judge. In either case, the proceeding shall include all the protections afforded in a typical lawsuit, such as the right to attorney, the right to present evidence, and the right to present and cross-examine witnesses].

(g) Hearings, findings and conclusions, order. [Subparts (1) and (2) set forth a time table for hearings and deciding these claims.]

   (3) If the administrative law judge finds that a respondent has engaged or is about to engage in a discriminatory housing practice, [the judge] shall promptly issue an order for such relief as may be appropriate, which may include actual damages [money to reimburse and compensate the victim] suffered by the aggrieved person and injunctive or other equitable relief [including, for example, an order to stop a discriminatory practice]. [The administrative law judge may also award attorneys fees to the prevailing party.] Such order may, to vindicate the public interest, assess a civil penalty against the respondent:

   (A) in an amount not exceeding $10,000 [for a first offense]; (B) in an amount not exceeding $25,000 if the respondent has [had a prior discriminatory housing offense within the last five years]; or

(C) in an amount not exceeding $50,000 if the respondent [committed two or more such offenses within the last seven years];

(o) Civil action for enforcement when election is made for such civil action.

(3) [Similarly,] in a civil action under this subsection, if the court finds that a discriminatory housing practice has occurred or is about to occur, the court may grant any relief [as provided in the section below, which essentially includes all typical types of relief].

Section 3613. Enforcement by private persons.

(a) Civil action.

(1)(A) An aggrieved person may commence a civil action in an appropriate United States district court or State court not later than 2 years after the occurrence or the termination of an alleged discriminatory housing practice, or the breach of a conciliation agreement. . . .

(b) Appointment of attorney by court.

Upon application by a person alleging a discriminatory housing practice or a person against whom such a practice is alleged, the court may appoint an attorney for such person and may waive the payment of fees, costs, or security, if in the opinion of the court such person is financially unable to bear the costs of such action.

(c) Relief which may be granted.

(1) . . . [I]f the court finds that a discriminatory housing practice has occurred or is about to occur, the court may award to the plaintiff actual and punitive damages, and . . . may grant as relief, as the court deems appropriate, any permanent or temporary injunction, temporary restraining order, or other order (including an order enjoining the defendant from engaging in such practice or ordering such affirmative action as may be appropriate). [Author's Note: "Punitive" damages are money damages levied against the violator in an effort to punish his or her bad behavior and to try to ensure that the behavior is not repeated. An "injunction" is an order given by the court to do a certain act or to refrain from doing a certain act.]

Section 3614. Enforcement by Attorney General.

(a) Pattern or practice cases. Whenever the Attorney General has reasonable cause to believe that any person or group of persons is engaged in a pattern or practice [to resist complying with this act], or that any group of persons has been denied any of the rights granted by this [act] and such denial raises an issue of general public importance, the Attorney General may commence a civil action in any appropriate United States district court. (b) [The Attorney General may also commence a civil action] [o]n referral [by the Secretary] of discriminatory housing practice or conciliation agreement for enforcement.

(d) Relief which may be granted in civil actions under subsections (a) and (b) [above]:

> (1) In a civil action under subsection (a) or (b) of this section, the court (A) may award such preventive relief, including a permanent or temporary injunction, restraining order, or other order against the [violator] as is necessary to assure the full enjoyment of [fair housing] rights; (B) may award such other relief as the court deems appropriate, including monetary damages to persons aggrieved; and (C) may, to vindicate the public interest, assess a civil penalty against the respondent in an amount not exceeding $50,000, for a first violation; and in an amount not exceeding $100,000, for any subsequent violation.

Section 3617. Interference, coercion, or intimidation.

It shall be unlawful to coerce, intimidate, threaten, or interfere with any person in the exercise or enjoyment of, or on account of his having exercised or enjoyed, or on account of his having aided or encouraged any other person in the exercise or enjoyment of, any right granted or protected by [this law].

PART III

EDUCATION LAWS

14

Head Start

1965

Lately Head Start has been a program with an identity crisis. Despite the fact that it has been around for nearly four decades and has served millions of America's underprivileged pre-school children, politicians continue to debate whether Head Start is, or should be, primarily a health program or primarily an education program.

The answer is that it is both. Head Start is the largest and most comprehensive program ever devised by the federal government to ensure the health and well-being of this nation's youngest citizens. It takes a multi-faceted approach to ensuring their proper development. Components of the program include providing medical and dental care, providing nutritional meals, developing social skills, offering psychological counseling, developing children's basic learning skills, and working closely with parents to ensure that their children thrive.

The key belief behind the program is that a healthy, well-balanced child will be better equipped to learn. Many poor children go without the basic necessities for a healthy and happy start to life. Consequently, Head Start aims to provide whatever it is that a young child needs to be well prepared for school. There is no one approach to creating a successful child; indeed, because Head Start is locally administered, different providers may take different approaches, within the guidelines set by Congress, toward early childhood development. The local focus of Head Start helps to ensure that the individual needs of the child within his or her family and community are met.

Head Start was not the brainchild of Congress. Credit for the development of this program goes to President Lyndon B. Johnson and his personal advisor Sargent Shriver, the first director of the Peace Corps and the brother-in-law of President John F. Kennedy. (Today's young readers probably know Sargent Shriver as the Chairman of the Special Olympics, which his wife Eunice Kennedy Shriver founded in 1968. The Shrivers are also the parents of NBC news correspondent Maria Shriver Schwarzenegger.) As part of his Great Society plans, Johnson announced his belief that America should fight a "War on Poverty." Johnson appointed Shriver to be the commander of this war and to develop legislation to assist America's underprivileged.

The first major piece of legislation in the War on Poverty was the Economic Opportunity Act (1964), which created the Office of Economic Opportunity. This office, headed by Shriver, gave federal grants to low-income communities. Shortly after its inception, Shriver considered what could be done specifically to help children in these communities. He asked his friend pediatrician Dr. Robert Cooke of Johns Hopkins University to help him develop a program. They formed a committee to investigate what type of program was needed and to determine how it should be structured and implemented. Included on the committee was Professor Edward Zigler, a renowned scholar of psychology and child development at Yale (who would later write a book about his experiences, noted in this book's bibliography). Another person who actively helped to champion this effort was Ladybird Johnson, the president's wife.

By early 1965 a pilot program was beginning to take shape. With congressional funding, it was implemented in the summer of 1965. The eight-week program served over one-half million American children. It was judged a success, and in 1966 Congress amended the Economic Opportunity Act to provide for a permanent Head Start Program, to be administered by Shriver's Office of Economic Opportunity. In 1969 the program was moved to the Department of Health, Education, and Welfare, which is a cabinet-level department. This Department is now called the Department of Health and Human Services, and it remains responsible for implementing and overseeing the program.

As was the case with much of the Great Society legislation, the first Head Start program legislation passed Congress with relative ease. The nation, still reeling from the death of President Kennedy, placed a lot of faith in President Johnson and the Democratic-controlled Congress. The nation seemed ready to embrace legislation aimed at fixing its flaws, including laws for civil and voting rights, equal employment and housing rights, and better educational opportunities for children and college students alike. Some estimates place the total number of Great Society laws passed during Johnson's four years in office at over one thousand. Many programs created at that time still exist and have grown significantly in size and popularity over the years, including Head Start.

Head Start is run by individual providers called "delegate agencies." These private or public agencies are all community-based and can include schools, universities, social welfare agencies, and even medical clinics. The federal government covers 80 percent of a provider's costs; each provider must match government funding by raising the remaining 20 percent. Agencies are authorized and approved by the Department of Health and Human Services and must follow the guidelines set by Congress in the Head Start Act and by the department in its regulations. The guidelines often are rather broad, indicating the types of services to be provided, but allowing for site-specific program and curriculum development that can be geared toward local needs.

Head Start is targeted to the nation's poorest children, those falling below the poverty line (although a small percentage of families above the poverty line also participate). Most children involved in the program are age three to five. In 1995, however, Congress created a supplement to Head Start called "Early Head Start," which targets infants and toddlers from birth through age two. Head Start does not require families to pay for enrollment in the program. (Families that can afford to pay for the program may do so.) Moreover, in keeping with the goals of the Individuals with Disabilities Education Act (discussed later in this book), Head Start has been recently directed to enroll a greater percentage of disabled children.

With regard to education, the Head Start Act requires measurable results. The Act specifies some of the skills that Head Start children should learn, including the ability to "know that letters of the alphabet are a special category of visual graphics that can be individually named; recognize a word as a unit of print; identify at least 10 letters of the alphabet; and associate sounds with written words." Other standards have been developed in coordination with the Department of Health and Human Services. Head Start Program Performance Standards, covering the program in general, were first adopted into law in 1975. They continue to be revised as expectations for the program change.

One of the most important goals of the Head Start Program is family participation. Head Start program agencies are required to involve parents intimately with their undertakings and, in fact, to provide services to parents, not just children. The agencies should offer parenting training and counseling, for example. They should also place parents in contact with other social service agencies that might be of help to the family and should assist parents with job placement. Congress has also mandated that the agencies provide transitional assistance to students and their parents as the children leave Head Start to enter elementary school. To this end, Head Start providers must work with school officials and parents to ensure that children are well prepared for and well adjusted to school life.

Over the years Head Start has proven to have bipartisan support. The program was expanded significantly during the Carter, Bush (Sr.), and Clinton administrations. During President Clinton's tenure in office, the funding for Head Start nearly doubled. Over ten million children have been served by the program since its inception. President Clinton wanted to increase the reach of the program to serve at least one million children per year, but this goal remains elusive. Indeed, many eligible children have not yet been able to take advantage of Head Start.

Despite its popularity, Head Start continues to have its share of sharp critics. As the program has matured, it has been subjected to scrutiny from members of Congress, educators, and taxpayers who want to ensure that the significant sums of money directed to Head Start are well spent. The basic question most often asked is: Does Head Start work? People want to know the specific advantages children gain from participation in the program and if it really prepares underprivileged children to succeed in school.

The answers to these questions are not conclusive, at least not yet. Many studies indicate the effectiveness of Head Start, and proponents of the program remain extremely loyal and dedicated to it. Opponents point to studies that suggest that, even if Head Start provides initial benefits to young children to prepare them for school, those benefits are erased by the time a student reaches middle or high school. Worried that program funds are not being well spent, opponents contend that Head Start has become a sacred cow of sorts, and has escaped close political and financial scrutiny because so many elected officials find it politically beneficial to support the program.

Part of the problem in determining Head Start's efficacy is in agreeing on what to measure. That's where the program's identity crisis becomes significant. To the extent that Head Start is a health, welfare, and early childhood socialization program, it seems unfair to judge it on the basis of future student academic performance. But the program clearly has an educational component, too, and this can and should be measured.

To solve this dilemma, in the last reauthorization of Head Start the Congress appropriated several million dollars to study the program's efficacy. It called for the creation of an independent panel of experts in program evaluation, education, and early childhood development to conduct research on several questions, including: Does Head Start "enhance the growth and development of children in cognitive, emotional, and physical health areas?" Does it "strengthen families as the primary nurturers of children?" Does it "ensure that children attain school readiness?" The researchers are required to compare Head Start children to those who have not gone through the program. Virtually all aspects of the program will be comprehensively reviewed, and the findings will be reported to Congress.

The current reauthorization of Head Start, passed in 1998, continues through fiscal year 2003. At that time Congress will have received the results of its independent research and will vote on whether and to what extent the Head Start Program deserves to be funded. Those interested in the future of Head Start should probably make their voices heard now, as Congress will begin considering the next reauthorization well in advance of that date.

14. Head Start

Section 9831. Statement of purpose.

It is the purpose of this subchapter to promote school readiness by enhancing the social and cognitive development of low-income children through the provision, to low-income children and their families, of health, educational, nutritional, social, and other services that are determined, based on family needs assessments, to be necessary.

Section 9832. Definitions.

For purposes of this subchapter:

(2) The term "delegate agency" means a public, private nonprofit, or for-profit organization or agency to which a grantee has delegated all or part of the responsibility of the grantee for operating a Head Start program.

(3) The term "family literacy services" means services that are of sufficient intensity in terms of hours, and of sufficient duration, to make sustainable changes in a family, and that integrate all of the following activities: interactive literacy activities between parents and their children; training for parents regarding how to be the primary teacher for their children and full partners in the education of their children; parent literacy training that leads to economic self-sufficiency; an age-appropriate education to prepare children for success in school and life experiences.

(7) The term "Head Start classroom" means a group of children supervised and taught by two paid staff members (a teacher and a teacher's aide or two teachers) and, where possible, a volunteer.

(11) The term "local educational agency" has the meaning given such term in the Elementary and Secondary Education Act of 1965.

Section 9833. Financial assistance for Head Start programs.

The Secretary may provide financial assistance to [an eligible Head Start] agency for the planning, conduct, administration, and evaluation of a Head Start program focused primarily upon children from low-income families who have not reached the age of compulsory school attendance which (1) will provide such comprehensive health, education, parental involvement, nutritional, social, and other services as will enable the children to attain their full potential and attain school readiness; and (2) will provide for direct participation of the parents of such children in the development, conduct, and overall program direction at the local level.

Section 9834. Authorization of appropriations.

(a) There are authorized to be appropriated for carrying out the provisions of this subchapter such sums as may be necessary for fiscal years 1999 through 2003.

(b) From the amount appropriated, the Secretary shall make available: (1) for each of fiscal years 1999 through 2003 to carry out [Head Start Program] activities, not more than $35,000,000 but not less than the amount that was made available for such activities for fiscal year 1998; (2) not more than $5,000,000 for each of fiscal years 1999 through 2003 to carry out impact studies; and (3) not more than $12,000,000 for fiscal year 1999, and such sums as may be necessary for each of fiscal years 2000 through 2003, to carry out other research, demonstration, and evaluation activities, including longitudinal studies. . . .

Section 9835. Allotment of funds.

[This lengthy section contains rather specific instructions to the Secretary of Health and Human Services on how to allocate Head Start funds. It concludes by noting that the federal share of Head Start costs] shall not exceed 80 percent of the approved costs of the assisted program or activities, except that the Secretary may approve assistance in excess of such percentage if the Secretary determines that such action is required [to further] the purposes of this [law]. [The section goes on to provide that:]

(d) Enrollment of children with disabilities and provision of services. The Secretary shall establish policies and procedures designed to assure that for fiscal year 1999 and thereafter no less than 10 percent of the total number of enrollment opportunities in Head Start programs in each State shall be available for children with disabilities and that services shall be provided to meet their special needs.

(e) Distribution of benefits between residents of rural and urban areas. The Secretary shall adopt appropriate administrative measures to assure that the benefits of this subchapter will be distributed equitably between residents of rural and urban areas.

(f) Guidelines for local service delivery models. The Secretary shall establish procedures to enable Head Start agencies to develop locally designed or specialized service delivery models to address local community needs.

Section 9836. Designation of Head Start agencies.

(a) Authorization; prerequisites. The Secretary is authorized to designate as a Head Start agency any local public or private nonprofit or for-profit agency, within a community, which (1) has the power and authority to carry out the purposes of this subchapter and perform the [required] functions within [its] community; and (2) is determined by the Secretary (in consultation with the chief executive officer of the State involved, if such State expends non-Federal funds to carry out Head Start programs) to be capable of planning, conducting, administering, and evaluating, either directly or by other arrangements, a Head Start program.

(b) Definition. For purposes of this subchapter, a community may be a city, county, or multi-city or multi-county unit within a State, an Indian reservation (including Indians in any off-reservation area designated by an appropriate tribal government in consultation with the Secretary), or a neighborhood or other area (irrespective of boundaries or political subdivisions) which provides a suitable organizational base and possesses the commonality of interest needed to operate a Head Start program.

Section 9836a. Quality standards; monitoring of Head Start agencies and programs.

(a) Quality standards.

(1) Establishment of standards. The Secretary shall establish by regulation standards, including minimum levels of overall accomplishment, applicable to Head Start agencies, programs, and projects under this subchapter, including:

(A) performance standards with respect to services required to be provided, including health, parental involvement, nutritional, social, transition activities described [below], and other services;

(B)(i) education performance standards to ensure the school readiness of children participating in a Head Start program, on completion of the Head Start program and prior to entering school; and

(ii) additional education performance standards to ensure that the children participating in the program, at a minimum, develop phonemic, print, and numeracy awareness; understand and use language to communicate for various purposes; understand and use increasingly complex and varied vocabulary; develop and demonstrate an appreciation of books; and [for non-English speaking children], progress toward acquisition of the English language.

(2) Considerations in developing standards. In developing the regulations required [above], Secretary shall consult with experts in the fields of child development, early childhood education, child health care, family services (including linguistically and culturally appropriate services to non-English language background children and their families), administration, and financial management, and with persons with experience in the operation of Head Start programs. . . .

(b) Results-based performance measures.

(1) In general. The Secretary, in consultation with representatives of Head Start agencies and with experts in the fields of early childhood education and development, family services, and program management, shall develop methods and procedures for measuring, annually and over longer periods, the quality and effectiveness of programs operated by Head Start agencies, and the impact of the services provided through the programs to children and their families.

(4) Educational performance measures. Such results-based performance measures shall include educational performance measures that ensure that children participating in Head Start programs: know that

letters of the alphabet are a special category of visual graphics that can be individually named; recognize a word as a unit of print; identify at least 10 letters of the alphabet; and associate sounds with written words.

(5) Additional local results-based performance measures. In addition to other applicable results-based performance measures, Head Start agencies may establish local results-based educational performance measures.

Section 9837. Powers and functions of Head Start agencies.

(b) Participation of parents in decisionmaking, implementation, etc. A Head Start agency shall:

(1) establish effective procedures by which parents and area residents concerned will be enabled to directly participate in decisions that influence the character of programs affecting their interests;

(2) provide for their regular participation in the implementation of such programs;

(3) provide technical and other support needed to enable parents and area residents to secure on their own behalf available assistance from public and private sources;

(4) seek the involvement of parents of participating children in activities designed to help such parents become full partners in the education of their children, and to afford such parents the opportunity to participate in the development, conduct, and overall performance of the program at the local level;

(5) offer to parents of participating children, family literacy services and parenting skills training;

(6) offer to parents of participating children substance abuse counseling (either directly or through referral to local entities), including information on drug-exposed infants and fetal alcohol syndrome;

(7) at the option of such agency, offer (directly or through referral to local entities), to such parents training in basic child development; assistance in developing communication skills; opportunities to share experiences with other parents; regular in-home visitation; or any other activity designed to help such parents become full partners in the education of their children;

(8) provide, with respect to each participating family, a family needs assessment that includes consultation with such parents about the benefits of parent involvement and about the activities described in paragraphs (4) through (7) in which such parents may choose to be involved (taking into consideration their specific family needs, work schedules, and other responsibilities);

(9) consider providing services to assist younger siblings of children

participating in its Head Start program to obtain health services from other sources;

(10) perform community outreach to encourage individuals previously unaffiliated with Head Start programs to participate in its Head Start program as volunteers; and

(11)(A) inform custodial parents in single-parent families that participate in programs, activities, or services carried out or provided under this subchapter about the availability of child support services for purposes of establishing paternity and acquiring child support and refer eligible parents to the child support offices of State and local governments.

Section 9837a. Head Start transition.

Each Head Start agency shall take steps to coordinate with the local educational agency serving the community involved and with schools in which children participating in a Head Start program operated by such agency will enroll following such program, including:

(1) developing and implementing a systematic procedure for transferring, with parental consent, Head Start program records for each participating child to the school in which such child will enroll;

(2) establishing channels of communication between Head Start staff and their counterparts in the schools (including teachers, social workers, and health staff) to facilitate coordination of programs;

(3) conducting meetings involving parents, kindergarten or elementary school teachers, and Head Start program teachers to discuss the educational, developmental, and other needs of individual children;

(4) organizing and participating in joint transition-related training of school staff and Head Start staff;

(5) developing and implementing a family outreach and support program in cooperation with entities carrying out parental involvement efforts under title I of the Elementary and Secondary Education Act of 1965;

(6) assisting families, administrators, and teachers in enhancing educational and developmental continuity between Head Start services and elementary school classes; and

(7) linking the services provided in such Head Start program with the education services provided by such local educational agency.

Section 9840. Participation in Head Start programs.

(a) Criteria for eligibility.

(1) The Secretary shall by regulation prescribe eligibility for the participation of persons in Head Start programs assisted under this sub-

chapter. Except as provided in paragraph (2), such criteria may provide:

(A) that children from low-income families shall be eligible for participation in programs assisted under this subchapter if their families' incomes are below the poverty line, or if their families are eligible or, in the absence of child care, would potentially be eligible for public assistance; and

(B) pursuant to such regulations as the Secretary shall prescribe, that programs assisted under this subchapter may include, to a reasonable extent, participation of children in the area served who would benefit from such programs but whose families do not meet the low-income criteria prescribed [above].

(2) Whenever a Head Start program is operated in a community with a population of 1,000 or less individuals and there is no other preschool program in the community; the community is located in a medically underserved area . . . the community is in a location which, by reason of remoteness, does not permit reasonable access to the types of services described [above] and not less than 50 percent of the families to be served in the community are eligible [to participate in Head Start], the Head Start program in each such locality shall establish the criteria for eligibility. [No eligible child shall be denied Head Start services.]

(b) Establishment of fee schedule or charging of fees; payment by families willing and able to pay. The Secretary shall not prescribe any fee schedule or otherwise provide for the charging of any fees for participation in Head Start programs, unless such fees are authorized by legislation hereafter enacted. Nothing in this subsection shall be construed to prevent the families of children who participate in Head Start programs and who are willing and able to pay the full cost of such participation from doing so. A Head Start agency that provides a Head Start program with full-working-day services in collaboration with other agencies or entities may collect a family co-payment to support extended day services. . . .

Section 9840a. Early Head Start programs for families with infants and toddlers.

(a) In general. The Secretary shall make grants, in accordance with the provisions of this section for programs providing family-centered services for low-income families with very young children designed to promote the development of the children, and to enable their parents to fulfill their roles as parents and to move toward self-sufficiency.

(b) Scope and design of programs. In carrying out a program described in subsection (a) of this section, an entity receiving assistance under this section shall:

(1) provide, either directly or through referral, early, continuous, intensive, and comprehensive child development and family support services that will enhance the physical, social, emotional, and intellectual development of participating children;

(2) ensure that the level of services provided to families responds to their needs and circumstances;

(3) promote positive parent-child interactions;

(4) provide services to parents to support their role as parents and to help the families move toward self-sufficiency (including educational and employment services as appropriate);

(5) coordinate services with services provided by programs in the State and programs in the community (including programs for infants and toddlers with disabilities) to ensure a comprehensive array of services (such as health and mental health services);

(6) ensure formal linkages with local Head Start programs in order to provide for continuity of services for children and families;

(7) in the case of a Head Start agency that operates a program and that also provides Head Start services through the age of mandatory school attendance, ensure that children and families participating in the program receive such services through such age;

(8) ensure formal linkages with the agencies and entities described in the Individuals with Disabilities Education Act and providers of early intervention services for infants and toddlers with disabilities [under that act]; and

(9) meet such other requirements concerning design and operation of the program as the Secretary may establish.

(c) Persons eligible to participate. Persons who may participate in [Early Head Start] include pregnant women and families with children under age 3 who meet the income criteria specified for families.

Section 9843a. Staff qualifications and development.

(2)(A) Degree requirements. The Secretary shall ensure that not later than September 30, 2003, at least 50 percent of all Head Start teachers nationwide in center-based programs have an associate, baccalaureate, or advanced degree in early childhood education; or an associate, baccalaureate, or advanced degree in a field related to early childhood education, with experience in teaching preschool children.

Section 9844. Research, demonstrations, and evaluation.

(a) In general.

(1) Requirement; general purposes. The Secretary shall carry out a continuing program of research, demonstration, and evaluation activities, in order to:

(A) foster continuous improvement in the quality of the Head Start programs under this subchapter and in their effectiveness in enabling participating children and their families to succeed in school and otherwise; and

(B) use the Head Start programs to develop, test, and disseminate new ideas and approaches for addressing the needs of low-income preschool children (including children with disabilities) and their families and communities. . . .

(d) Specific objectives [of this research]. The research, demonstration, and evaluation activities shall include components designed to:

(1) permit ongoing assessment of the quality and effectiveness of the programs under this subchapter;

(2) establish evaluation methods that measure the effectiveness and impact of family literacy services program models, including models for the integration of family literacy services with Head Start services;

(4) assist in developing knowledge concerning the factors that promote or inhibit healthy development and effective functioning of children and their families both during and following participation in a Head Start program;

(5) permit comparisons of children and families participating in Head Start programs with children and families receiving other child care, early childhood education, or child development services and with other appropriate control groups;

(9) [and] study the experiences of small, medium, and large States with Head Start programs in order to permit comparisons of children participating in the programs with eligible children who did not participate in the programs. . . .

15

Elementary and Secondary Education Act (ESEA)

1965

If Congress can be criticized for under-legislating on behalf of children during the first half of the twentieth century, it certainly made up for much of its past inaction with the Elementary and Secondary Education Act (ESEA). First passed as a Great Society law in 1965, the act has grown so large over the years that it needs volumes of the U.S. Code and Code of Federal Regulations (CFR) to contain it. The original version of the act was in force for five years; it has been reauthorized, amended, and expanded by Congress every five years since that time. Today nearly every school district in the country is touched in some way by the ESEA, which contains a virtually uncountable array of federally sponsored undertakings on behalf of preschool, elementary, middle, and high school students.

The original ESEA, passed by President Lyndon B. Johnson's Democratic-controlled Congress, targeted efforts to underprivileged children in poor schools. It sought to enhance learning opportunities for these children, primarily through the first and most famous part of the act, Title I. Title I provides federal grant money to states and local school districts. The funds are to be used to assist low-income and underachieving students to improve their educational performance. Over the years Title I has grown into a multi-billion dollar program, and school districts today continue to rely heavily on its funds.

Shortly after the passage of the original act, Congress added disabled children to the list of its beneficiaries, passing Title VI. Similar to Title I, Title VI provided federal funds to states and local school districts for programs to establish or improve learning opportunities for disabled children. Title VI represented Congress' first comprehensive commitment to the education of disabled children. As that commitment grew, Title VI was taken out of the ESEA and made a separate law. It eventually became known as the Education for All Handicapped Children Act, and then as the Individuals with Disabilities Education Act (IDEA). The IDEA is discussed in full later in this book.

As these first titles may indicate, the history of the ESEA has largely been one of identifying groups in need of federal assistance and targeting federal programs and funds toward them. Over time Congress has expanded the ESEA to include assistance for American Indian, Native Hawaiian, and Native Alaskan children. It has special programs for the children of migratory workers and for bilingual students. It now includes programs for delinquent youths and dropouts, as well as programs for gifted and talented students.

In addition to targeting particular audiences, the ESEA targets particular problems facing school children. As new problems have been identified, Congress has amended the ESEA to address them. The 1994 version of the act, for example, included special funding to encourage drug-free schools, gun-free schools, and violence-free schools. Also added was Even Start, a literacy program where parents and children participate as a family to improve the children's reading skills. The current reauthorization of the act, described more fully below, targets federal funds to underperforming schools and provides extensive assistance to improve reading skills.

The ESEA also funds educational experiments and alternative schooling methods, such as public charter schools and magnet schools. It funds professional development and training activities for teachers. It supports school arts programs, civic education programs, and national writing projects. A relatively new title is dedicated to providing and improving technology in schools. Among other goals, this title seeks to improve students' access to the latest technology by providing grants to school districts and schools that use technology in unique and creative ways.

The ESEA is, in a word, huge. It is also very controversial. Because the ESEA has grown so large, and so expensive, members of Congress, as well as parents, school officials, educational reformers, and taxpayers, want to know if they are receiving their money's worth from the act. Critics charge that the billions of dollars spent on the ESEA each year do not produce the desired results. They argue that, despite all of the act's programs and resources, students are not better prepared for school and are not achieving at significantly higher levels now than when the act was first adopted. Many view the ESEA programs as creating a dependency of sorts: education, which was once a singularly local endeavor, has become nationalized, and local school districts now depend on Congress for their sustenance.

Former Secretary of Education William J. Bennett, for example, has been a leading critic of the ESEA, which he believes has failed the disadvantaged low-income and minority children that it was originally designed to serve. He and other opponents of the ESEA argue that federal funds should be given not to the school districts and other educational institutions, which tend to grow complacent, but directly to students and their parents, who can create competition among schools by choosing which ones to attend. They argue that federal educational initiatives should give greater flexibility to states and school districts and offer enhanced opportunities for school choice.

Critics also point out that ESEA money is not freely given by Congress. States and school districts must jump through a variety of regulatory hoops to receive ESEA funds. The regulations generated by the ESEA are several inches thick in the Code of Federal Regulations (CFR). Complying with the rules for various ESEA programs is expensive; meeting the paperwork requirements alone can be daunting.

Many of the disagreements over ESEA are party-based, with Republicans tending to support more block grants and more local control for school districts and parents. (A block grant is a large sum of money given to a state for a general purpose, such as elementary education. The state is then free to use the money as it wishes, devising its own programs rather than following federal ones.) Republicans also tend to support school voucher programs, where a sum of money (usually for tuition) is given directly to low-income parents and students in an effort to give them a wider choice of schools, including private ones.

Democrats, on the other hand, largely reject school vouchers, believing that they will undermine the public school system and that they violate the First Amendment's establishment clause, commonly known as the "separation of church and state," because federal money will be used by parents to send their children to faith-based private schools. Democrats also believe that many of the programs sponsored by the ESEA are working; while they support reform of ineffective programs, they do not believe in the wholesale reform of the act.

The ESEA also has powerful supporters within the education system, most notably from the National Education Association, the National School Boards Association, and the National PTA. Because ESEA funding is so widespread, many institutions have come to rely on it not just to fund programs, but as part of overall school budgets. Therefore, cutting back the ESEA could very well mean the loss of jobs as well as programs, as school districts struggle to do more with less. For that reason many interest groups across the nation support continuation of the ESEA or the various programs within it that affect them. These groups have pressured Congress to preserve the act, just as skeptics have asked Congress to reconsider it.

But the debate over the ESEA is more than just party- and interest-group-based. To say that it is also ideological is true, but still somewhat misleading, because ideologies are not always clear cut where education is concerned. It would be difficult to find a politician who does not support improving the education of America's children. *How* to do so is the sticking point.

For example, within days of taking office in 2001, President George W. Bush (Jr.), a Republican, offered Congress a plan for education called "No Child Left Behind." His plan provided for more local control over school spending and called for national educational testing of students. The president, whose wife was a teacher and librarian, ardently supports family literacy programs such as Even Start; his proposal called for an expansion of such programs. Critics of the Bush plan, however, immediately argued that it provided too little money for education. They objected to national testing as a measure of school quality and rejected the idea that improvement in test scores should be used to determine whether a school deserves federal funds. They also ardently opposed school vouchers.

Given the widely differing views about the best way to provide quality education and to make schools accountable for student achievement, it took Congress nearly a year to agree on a bipartisan compromise measure. President Bush signed this reauthorization of the ESEA into law on January 8, 2002. Called the No Child Left Behind Act, it stresses four main goals: accountability of educational institutions, school choice for students and parents, flexibility in implementing programs and spending federal funds, and a commitment to enhancing children's reading skills.

Under the new act, states and local educational agencies must demonstrate greater accountability in their efforts to educate students. In other words, they must demonstrate that their efforts are working, and that children are learning—or, more precisely, that *all* children are learning. President Bush's call for national testing was rejected by Congress. Instead, states must develop systems to assess the performance of both schools and children. The act calls for annual statewide testing of all public school children in grades three through eight. The results of this testing and of other required assessment measures must be presented to the government, as well as to parents and the public, by using various categories, including the economic status of the students, their race or ethnicity, and their English proficiency. When educational results are broken down in this way, educators and parents will be better able to tell if a particular group of students is failing. Once such groups are identified, federal funds can be targeted to failing or underachieving schools, or alternatively to those groups of failing or underachieving students.

States and local school districts are required to submit yearly "report cards" on their progress so that failing schools and programs can be quickly identified and improved. The act provides financial incentives for schools that improve, or that perform so well as to be considered "model" schools. If a failing school does not improve, parents have the right to remove their children from it and place them in another public school. Alternatively, they can use Title I money to purchase outside educational services such as tutoring for their children. These supplemental services can be provided by any approved entity, whether public or private.

But do "private" schools include religious ones? School vouchers, for example, proved too controversial for inclusion in the reauthorization act. President Bush, in frustration, publicly expressed his wish that the Supreme Court decide once and for all whether school voucher programs are constitutional.

The president recently got his wish. In late June of 2002, the Supreme Court decided by a vote of five to four that school voucher programs can be constitutional. *Zelman v. Simmons-Harris* involved the use of vouchers in the Cleveland school system. Faced with widespread educational performance failure across the district, the Ohio legislature authorized tuition payments to the parents of children in failing schools, which they could use to move their children to new schools of their choosing. Almost all of the alternative schools participating in the program, however, were faith-based, leading to this constitutional challenge. The Court majority determined that the structure of the Cleveland voucher program did not unconstitutionally entangle the government with religion, despite the fact that the lion's share of voucher money was directed to religious schools. It reasoned that the money was not given to the schools, but to the parents, who then had the choice of where to place their children. As constructed, the program did not directly subsidize or advance faith-based schools, because the parents ultimately controlled which schools received the funds, and public and non-religious private schools were able to participate in the program.

The Supreme Court's decision was a victory for advocates of school vouchers and school choice. However, not every school voucher program is going to pass constitutional muster. The program must be carefully crafted to ensure that funds are not provided directly to faith-based schools. The more direct the connection between the vouchers and such schools, the greater the chance that the program violates the First Amendment's requirement of separation of church and state. Moreover, the decision in *Simmons-Harris* was a close one; the appointment of one new justice could lead to its reversal. The Supreme Court has spoken, as President Bush desired, but it is unlikely that it has resolved this sensitive legal and political issue once and for all.

Although the new ESEA imposes tough new achievement standards on states and school districts, it relieves some of the administrative burdens on them by providing more flexibility in how they spend federal money. States and school districts can now shift up to fifty percent of the money they receive under certain grant programs to other programs, including Title I. For example, a district that receives money to make its schools drug free, and does not need funds for this purpose, can use them to address more pressing concerns. This relaxing of rules allows states, and more importantly local school districts, the ability to target their funds to the areas they have identified as most in need of support.

Finally, the newly reauthorized ESEA provides significant additional funding for reading programs. It expands the Even Start and Family Literacy programs implemented in the previous version of the act, and creates a new program called Reading First. The goal of this program is to ensure that every child in the United States can read by the end of the third grade. Given this goal, funds are targeted to preschool and early childhood reading programs. States and local educational providers are eligible to apply for six-year grants to develop reading skills, particularly those of students at risk of failure.

Beyond Title I, the ESEA reauthorization continues to offer a diverse and complex array of programs for the improvement of elementary and secondary schools. Title II is directed at recruiting and training excellent teachers and educational paraprofessionals such as teachers' aides. Title III aims to improve English language proficiency. Title IV is dedicated to preparing schools technologically for the twenty-first century. Title V encourages parental participation and choice as well as the creation of innovative educational programs. Other titles provide for the education of specific groups of children, including homeless children.

As the current widespread bipartisan support for the No Child Left Behind Act indicates, the ESEA is simply too large to disappear from the legislative map, despite increasingly louder cries for major federal education reform. But just as the ESEA will not go away, the issue of its reform will not go away either. In another five years, Congress will again be called on to judge the success of the ESEA and its new reforms and to determine which parts of the act merit reauthorization. Everyone agrees that our nation's children deserve the best possible education, and millions of people, from the highest elected official in the land to the kindergarten teacher in the poorest inner-city school, are struggling to make that happen. But there are many different views on and approaches to this issue, and reaching a consensus is nearly impossible. That fact, of course, is both the blessing and the curse of a democracy.

15. Elementary and Secondary Education Act (ESEA)

[Author's note: When an act of Congress is reauthorized, it is common for Congress to give the reauthorizing legislation a different name. This is the 2002 reauthorization of the ESEA, signed into law by President George W. Bush (Jr.) on January 8, 2002. It is called the No Child Left Behind Act. Because the ESEA is so large, the following excerpt is limited to Title I of the act. Moreover, this excerpt is taken from the "enrolled bill"—the final version passed by both houses of Congress and sent to the president for signature. The act is so new that is has not yet been officially printed by the Government Printing Office.]

[The Elementary and Secondary Education Act of 1965 is amended to read as follows:]

TITLE I: IMPROVING THE ACADEMIC ACHIEVEMENT OF THE DISADVANTAGED

Section 1001. Statement of Purpose.

The purpose of this title is to ensure that all children have a fair, equal, and significant opportunity to obtain a high-quality education and reach, at a minimum, proficiency on challenging State academic achievement standards and state academic assessments. This purpose can be accomplished by:

(1) ensuring that high-quality academic assessments, accountability systems, teacher preparation and training, curriculum, and instructional materials are aligned with challenging State academic standards so that students, teachers, parents, and administrators can measure progress against common expectations for student academic achievement;

(2) meeting the educational needs of low-achieving children in our Nation's highest-poverty schools, limited English proficient children, migratory children, children with disabilities, Indian children, neglected or delinquent children, and young children in need of reading assistance;

(3) closing the achievement gap between high- and low-performing children, especially the achievement gaps between minority and non-minority students, and between disadvantaged children and their more advantaged peers;

(4) holding schools, local educational agencies, and States accountable for improving the academic achievement of all students, and identifying and turning around low-performing schools that have failed to provide a high-quality education to their students, while providing alternatives to students in such schools to enable the students to receive a high-quality education;

(5) distributing and targeting resources sufficiently to make a difference to local educational agencies and schools where needs are greatest;

(6) improving and strengthening accountability, teaching, and learning by using State assessment systems designed to ensure that students are meeting challenging State academic achievement and content standards and increasing achievement overall, but especially for the disadvantaged;

(7) providing greater decision-making authority and flexibility to schools and teachers in exchange for greater responsibility for student performance;

(8) providing children an enriched and accelerated educational program, including the use of school-wide programs or additional services that increase the amount and quality of instructional time;

(9) promoting school-wide reform and ensuring the access of children to effective, scientifically based instructional strategies and challenging academic content;

(10) significantly elevating the quality of instruction by providing staff in participating schools with substantial opportunities for professional development;

(11) coordinating services under all parts of this title with each other, with other educational services, and, to the extent feasible, with other agencies providing services to youth, children, and families; and

(12) affording parents substantial and meaningful opportunities to participate in the education of their children.

Section 1002. Authorization of Appropriations.

(a) Local Educational Agency Grants. For the purpose of carrying out part A [below], there are authorized to be appropriated: (1) $13,500,000,000 for fiscal year 2002; (2) $16,000,000,000 for fiscal year 2003; (3) $18,500,000,000 for fiscal year 2004; (4) $20,500,000,000 for fiscal year 2005; (5) $22,750,000,000 for fiscal year 2006; and (6) $25,000,000,000 for fiscal year 2007.

(b) Reading First [and related programs]: For the purpose of carrying out [the Reading First program], there are authorized to be appropriated $900,000,000 for fiscal year 2002 and such sums as may be necessary for each of the 5 succeeding fiscal years. For the purpose of carrying out [the Early Reading First program], there are authorized to be appropriated $75,000,000 for fiscal year 2002 and such sums as may be necessary for each of the 5 succeeding fiscal years. For the purpose of carrying out [the Even Start program], there are authorized to be appropriated $260,000,000 for fiscal year 2002 and such sums as may be necessary for each of the 5 succeeding fiscal years. For the purpose of carrying out [the Improving Literacy Through School Libraries program], there are authorized to be appropriated $250,000,000 for fiscal year 2002 and such sums as may be necessary for each of the 5 succeeding fiscal years. For the purpose of carrying out [the Education of Migratory Children program], there are authorized to be appropriated $410,000,000 for fiscal year 2002 and such sums as may be necessary for each of the 5 succeeding fiscal years. [For programs directed toward neglected, delinquent, or at-risk youth], there are authorized to be appropriated $50,000,000 for fiscal year 2002 and such sums as may be necessary for each of the 5 succeeding fiscal years.

(f) Comprehensive School Reform. For the purpose of carrying out [this goal], there are authorized to be appropriated such sums as may be necessary for fiscal year 2002 and each of the 5 succeeding fiscal years.

(g) Advanced Placement. For the purposes of carrying out [advanced placement programs], there are authorized to be appropriated such sums for fiscal year 2002 and each of the 5 succeeding fiscal years.

(h) School Dropout Prevention. For the purpose of carrying out [this goal], there are authorized to be appropriated $125,000,000 for fiscal year 2002 and such sums as may be necessary for each of the 5 succeeding fiscal years.

(i) School Improvement. For the purpose of carrying out [this goal], there are authorized to be appropriated $500,000,000 for fiscal year 2002 and such sums as may be necessary for each of the 5 succeeding fiscal years.

Section 1003. School Improvement.

(a) [State educational agencies shall be required to reserve a portion of the funds they receive for the following purposes.]

(b) Uses. Of the amount reserved for any fiscal year, the State educational agency: (1) shall allocate not less than 95 percent of that amount directly to local educational agencies for schools identified for school improvement, corrective action, and restructuring . . . or (2) may, with the approval of the local educational agency, directly provide for these activities or arrange for their provision through other entities such as school support teams or educational service agencies.

(c) Priority. The State educational agency, in allocating funds to local educational agencies under this section, shall give priority to local educational agencies that: (1) serve the lowest-achieving schools; (2) demonstrate the greatest need for such funds; and (3) demonstrate the strongest commitment to ensuring that such funds are used to enable the lowest-achieving schools to meet the progress goals in school improvement plans. . . .

Part A: Improving Basic Programs Offered by Local Educational Agencies

Subpart 1: Basic Program Requirements.

Section 1111. State Plans.

(a) Plans required: For any State desiring to receive a grant under this part, the State educational agency shall submit to the Secretary a plan, developed by the State educational agency, in consultation with local educational agencies, teachers, principals, pupil services personnel, administrators (including administrators of programs described in other parts of this title), other staff, and parents, that satisfies the requirements of this section and that is coordinated with other programs under this Act, the Individuals with Disabilities Education Act, the Carl D. Perkins Vocational and Technical Education Act of 1998, the Head Start Act, the Adult Education and Family Literacy Act, and the McKinney-Vento Homeless Assistance Act.

(b) Academic Standards, Academic Assessments, and Accountability.

(1) Challenging academic standards.

(A) Each State plan shall demonstrate that the State has adopted challenging academic content standards and challenging student academic achievement standards that will be used by the State, its local educational agencies, and its schools to carry out this part. . . .

(B) The academic standards shall be the same academic standards that the State applies to all schools and children in the State.

(C) The State shall have such academic standards for all public elementary school and secondary school children in subjects determined by the State, but including at least mathematics, reading or language arts, and (beginning in the 2005–2006 school year) science. . . .

(D) Standards under this paragraph shall include challenging academic content standards in academic subjects that specify what children are expected to know and be able to do; contain coherent and rigorous content; and encourage the teaching of advanced skills.

(2) Accountability.

(A) Each State plan shall demonstrate that the State has developed and is implementing a single, statewide State accountability system that will be effective in ensuring that all local educational agencies, public elementary schools, and public secondary schools make adequate yearly progress as defined under this paragraph. Each State accountability system shall (i) be based on the academic standards and academic assessments [adopted by the states]; shall take into account the achievement of all public elementary school and secondary school students; (ii) be the same accountability system the State uses for all public elementary schools and secondary schools or all local educational agencies in the State . . . ; and, (iii) include sanctions and rewards, such as bonuses and recognition, the State will use to hold local educational agencies and public elementary schools and secondary schools accountable for student achievement and for ensuring that they make adequate yearly progress. . . .

(B) Each State plan shall demonstrate adequate yearly progress of all public elementary schools, secondary schools, and local educational agencies in the State, toward enabling all public elementary school and secondary school students to meet the State's student academic achievement standards, while working toward the goal of narrowing the achievement gaps in the State, local educational agencies, and schools.

(C) "Adequate yearly progress" [means that the state must apply] the same high standards of academic achievement to all public elementary school and secondary school students in the State; [must be] statistically valid and reliable; [these standards must result] in continuous and substantial academic improvement for all students; [must measure] the progress of public elementary schools, secondary schools and local educational agencies; [and must include] separate measurable annual objectives for continuous and substantial improvement for all public elementary school and secondary school students. [The achievement of the following groups must be measured: economically disadvantaged students; students from major racial and ethnic groups; students with disabilities; and students with limited English proficiency.]

(G–H) Each State shall establish statewide annual measurable objectives [and shall also set] intermediate goals for meeting the requirements [of this act]. Each group of students described [above] must meet or exceed the [annual] objectives set by the State.

(3) Academic Assessments.

(A–C) Each State plan shall demonstrate that the State educational agency, in consultation with local educational agencies, has implemented a set of high-quality, yearly student academic assessments that include, at a minimum, academic assessments in mathematics, reading or language arts, and science. . . . These assessments shall be . . . used to measure the achievement of all children; be aligned with the State's challenging academic content and student academic achievement standards; . . . be consistent with relevant, nationally recognized professional and technical standards; . . . be of adequate technical quality for each purpose required under this Act; and, . . . [annually] measure the proficiency of students in, at a minimum, mathematics and reading or language arts.

(6) Parents' right to know.

(A–B) At the beginning of each school year, a local educational agency that receives funds under this part shall notify the parents of each student attending any school receiving funds under this part that the parents may request, and the agency will provide the parents on request (and in a timely manner), information regarding the professional qualifications of the student's classroom teachers . . . ; information on the level of achievement of the parent's child in each of the State academic assessments as required under this part; and . . . timely notice that the parent's child has been assigned, or has been taught for four or more consecutive weeks by, a teacher who is not highly qualified.

Section 1112. Local Educational Agency Plans.

(a) A local educational agency may receive a subgrant under this part for any fiscal year only if such agency has on file with the State educational agency a plan, approved by the State educational agency, that is coordinated with other programs under this Act, the Individuals with Disabilities Education Act, the Carl D. Perkins Vocational and Technical Education Act of 1998, the McKinney-Vento Homeless Assistance Act, and other Acts, as appropriate.

(b) In order to help low-achieving children meet challenging achievement academic standards, each local educational agency plan shall include [among other things, high quality academic assessments as described for State plans.]

Section 1114. Schoolwide Programs.

(a) A local educational agency may consolidate and use funds under this part, together with other Federal, State, and local funds, in order to upgrade the entire educational program of a school that serves an eligible school attendance area in which not less than 40 percent of the children are from low-income families, or not less than 40 percent of the children enrolled in the school are from such families.

(b) A schoolwide program shall include [a] comprehensive needs assessment of the entire school; schoolwide reform strategies that provide opportunities for all children to meet the State's proficient and advanced levels of student academic achievement provide an enriched and accelerated curriculum; . . . strategies [that particularly] address the needs of low-achieving children and those at risk of not meeting the State student academic achievement standards; address how the school will determine if such needs have been met; and are consistent with, and are designed to implement, the State and local improvement plans, if any. . . . [These schoolwide programs should attempt to incorporate] Federal, State, and local services and programs, including programs supported under this Act, violence prevention programs, nutrition programs, housing programs,

Head Start, adult education, vocational and technical education, and job training.

Section 1115. Targeted Assistance Schools.

(a) In all schools that are ineligible for a schoolwide program or that choose not to operate such a schoolwide program, a local educational agency serving such school may use funds received under this part only for programs that provide services to eligible children identified as having the greatest need for special assistance.

(b) Eligible children [include those children under age 21 who are] identified by the school as failing, or most at risk of failing, to meet the State's challenging student academic achievement standards on the basis of multiple, educationally related, objective criteria established by the local educational agency and supplemented by the school, except that children from preschool through grade 2 shall be selected solely on the basis of such criteria as teacher judgment, interviews with parents, and developmentally appropriate measures.

(c) To assist targeted assistance schools and local educational agencies to meet their responsibility to provide for all their students served under this part the opportunity to meet the State's challenging student academic achievement standards in subjects as determined by the State, each targeted assistance program under this section shall . . . use such program's resources to help participating children meet such State's challenging student academic achievement standards; ensure that planning for students served under this part is incorporated into existing school planning; use effective methods and instructional strategies; give primary consideration to providing extended learning time, such as an extended school year, before- and after-school, and summer programs and opportunities; help provide an accelerated, high-quality curriculum, including applied learning; and minimize removing children from the regular classroom during regular school hours for instruction provided under this part. [Among other things, they shall also provide] strategies to increase parental involvement . . . and coordinate and integrate Federal, State, and local services and programs, including programs supported under this Act, violence prevention programs, nutrition programs, housing programs, Head Start, adult education, vocational and technical education, and job training.

Section 1116. Academic Assessment and Local Agency and School Improvement.

(a) Each local educational agency receiving funds under this part shall use the State academic assessments and other indicators described in the State plan to review annually the progress of each school to determine whether the school is making adequate yearly progress, . . . publicize and disseminate the results of the local annual review, . . . and review the effectiveness of the actions and activities the schools are carrying out under this part with respect to parental involvement, professional development, and other activities.

(b) School Improvement.

(1) General requirements. (A) A local educational agency shall identify for school improvement any elementary school or secondary school served under this part that fails, for 2 consecutive years, to make adequate yearly progress as defined in the State's plan. . . . (E) In the case of a school identified for school improvement, the local educational agency shall, not later than the first day of the school year following such identification, provide all students enrolled in the school with the option to transfer to another public school served by the local educational agency, which may include a public charter school, unless such an option is prohibited by State law. In providing students the option to transfer to another public school, the local educational agency shall give priority to the lowest achieving children from low-income families.

(3) School plan. (A) Each school identified for improvement shall, not later than 3 months after being so identified, develop or revise a school plan, in consultation with parents, school staff, the local educational agency serving the school, and outside experts, for approval by such local educational agency. The school plan shall cover a 2-year period. [It shall] strengthen the core academic subjects in the school and address the specific academic issues that caused the school to be identified for school improvement. . . . [It shall also include] policies and practices concerning the school's core academic subjects that have the greatest likelihood of ensuring that all groups of students enrolled in the school will meet the State's proficien[cy] level[s] of achievement. . . .

(5) Failure to make adequate yearly progress after identification. In the case of any school that fails to make adequate yearly progress by the end of the first full school year after identification [as a school needing improvement], the local educational agency serving such school shall continue to provide all students enrolled in the school with the option to transfer to another public school [and] shall make supplemental educational services available [to students].

(6) Notice to parents. A local educational agency shall promptly provide parents of students enrolled in [a school identified for improvement, corrective action, or restructuring] with an explanation of what the identification means, and how the school compares in terms of academic achievement to other elementary schools or secondary

schools. [It shall also give them] an explanation of what the school [needs to improve and how it intends to do so], and [invite them] to become involved in addressing the academic issues that caused the school to be identified for school improvement. [It shall] explain the parents' option to transfer their child to another public school . . . or to obtain supplemental educational services for the child in accordance with this act.

(7) Corrective action. Corrective action [must] substantially and directly respond to the consistent academic failure of a school, [including] . . . any underlying staffing, curriculum, or other problems in the school. . . . [If a school fails to take corrective action or to make adequate progress, it shall] continue to provide all students enrolled in the school with the option to transfer to another public school, continue to make supplemental educational services available [to its students], and take at least one of the following measures: replace the school staff who are relevant to the failure to make adequate yearly progress; institute and fully implement a new curriculum, including providing appropriate professional development for all relevant staff, that is based on scientifically based research and offers substantial promise of improving educational achievement for low-achieving students and enabling the school to make adequate yearly progress; significantly decrease management authority at the school level; appoint an outside expert to advise the school on its progress toward making adequate yearly progress, based on its school plan; extend the school year or school day for the school; [and] restructure the internal organizational structure of the school.

(8) Restructuring. If, after one full school year of corrective action under paragraph (7) [above], a school subject to such corrective action continues to fail to make adequate yearly progress, then the local educational agency shall continue to provide all students enrolled in the school with the option to transfer to another public school, continue to make supplemental educational services available [to students, and] prepare a plan and make necessary arrangements to [restructure the school]. [Means of restructuring include] reopening the school as a public charter school; replacing all or most of the school staff (which may include the principal) who are relevant to the failure to make adequate yearly progress; entering into a contract with an entity, such as a private management company, with a demonstrated record of effectiveness, to operate the public school; turning the operation of the school over to the State educational agency, if permitted under State law and agreed to by the State; [and any other approach to] major

restructuring of the school's governance arrangement that makes fundamental reforms. . . .

(c) State review and local educational agency improvement. [The requirements for State review of local educational agencies resemble those given to local educational agencies in reviewing their schools (described above). The states have similar powers to improve and if necessary restructure failing local educational agencies.]

(e) Supplemental educational services.

(1) The local educational agency serving [a failing school] shall, subject to this subsection, arrange for the provision of supplemental educational services to eligible children in the school from a provider with a demonstrated record of effectiveness, that is selected by the parents and approved for that purpose by the State educational agency.

(2) Each local educational agency shall provide, at a minimum, annual notice to parents of the availability of services under this subsection; the identity of approved providers of those services that are within the local educational agency or whose services are reasonably available in neighboring local educational agencies; and a brief description of the services, qualifications, and demonstrated effectiveness of each such provider;

(5) In order for a provider to be included on the State list, it shall agree to provide a progress report to parents of children receiving supplemental educational services and to the appropriate local educational agency; ensure that instruction provided and content used [are consistent with established] student academic achievement standards; meet all applicable Federal, State, and local health, safety, and civil rights laws; and, ensure that its instruction and content are secular, neutral, and non-ideological.

Section 1117. School Support and Recognition.

(a) Each State shall establish a statewide system of intensive and sustained support and improvement for local educational agencies and schools receiving funds under this part, in order to increase the opportunity for all students served by those agencies and schools to meet the State's academic content standards and student academic achievement standards. . . . [School support teams] shall be composed of persons knowledgeable about scientifically based research and practice on teaching and learning and about successful schoolwide projects, school reform, and improving educational opportunities for low-achieving students. [These persons may include] highly qualified or distinguished teachers and principals, pupil services personnel, parents, representatives of institutions of higher education, [outside educational consultants, and others that the State deems appropriate].

(b) Each State receiving a grant under this part shall establish a program for making academic achievement awards to recognize schools that meet the criteria [of this act]. [It shall also] designate as distinguished schools those schools that have made the greatest gains in closing the achievement gap [of its students] or exceeding adequate yearly progress [goals]. Such distinguished schools may serve as models for and provide support to other schools. [A State] may also recognize and provide financial awards to teachers or principals [in such schools].

Section 1118. Parental Involvement.

(a) A local educational agency may receive funds under this part only if such agency implements programs, activities, and procedures for the involvement of parents. . . .

(b) Each local educational agency that receives funds under this part shall develop jointly with, agree on with, and distribute to, parents of participating children a written parent involvement policy. [The policy should describe how the agency will] involve parents in the joint development of the [agency's educational] plan [and] provide the coordination, technical assistance, and other support necessary to assist participating schools in planning and implementing effective parent involvement activities to improve student academic achievement and school performance. . . . [The policy should explain how the agency intends to] involve parents in the activities of the schools served [by its plan].

(d) As a component of the school-level parental involvement policy [explained above], each school served under this part shall jointly develop with parents for all children served under this part a school-parent compact that outlines how parents, the entire school staff, and students will share the responsibility for improved student academic achievement and the means by which the school and parents will build and develop a partnership to help children achieve the State's high standards.

Section 1120. Participation of Children Enrolled in Private Schools.

(a) (1) A local educational agency shall, after timely and meaningful consultation with appropriate private school officials, provide such children, on an equitable basis, special educational services or other benefits under this part (such as dual enrollment, educational radio and television, computer equipment and materials, other technology, and mobile educational services and equipment) that address their needs, and shall ensure that teachers and families of the children participate, on an equitable basis, in services and activities developed [under this act]. (2) Such educational services or other benefits, including materials and equipment, shall be secular, neutral, and nonideological. . . . (5) The local educational agency may provide services under this section directly or through contracts with public and private agencies, organizations, and institutions.

Part B: Student Reading Skills Improvement Grants

Section 1201. Purposes. The purposes of [the Reading First and related reading programs] are as follows:

(1) To provide assistance to State educational agencies and local educational agencies in establishing reading programs for students in kindergarten through grade 3 that are based on scientifically based reading research, to ensure that every student can read at grade level or above not later than the end of grade 3.

(2) To provide assistance to State educational agencies and local educational agencies in preparing teachers, including special education teachers, through professional development and other support, so the teachers can identify specific reading barriers facing their students and so the teachers have the tools to effectively help their students learn to read.

(3) To provide assistance to State educational agencies and local educational agencies in selecting or administering screening, diagnostic, and classroom-based instructional reading assessments.

(4) To provide assistance to State educational agencies and local educational agencies in selecting or developing effective instructional materials (including classroom-based materials to assist teachers in implementing the essential components of reading instruction), programs, learning systems, and strategies to implement methods that have been proven to prevent or remediate reading failure within a State.

(5) To strengthen coordination among schools, early literacy programs, and family literacy programs to improve reading achievement for all children.

[To achieve these purposes, Part B of Title I authorizes and funds the following programs: Reading First, Early Reading First, William F. Goodling Even Start Family Literacy Programs, and the Improving Literacy Through School Libraries Program.]

[Part C of Title I authorizes and funds the Education of Migratory Children Program; Part D authorizes and funds the Prevention and Intervention Programs for Children and Youth who are Neglected, Delinquent, or At-Risk as well as state and local programs to assist these children; and Parts E-H provide for, among other things, a national assessment program, a comprehensive school reform program, advanced placement programs, and a program to prevent school dropouts.]

16

Higher Education Act (HEA)

1965

Federal aid to higher education can be traced back to before the Civil War in the nineteenth century. Although a number of private colleges and universities were already well established in the nation by that time, many states wished to expand educational opportunities by creating their own institutes of higher learning for their citizens. Congress responded by providing many states with a resource it had in abundance: land. The states used this land to create public colleges and universities, which are commonly called "land grant colleges" or "land grant universities."

The first major federal land grant program led to the establishment of the University of Michigan in 1836 and the University of Wisconsin in 1848. In 1862 President Abraham Lincoln signed into law the Morrill Act, which awarded every state that had stayed in the Union with 30,000 acres of federal land for each representative and senator it had in Congress. (Given that the minimum number of federal legislators a state has is three, that meant at least 90,000 acres of land per eligible state!) The states were able to build their educational institutions on this land or to sell all or part of the land to raise the money to do so. Under the original Morrill Act approximately six dozen institutions of higher learning were founded.

In 1890 Congress extended the act to cover historically black colleges and universities as well. But these schools were sometimes discriminated against in the application of the Second Morrill Act, and the effects of this discrimination persist. In fact, in the 1998 amendments to the Higher Education Act, Congress specifically acknowledged this discrimination and provided special funding and programs for these schools.

Although the federal government provided the land for these public colleges and universities, building and operating the schools was left up to the states, as was the task of attracting students. Students and their families generally paid for higher education. Some received private scholarships or stipends, of course, but federal student financial aid, used so extensively by today's students, was unheard of until the last half of the twentieth century. Consequently, higher education largely remained a privilege of the children of higher income families.

One of the first and certainly the most famous federal program for college-bound students was the G.I. Bill, which sent an entire generation of young men to college after their service in World War II. First passed into law in 1944, the G.I. Bill still exists to help the nation's military servicepersons to pursue their educational plans. In the 1940s and 1950s the bill helped men and women returning from overseas to ease their way back into their communities and back into the economy. Many of the millions of veterans who attended college on the G.I. Bill would never have gone otherwise. The bill was not only a way to compensate people for their military service, it also opened the doors of higher education, showing that it was not the exclusive purview of the rich.

The success of the G.I. Bill, the growing desire by employers for college-educated employees, and the nation's increased awareness of the value of higher education soon caused Congress to consider granting student financial aid that was not tied to some type of military service. As part of his Great Society Program, President Lyndon Johnson initiated and Congress passed a revolutionary piece of legislation designed to make higher education more affordable to Americans. This law, called the Higher Education Act (HEA), remains in place today and, in fact, has been significantly expanded over its history. The act faces reauthorization every five years and has been strongly supported each time. It and related laws have made the federal government by far the largest single provider of higher education funding and student financial aid in the nation.

The HEA is a very long and very complicated law. It is broken into sections called "titles," and contains numerous programs under its rubric. Title IV concerns student financial aid. Some of the financial aid programs that we are familiar with today, such as the

Work-Study Program, were first introduced in the original 1965 legislation. Other popular programs, such as the Pell Grant Program, were introduced in subsequent reauthorizations. A description of the most popular HEA financial aid programs is provided at the end of this discussion.

It is impossible to review the entire history of Title IV, let alone of the entire act, but a few important developments bear mentioning before its current provisions are outlined. The original legislation was targeted to needy students, who had to qualify to receive aid. The qualification process is known as "needs-based testing," and it still exists for most forms of federal aid. Some provisions were made in the original act for middle-class students as well, in the form of student loans. The original program was called the "Guaranteed Student Loan Program"; it has since been replaced by other loan programs. In offering grants and loans to students, it was largely expected that they would attend traditional four-year colleges or universities. That presumption quickly struck many legislators as elitist, or at least unfair, and in response Congress passed amendments to the HEA in 1972 that expanded the types of educational institutions that a student could attend. Students can use federal monies to enroll in two-year and community colleges, technical or vocational schools, and career-based training programs.

It is probably fair to say that, when they were first adopted, no one had any idea how large the federal student aid programs would become, how many students would come to use them, and how student loans would come to comprise such a significant part of federal aid. In 1972 Congress created "Sallie Mae" (the Student Loan Marketing Association), a private corporation that administers federal student loan programs and works to ensure that they are financially sound. Over the years the original Guaranteed Student Loan program grew, and new types of loan programs were added. Moreover, student loans have been made increasingly easier to obtain, and in higher amounts, making it an attractive means of funding education after high school. For many students today there is no choice: student loans are necessary to cover the costs of their education, particularly given the steadily rising tuition rates at many post-secondary institutions.

But if using loans is attractive, it can also be seductive. Federal loans, unlike grants or scholarships, have to be paid back. Today's students often find themselves with significant student loan debt that will take them ten years or more to repay. Default rates on federal student loans have been increasing in recent years, as students find themselves unable to obtain jobs with salaries high enough to pay for their indebtedness.

Nevertheless, Congress has repeatedly reauthorized the HEA to provide for new and different loan programs and to raise the ceilings on the amounts that students may borrow. It has created at least one program where students may borrow money without establishing financial need and another program permitting parents to borrow on their children's behalf. Loans can be taken out not only for college, but also to attend graduate or professional schools, such as medical and law schools. (Interestingly, a student cannot avoid paying back student loans by filing bankruptcy; Congress has decided that such debts cannot be forgiven by the bankruptcy court.)

Despite the drawbacks, student loans have opened the door of higher education to more students than ever before and particularly to minority and nontraditional students. Federal aid programs have also contributed to the increased number of educational institutions offering degree or certificate programs and particularly technical, vocational, and career-based specialty schools. And the question of the affordability of higher education continues to be debated before Congress. In the early 1990s, for example, President Bill Clinton proposed the creation of "loan forgiveness" programs for graduates who participated in certain types of community service, such as teaching in inner-city public schools. Many schools have created their own loan forgiveness programs, too, for certain types of public service, but all of these programs combined only reach a small percentage of indebted students. In the coming years, no doubt, Congress will have to revisit the issue of mounting student loan debt and devise creative ways to solve this problem. Therefore, continuing student and parental input to Congress on this issue is crucial.

Congress remains aware of this and other problems in its funding of higher education. In 1998 Congress passed sweeping amendments to the Higher Education Act in an effort to make its programs work more efficiently and effectively. The 1998 amendments are the most comprehensive package of amendments passed to date. This reauthorization of the HEA was overwhelmingly embraced by Congress: it passed by a vote of 96 to 1 in the Senate and 414 to 4 in the House.

For Title IV, the amendments authorized the extension of the Pell

Grant Program and increased its maximum award. With regard to student loans Congress passed provisions to streamline the lending process by allowing students to apply for long-term lines of credit. The idea is that instead of applying for loans every year, with all the paperwork and delay that process entails, a student should eventually be able to apply only once and have his or her financial aid continue through his or her schooling, so long as the student remains eligible. Another provision requires lending institutions to inform students that they may be able to take advantage of an income-sensitive repayment program. Under such a program a student who graduates and obtains an entry-level or low-paying job may have his minimum loan payments reduced accordingly. The amendments ended certain loan forgiveness programs (for nurses and community servants), revised the one for teachers, and created a new one for child care providers. The amendments also reauthorized existing loan programs and the Work-Study Program. The needs-based testing methods for loans were also simplified. Finally, loan interest rates were lowered.

The 1998 reauthorization also created a new Title IV program called "GEAR UP," or Gaining Early Awareness and Readiness for Undergraduate Programs, which aims to identify students in elementary, middle, and secondary schools that are at risk for dropping out, and provide them with information, activities, and scholarships to encourage them to stay in school and pursue education after high school. The amendments also provided for a new academic achievement scholarship program for freshmen and sophomores in college who graduated at the top of their high school classes. In fact, assistance to high school students has been in place since the adoption of the HEA. The original Great Society War on Poverty legislation included three programs, Talent Search, Upward Bound, and Student Support Services, designed to improve the prospects for low-income students, including those from historically underrepresented racial and ethnic groups, to pursue higher education. These programs, which all quickly found themselves administered under the HEA, were nicknamed the "TRIO Programs." Although revised over the years, they still exist in the HEA, and similar programs, like GEAR UP, have been added. The programs now reach not only disadvantaged middle school and high school students, but adults as well, including nontraditional students such as older students, returning students, and single parents with young children.

Other HEA titles (there are eight in all) were also significantly amended. These titles concern, among other things, teacher quality and training, aid to post-secondary institutions (including especially historically black, American Indian, and Hispanic institutions), international education programs, and programs to improve post-secondary and graduate education. Because these programs are less directly relevant to the reader, they will not be discussed. However, one new general provision might raise the eyebrows of many college students: Congress included in the 1998 amendments a provision to address underage drinking and particularly binge drinking on campus. Concerned with the illegal consumption of alcohol by underage students, Congress funded an initiative to discourage this practice and to have educational institutions adopt a "zero-tolerance" policy for underage drinking. While Congress stopped short of denying aid to underage drinkers, students should be aware that many institutions already have provisions in place to deny financial aid to students who commit alcohol-related offenses and that, given this initiative, many more institutions will likely follow.

Students should also be aware that under current federal law a person convicted of a drug offense (for example, selling or possessing) is ineligible for federal financial aid. The author of this provision, Congressman Mark Souder (R-IN), has stated that he intended it to apply to currently enrolled students only, but it has been recently interpreted by the Department of Education as applying to anyone. Thus, someone with a drug conviction in his or her past, who now wishes to attend college, may be ineligible for federal aid for a year from conviction; two convictions renders the offender ineligible for two years, and three or more convictions makes the offender permanently ineligible. Many in Congress find this application of the law unfair, because it punishes people who have reformed and are seeking to better themselves, and it also has a disparate impact on low-income groups. It seems likely that this provision will be repealed or at least significantly changed in the near future. Finally, male college-bound students are required to register with the Selective Service to receive any form of federal student financial aid; typically, they must certify that they have registered in their applications for assistance.

Students may wonder whether it is constitutional to place such limitations on their eligibility to receive grants or to borrow funds. The answer is, of course, yes. Unlike Social Security, which is widely

considered politically untouchable by the federal government because it is viewed by Americans as an entitlement, the various student aid programs, like other federal laws, can be conditioned,
revised, and even eliminated, as Congress sees fit. In fact, there have
been calls over the years to cut back on federal funding of higher
education and to eliminate some student loan programs entirely.
These arguments have met with resistance, and it is likely that, as
more and more Americans take advantage of these federal programs (including more and more of our elected officials), federal
financial aid may in fact one day prove as untouchable as Social
Security. But that day is not here yet.

A SUMMARY OF POPULAR FINANCIAL AID PROGRAMS UNDER THE HEA

Because this book is aimed at high school and college students,
a brief summary of the most popular financial aid opportunities
provided under the HEA might prove useful. As the deadlines and
requirements for financial aid change often, a student would be
well advised to contact his or her prospective school well in advance
of enrollment to find out exactly how to apply for the various types
of federal, state, and private aid. This list includes the largest federal
aid programs, the ones that are used most commonly. However,
other more specific federal aid programs are available, including
numerous scholarship programs. Even a school's financial aid office
might not be familiar with all of them. Therefore, students seeking
aid would be wise to do their own research. A lot of useful information about paying for college is available in books on the topic
or now on the Internet.

1. The Pell Grant Program

Named after long-time Rhode Island congressman Claiborne
Pell, this program awards several million dollars per year to students
based on need. Because it is a grant, it does not have to be repaid.
It is awarded to undergraduates or to college graduates in teacher
certification programs. The amount of a grant varies; under the
current reauthorization, the maximum grant ranges from $4,500
(1999–2000 level) to $5,800 (2003–2004 level).

2. Stafford Loans, now commonly called Direct Loans or FFEL Loans

These loans come in two types: Direct Stafford Loans and FFEL Stafford loans. As far as the student is concerned, the loans are virtually identical; the main difference is in who provides the funds. In the Direct Loan program, the federal government provides the loan; in the FFEL (which stands for Federal Family Education Loan), a bank or other private lender provides the loan. Both of these loans may be subsidized by the federal government, which means that your loan will not accrue interest while you are in school, or they may be unsubsidized, which means that you must make interest payments as your loan matures, even if you are still in school. (With an unsubsidized loan, you can choose to tack on your interest payments to the loan balance rather than pay while you are still in school; unfortunately, this approach increases the amount of your total indebtedness.)

The unsubsidized Stafford, although less desirable of the two because of the immediately accruing interest, is awarded without regard to a student's financial need. An undergraduate student may borrow anywhere from $2,625 to $10,500 per year, depending on various factors such as his or her year in school and the costs of attending a particular institution. Graduate students may currently borrow up to $18,500 per year.

3. Plus Loans

Plus Loans are taken out by parents or guardians on behalf of their dependent children. These loans are usually taken out through the Direct and FFEL loan programs discussed above. A Plus Loan is obtained to cover expenses in excess of those for which financial aid has already been obtained. The amount to be borrowed depends to a large extent on the amount of a student's unmet financial need. Generally, parents must have good credit (although exceptions can be made), as they are liable for repayment of this loan.

4. Federal Supplemental Educational Opportunity Grants (FSEOG)

These grants are administered by educational institutions that choose to participate in this federal program. These grants are awarded to undergraduates with the greatest financial need and do not have to be paid back.

5. Work-Study

This program funds jobs for undergraduate and graduate students with financial need. A sum of money is given to each participating institution, which uses it to pay the salaries for a variety of positions on campus or, sometimes, off campus as well. Undergraduates are generally paid by the hour, and the number of hours they work is determined by the amount of money available and their academic standing. Usually work-study jobs are part time, perhaps ten or fifteen hours per week. Work-study is awarded by the institutions based on a variety of factors, including financial need.

6. Perkins Loans

A Perkins Loan is granted by the institution. It is a low-interest loan that is paid back directly to the school. These loans are reserved for students with greatest financial need. They can borrow up to $4,000 per year as undergraduates and $6,000 per year as graduate students. Again, as with the last two programs, Perkins Loans are awarded and administered by participating educational institutions.

16. Higher Education Act (HEA)

[TITLE I: GENERAL PROVISIONS]

Section 1001. General definition of institution of higher education.

(a) Institution of higher education. For purposes of this chapter, other than subchapter IV, the term "institution of higher education" means an educational institution in any State that (1) admits as regular students only persons having a certificate of graduation from a school providing secondary education, or the recognized equivalent of such a certificate; (2) is legally authorized within such State to provide a program of education beyond secondary education; (3) provides an educational program for which the institution awards a bachelor's degree or provides not less than a 2-year program that is acceptable for full credit toward such a degree; (4) is a public or other nonprofit institution; and (5) is accredited by a nationally recognized accrediting agency or association, or if not so accredited, is an institution that has been granted pre-accreditation status. . . .

(b) Additional institutions included. For purposes of this chapter, other than subchapter IV, the term "institution of higher education" also includes (1) any school that provides not less than a one-year program of training to prepare students for gainful employment in a recognized occupation and (2) a public or nonprofit private educational institution in any State that admits as regular students persons who are beyond the age of compulsory school attendance in the State in which the institution is located.

Section 1002. Definition of institution of higher education for purposes of student assistance [financial aid] programs.

. . . [T]he term "institution of higher education" includes, in addition to the institutions covered [above], (A) a proprietary institution of higher education [and] (B) a postsecondary vocational institution.

Section 1011a. Protection of student speech and association rights.

(a) Protection of [free speech] rights. Congress [believes] that no student attending an institution of higher education should [be punished for] participation in protected speech or protected association [under the First Amendment]. [For example, no student should] be excluded from participation in, be denied the benefits of, or be subjected to discrimination or official sanction under any education program, activity, or division of the institution directly or indirectly receiving financial assistance under this chapter, whether or not such program, activity, or division is sponsored or officially sanctioned by the institution.

Section 1018. Performance-Based Organization for delivery of federal student financial assistance.

(a) Establishment and purpose.

(1). Establishment. There is established in the Department a Performance-Based Organization (hereafter referred to as the "PBO") which shall be a discrete management unit responsible for managing the operational functions supporting the [financial aid] programs authorized under subchapter IV of this chapter.

(2). Purposes. The purposes of the PBO are:

(A) to improve service to students and other participants in the student financial assistance programs . . . including making those programs more understandable to students and their parents; (B) to reduce the costs of administering [these] programs; (C) to increase the accountability of the officials responsible for administering [these] programs; (D) to provide greater flexibility in the management [of these] programs; (E) to integrate the information systems [of various] Federal student financial assistance programs; (F) to implement an open, common, [single] integrated system for the delivery of student financial assistance . . . and (G) to develop and maintain a student financial assistance system that contains complete, accurate, and timely data to ensure program integrity.

[TITLE II: TEACHER QUALITY ENHANCEMENT]

Section 1021. Purposes; definitions.

(a) Purposes. The purposes of this subchapter are to (1) improve student achievement; (2) improve the quality of the current and future teaching force by improving the preparation of prospective teachers and enhancing professional development activities; (3) hold institutions of higher education accountable for preparing teachers who have the necessary teaching skills and are highly competent in the academic content areas in which the teachers plan to teach, such as mathematics, science, English, foreign languages, history, economics, art, civics, Government, and geography, including training in the effective uses of technology in the classroom; and (4) recruit highly qualified individuals, including individuals from other occupations, into the teaching force.

[TITLE III: INSTITUTIONAL AID]

Section 1051. Findings and purpose.

(a) Findings. The Congress finds that:

(1) there are a significant number of institutions of higher education serving high percentages of minority students and students from low-income backgrounds, that face problems that threaten their ability to survive;

(4) the subchapter III program prior to 1985 did not always meet the specific development needs of historically Black colleges and universities and other institutions with large concentrations of minority, low-income students;

(6) providing assistance to eligible institutions will enhance the role of such institutions in providing access and quality education to low-income and minority students;

(7) these institutions play an important role in the American system of higher education, and there is a strong national interest in assisting them in solving their problems and in stabilizing their management and fiscal operations, and in becoming financially independent; and

(8) there is a particular national interest in aiding those institutions

of higher education that have historically served students who have been denied access to postsecondary education because of race or national origin and whose participation in the American system of higher education is in the Nation's interest so that equality of access and quality of postsecondary education opportunities may be enhanced for all students.

(b) Purpose. It is the purpose of this subchapter to assist such institutions in equalizing educational opportunity through a program of Federal assistance.

Section 1060. Findings and purposes. The Congress finds that . . . :

(2) States and the Federal Government have discriminated in the allocation of [public] land and [public funds] to support Black public institutions under the Morrill Act of 1862 and its progeny, and against public and private Black colleges and universities in the award of federal grants and contracts, and the distribution of federal resources under this chapter and other federal programs which benefit institutions of higher education;

(3) the current state of Black colleges and universities is [in part due to] the discriminatory action of the States and the Federal Government. This [discrimination must be remedied. Consequently, Congress wishes to enhance] Black postsecondary institutions to ensure their continuation and participation in fulfilling the Federal mission of equality of educational opportunity; and

(4) [to provide] financial assistance to establish or strengthen the physical plants, financial management, academic resources, and endowments of the historically Black colleges and universities are appropriate methods to enhance these institutions and facilitate a decrease in reliance on governmental financial support and to encourage reliance on endowments and private sources.

Section 1059c. American Indian tribally controlled colleges and universities.

(a) Program authorized.

The Secretary shall provide grants and related assistance to Indian Tribal Colleges and Universities to enable such institutions to improve and expand their capacity to serve Indian students.

(c) Authorized activities.

(1) In general. Grants awarded under this section shall be used by Tribal Colleges or Universities to assist such institutions to plan, develop, undertake, and carry out activities to improve and expand such institutions' capacity to serve Indian students.

(2) [The funds may be used for: obtaining laboratory equipment;

construction and maintenance of school facilities; faculty development and fellowships; academic instruction; obtaining library books and other materials; tutoring, counseling, and other student services; management of institutional funds; alumni fundraising; teacher education programs; community outreach; and other approved activities.]

[TITLE IV: STUDENT ASSISTANCE]

Section 1070. Statement of purpose; program authorization.

(a) Purpose. It is the purpose of this part, to assist in making available the benefits of postsecondary education to eligible students in institutions of higher education by: (1) providing Federal Pell Grants to all eligible students; (2) providing supplemental educational opportunity grants to those students who demonstrate financial need; (3) providing for payments to the States to assist them in making financial aid available to such students; (4) providing for special programs and projects designed (A) to identify and encourage qualified youths with financial or cultural need with a potential for postsecondary education, (B) to prepare students from low-income families for postsecondary education, and (C) to provide remedial (including remedial language study) and other services to students; and (5) providing assistance to institutions of higher education.

(b) Secretary [of Education] required to carry out purposes. The Secretary shall . . . carry out programs to achieve the purposes of this part.

Section 1070a. Federal Pell Grants: amount and determinations; applications.

(a) Program authority and method of distribution.

(1) For each fiscal year through fiscal year 2004, the Secretary shall pay to each eligible institution such sums as may be necessary to pay to each eligible student (defined in accordance with section 1091 of this title) for each academic year during which that student is in attendance at an institution of higher education, as an undergraduate, a Federal Pell Grant in the amount for which that student is eligible. . . .

(3) Grants made under this subpart shall be known as "Federal Pell Grants."

(b) Purpose and amount of grants. (1) The purpose of this subpart is to provide a Federal Pell Grant that in combination with reasonable family and student contribution and supplemented by the programs authorized under subparts 3 and 4 of this part, will meet at least 75 percent of a student's cost of attendance, unless the institution determines that a greater amount of assistance would better serve the purposes of [this title]. . . .

(2)(A) The amount of the Federal Pell Grant for a student eligible under this part shall be: (i) $4,500 for academic year 1999–2000; (ii) $4,800 for academic year 2000–2001; (iii) $5,100 for academic year 2001–2002; (iv) $5,400 for academic year 2002–2003; and (v) $5,800 for academic year 2003–2004, less an amount equal to the amount determined to be the expected family contribution with respect to that student for that year.

(B) In any case where a student attends an institution of higher education on less than a full-time basis (including a student who attends an institution of higher education on less than a half-time basis) during any academic year, the amount of the Federal Pell Grant to which that student is entitled shall be reduced in proportion to the degree to which that student is not so attending on a full-time basis. . . .

Section 1070a-11. Program authority; authorization of appropriations [for federal TRIO Programs].

(a) Grants and contracts authorized. The Secretary shall, in accordance with the provisions of this division, carry out a program of making grants and contracts designed to identify qualified individuals from disadvantaged backgrounds, to prepare them for a program of postsecondary education, to provide support services for such students who are pursuing programs of postsecondary education, to motivate and prepare students for doctoral programs, and to train individuals serving or preparing for service in programs and projects so designed.

Section 1071. [Federal Family Education Loan Program] Statement of purpose; nondiscrimination; and appropriations authorized.

(a) Purpose; discrimination prohibited.

(1) Purpose. The purpose of this part is to enable the Secretary: (A) to encourage States and nonprofit private institutions and organizations to establish adequate loan insurance programs for students in eligible institutions, (B) to provide a Federal program of student loan insurance for students or lenders who do not have reasonable access to a State or private nonprofit program of student loan insurance covered by an agreement under this title, (C) to pay a portion of the interest on loans to qualified students which are insured under this part, and (D) to guarantee a portion of each loan insured under a program of a State or of a nonprofit private institution or organization.

(2) Discrimination by creditors prohibited. No agency, organization, institution, bank, credit union, corporation, or other lender who regularly extends, renews, or continues credit or provides insurance under this part shall exclude from receipt or deny the benefits of, or discriminate against any borrower or applicant in obtaining, such credit or

insurance on the basis of race, national origin, religion, sex, marital status, age, or handicapped status.

(c) Designation. The program established under this part shall be referred to as the "Robert T. Stafford Federal Student Loan Program." Loans made pursuant to sections 1077 and 1078 of this title shall be known as "Federal Stafford Loans."

Section 1077. Eligibility of student borrowers and terms of federally insured student loans.

(a) List of requirements.

Except as provided in section 1078–3 of this title, a loan by an eligible lender shall be insurable by the Secretary under the provisions of this part only if [it is]:

(1) made to [an eligible] student who has agreed to notify promptly the holder of the loan concerning any change of address, and is carrying at least one-half the normal full-time academic workload for the course of study the student is pursuing (as determined by the institution); and

(2) evidenced by a note or other written agreement which (A) is made without security and without endorsement; (B) provides for repayment of the principal amount of the loan in installments over a period of not less than 5 years nor more than 10 years [and includes a six-month grace period after the student graduates or quits school]; (C) provides that periodic installments of principal need not be paid, but interest shall accrue and be paid, during any period during which the borrower is pursuing at least a half-time course of study as determined by an eligible institution . . . ; (D) provides for interest on the unpaid principal balance of the loan at a yearly rate, not exceeding the applicable maximum rate prescribed [under] this title, which interest shall be payable in installments over the period of the loan [or deferred while the student remains in school, in which case it is added to the principal balance of the loan]; (F) entitles the student borrower to accelerate [pay off the loan early] without penalty repayment of the whole or any part of the loan; [and] (H) provides that, no more than 6 months prior to the date on which the borrower's first payment on a loan is due, the lender shall offer the borrower the option of repaying the loan in accordance with a graduated or income-sensitive repayment schedule established by the lender and in accordance with the regulations of the Secretary. . . .

Section 1087–2. Student Loan Marketing Association [SALLIE MAE].

(a) Purpose. Congress [establishes the Student Loan Marketing Association (Sallie Mae)] as a private corporation which will be financed by private capital. [It will manage federal] student loans . . . and will provide liquidity for student loan investments; (2) [It will also handle the collection of student loan monies, and the purchase or sale of student loans with other financial institutions]; (3) [It will also provide] . . . an additional program of loan insurance [for student loans].

Section 1087a. [William D. Ford Federal Direct Loan] Program authority.

(a) In general. [Congress appropriates] such sums as may be necessary to make [these] loans to all eligible students (and the eligible parents of such students) in attendance at participating institutions of higher education selected by the Secretary, to enable such students to pursue their courses of study at such institutions. [These] loans shall be made by participating institutions, or consortia thereof, that have agreements with the Secretary to [make] loans . . . for students in attendance at participating institutions (and their parents).

(b) Designation.

(1) Program. The program established under this part shall be referred to as the "William D. Ford Federal Direct Loan Program."

(2) Direct loans. Notwithstanding any other provision of this part, loans made to borrowers under this part . . . shall be known as "Federal Direct Stafford/Ford Loans."

Section 1087e. Terms and conditions of loans.

(a) In general.

(1) Parallel terms, conditions, benefits, and amounts. Unless otherwise specified in this part, loans made to borrowers under this part shall have the same terms, conditions, and benefits, and be available in the same amounts, as [the FFEL Loans, described above].

(2) Designation of loans. Loans made to borrowers under this part that, except as otherwise specified in this part, have the same terms, conditions, and benefits as loans made to borrowers under (A) section 1078 of this title shall be known as "Federal Direct Stafford Loans"; (B) section 1078–2 of this title shall be known as "Federal Direct PLUS Loans"; and (C) section 1078–8 of this title shall be known as "Federal Direct Unsubsidized Stafford Loans."

Section 1087aa. [Perkins Loan] Appropriations authorized.

(a) Program authority. The Secretary shall carry out a program of stimulating and assisting in the establishment and maintenance of funds at institutions of higher education for the making of low-interest loans to students in need thereof to pursue their courses of study in such institutions or while engaged in programs of study abroad approved for credit by such institutions. Loans made under this part shall be known as "Federal Perkins Loans."

Section 1087kk. Amount of need [Needs Analysis].

Except as otherwise provided, the amount of need of any student for financial assistance under [Title IV] is equal to (1) the cost of attendance of such student, minus (2) the expected family contribution for such student, minus (3) estimated financial assistance not received under this [title].

Section 1087nn. Determination of expected family contribution; data elements.

(b) Data elements. The following data elements are considered in determining the expected family contribution [toward the student's higher education]: (1) the available income of the student and the student's spouse, or the student and the student's parents, in the case of a dependent student; (2) the number of dependents in the family of the student; (3) the number of dependents in the family of the student [generally siblings] who are enrolled or accepted for enrollment, on at least a half-time basis, in a degree, certificate, or other program leading to a recognized educational credential at an institution of higher education and for whom the family may reasonably be expected to contribute to their postsecondary education; (4) the net assets of the student and the student's spouse, [or] the student and the student's parents, in the case of a dependent student; (5) the marital status of the student; (6) the age of the older parent, in the case of a dependent student; and (7) the additional expenses incurred [by the student's employed spouse or parents].

Section 1078–2. Federal PLUS loans.

(a) Authority to borrow.

(1) Authority and eligibility. Parents of a dependent student shall be eligible to borrow funds under this section in amounts specified in subsection (b) of this section, if the parents do not have an adverse credit history and the parents meet such other eligibility criteria as the Secretary [of Education] may establish by regulation.

(2) Terms, conditions, and benefits. [With minor exceptions, the] loans made under this section shall have the same terms, conditions, and benefits as all other loans made under this part.

(b) Limitation based on need. . . . [N]o loan may be made to any parent under this section for any academic year in excess of (A) the student's estimated cost of attendance, minus (B) other financial aid as certified by the eligible institution under this title, [including other federal student loans].

Section 1078–8. Unsubsidized Stafford loans for middle-income borrowers.

(a) In general. It is the purpose of this section to authorize insured loans under this part for borrowers who do not qualify for Federal interest subsidy payments. Except as provided in this section, all terms and conditions for Federal Stafford loans established [above] shall apply to loans made pursuant to this section.

(b) Eligible borrowers. Any student meeting the requirements for student eligibility of this title (including graduate and professional students as defined in regulations [created] by the Secretary) shall be entitled to borrow an unsubsidized Federal Stafford Loan if the eligible institution at which the student has been accepted for enrollment, or at which the student is in attendance, has determined and documented the student's need for the loan based on the student's estimated cost of attendance and the student's estimated financial assistance. . . .

(c) Determination of amount of loan. The determination of the amount of a loan by an eligible institution shall be calculated by subtracting from the estimated cost of attendance at the eligible institution any estimated financial assistance reasonably available to such student.

(d) Loan limits.

(1) In general. [The] annual and aggregate limits for loans under this section shall be the same as those [for Stafford loan programs described above].

(2) Annual limits for independent, graduate, and professional students. The maximum annual amount of loans under this section an independent student may borrow in any academic year [is] $4,000, if such student is enrolled in a program whose length is at least one academic year in length; or $5,000, in the case of a student who has successfully completed such first and second years but has not successfully completed the remainder of a program of undergraduate education. . . . [In] the case of a graduate or professional student, the limit is $10,000; and for . . . a student who has obtained a baccalaureate degree who wishes to complete the coursework necessary for a professional credential or certification from a State required for employment as a teacher, the limit is $5,000.

[Author's Note: Loan eligibility requirements, application procedures, and maximum amounts that can be borrowed change frequently. Students can find out about current financial aid opportunities and rates through the Department of Education's website. The url for this website is listed in the appendix.]

[TITLE V: DEVELOPING INSTITUTIONS]

Part A

Section 1101. [Hispanic-Serving Institutions] Findings; purpose; and program authority.

(a) Findings. Congress makes the following findings:

(1) Hispanic Americans are at high risk of not enrolling or graduating from institutions of higher education.

(3) Despite significant limitations in resources, Hispanic-serving Institutions provide a significant proportion of postsecondary opportunities for Hispanic students.

(4) Relative to other institutions of higher education, Hispanic-serving institutions are underfunded. Such institutions receive significantly less in State and local funding, per full-time equivalent student, than other institutions of higher education.

(6) There is a national interest in remedying disparities and ensuring that Hispanic students have an equal opportunity to pursue postsecondary opportunities.

(b) Purpose. The purpose of this subchapter is to: (1) expand educational opportunities for, and improve the academic attainment of, Hispanic students; and (2) expand and enhance the academic offerings, program quality, and institutional stability of colleges and universities that are educating the majority of Hispanic college students and helping large numbers of Hispanic students and other low-income individuals complete postsecondary degrees.

(c) Program authority. The Secretary shall provide grants and related assistance to Hispanic-serving institutions to enable such institutions to improve and expand their capacity to serve Hispanic students and other low-income individuals.

[TITLE VII: GRADUATE AND POSTSECONDARY IMPROVEMENT PROGRAMS]

Section 1133. Purpose.

It is the purpose of this subchapter:

(1) to authorize national graduate fellowship programs (A) in order to attract students of superior ability and achievement, exceptional promise, and demonstrated financial need, into high-quality graduate programs and provide the students with the financial support necessary

to complete advanced degrees; and (B) that are designed to sustain and enhance the capacity for graduate education in areas of national need; and encourage talented students to pursue scholarly careers in the humanities, social sciences, and the arts; and to promote postsecondary programs.

17

Rehabilitation Act of 1973

1973

Although Congress had adopted legislation in the past to assist certain classes of disabled citizens, all of its prior efforts combined could not match the scope of the Rehabilitation Act of 1973. With this one law disabled persons gained significant new rights and new powers to enforce them, ones that remain in full force today.

The Rehabilitation Act contains several sections. Among other things, it prohibits discrimination against the disabled in federal employment or by the federal government's contractors and subcontractors. With regard to young people, Section 504 of the Rehabilitation Act proves most important. In a nutshell, Section 504 requires that any program or activity that receives federal funds must be accessible to the disabled. This directive seems and is straightforward. What may not be so obvious is how many institutions, both then and now, receive federal funds and are therefore obligated to follow the Rehabilitation Act.

For example, virtually every college and university in the United States, public or private, receives federal funding of some sort, whether through land or construction grants, research fellowships, or student financial aid. Consequently, they must open their doors to the disabled and ensure that disabled students can participate in the same educational and extracurricular activities enjoyed by non-disabled students.

But colleges and universities are not the only entities receiving federal funds. School districts across the nation routinely receive these funds. Virtually every state or charitable social service agency relies on some amount of federal funding to function, whether it provides welfare, low-income housing, health care, child care, job training, legal services, or some other federally subsidized service. Even private businesses that receive federal funds must make sure that their programs and activities are accessible to the disabled.

Under Section 504 a typical disabled student is assured that he or she will not be discriminated against in admissions and that the school will not use the disability to limit financial aid. The school's classrooms must be accessible to the disabled. Dormitories must include housing for disabled students. Cafeterias, bathrooms, student centers, and other common areas must be made accessible as well. In addition to providing accessible facilities, a university must provide certain accommodations to disabled students, such as sign language interpreters, special transportation, extra time on assignments and examinations if necessary, transcribers, and other assistance, as needed.

In addition, the school cannot hold the disabled student to a standard higher than that expected of other students, nor can it exclude the student from courses or other educational programs or activities, including academic field trips and extracurricular activities. In short, the school must make accommodations to ensure that the needs of the disabled student are met and that the student enjoys the same opportunities that other students receive.

If a disabled person is denied participation in a program or activity, or if appropriate accommodations are not forthcoming, the act provides that person many avenues of redress. First, the disabled person can ask for an impartial review or hearing of his or her complaint. The complaint is usually addressed to and handled by the institution that allegedly has denied the services. Second, he or she can file a separate complaint with the U.S. Department of Education, which is charged with investigating violations of this law. Finally, the person can bring a lawsuit in federal court and, if successful, can receive typical types of relief, including money damages and an order or injunction from the court.

Clearly, the Rehabilitation Act was, and remains, sweeping in its protection of the disabled, including disabled students. But this act simply mandates that other entities—state, local, or private—adhere to Congress' directive. The act itself did not create any federal programs for the disabled or provide special funding to achieve its nondiscrimination goals. So while the act was groundbreaking, it did not really represent a comprehensive federal commitment to eradicating discrimination against disabled persons. But it was an important effort, and Congress was not done yet. In the following two decades Congress passed two more sweeping pieces of legislation, the Individuals with Disabilities Education Act and the Americans with Disabilities Act. Together with the Rehabilitation Act of 1973, these three laws provide extensive, and sometimes even overlapping, rights and protections to the disabled.

17. Rehabilitation Act of 1973

Section 794. Nondiscrimination under Federal grants and programs; promulgation of rules and regulations. [In the original act, this excerpt was Section 504. It was recodified as Section 794. Despite this fact, this excerpt is still commonly referred to as Section 504.]

(a) Promulgation of rules and regulations.

No otherwise qualified individual with a disability in the United States shall, solely by reason of his or her disability, be excluded from the participation in, be denied the benefits of, or be subjected to discrimination under any program or activity receiving Federal financial assistance or under any program or activity conducted by any Executive agency or by the United States Postal Service.

(b) "Program or activity" defined.

For the purposes of this section, the term "program or activity" means all of the operations of:

(1) (A) a department, agency, special purpose district, or other instrumentality of a State or of a local government; or (B) the entity of such State or local government that distributes [or receives federal assistance];

(2) (A) a college, university, or other postsecondary institution, or a public system of higher education; or (B) a local educational agency, system of vocational education, or other school system;

(3) (A) an entire corporation, partnership, or other private organization, or an entire sole proprietorship, [including, but not limited to, any] business of providing education, health care, housing, social services, or parks and recreation. . . .

(d) Standards used in determining violation of section.

The standards used to determine whether this section has been violated in a complaint alleging employment discrimination under this section shall be the standards applied under title I of the Americans with Disabilities Act. . . .

Section 794a. Remedies and attorney fees.

(a) (1) The remedies, procedures, and rights [that are described] in section 717 of the Civil Rights Act of 1964 shall be available . . . to any employee or applicant for employment [who filed a complaint but is not satisfied with its disposition]. In fashioning an equitable or affirmative action remedy [for the employee], a court may take into account the reasonableness of the cost of any necessary work place accommodation, and the availability [of] . . . other appropriate relief in order to achieve an equitable and appropriate remedy. (2) The remedies, procedures, and rights set forth in title VI of the Civil Rights Act of 1964 shall be available to any person aggrieved by any act or failure to act by any recipient of Federal assistance or Federal provider of such assistant under [this act].

(b) In any action or proceeding to enforce or charge a violation of a provision of this subchapter, the court, in its discretion, may allow the prevailing party . . . a reasonable attorney's fee as part of the costs.

18

Individuals with Disabilities Education Act (IDEA)

1975

The Rehabilitation Act of 1973 proved a significant step in Congress' protection of disabled individuals. But it was just a first step. Congress' next two major pieces of disability legislation, the Individuals with Disabilities Education Act and the Americans with Disabilities Act, would greatly expand the rights of disabled persons and especially disabled children.

In 1975 Congress passed the Education for All Handicapped Children Act, which sought to encourage and assist local governments in providing educational services to disabled children. This act was amended and underwent a name change in 1983 and became known as the Individuals with Disabilities Education Act, or "IDEA." In 1997 the IDEA was amended again to make it an even more powerful tool for disabled students and their parents. Although the 1997 amendments are relatively new, the IDEA legislation has been in effect in some form or another for over twenty-five years.

The key provision of the original act still represents the heart of the IDEA: disabled children are entitled to a "free appropriate" public school education. The provision of free public education is not new; the states have traditionally undertaken this important responsibility, and many state constitutions even recognize public education as a right of its citizens. But despite this fact, disabled children were historically turned away from public schools. Disabled children lucky enough to be allowed to attend school were often simply warehoused there and did not participate in meaningful educational activities. Moreover, schools in the past rarely checked or tested for latent (undetected) disabilities. Consequently, many children attended public schools but performed poorly—only to find out later that they had an undiagnosed disability that had adversely affected their performance. They had received a free education while in school but certainly not an appropriate one. And, unfortunately, poor or failing students were often labeled as lazy, apathetic, or uncooperative, when in fact their disabilities had contributed to their problems in school.

The act sought to change these unacceptable conditions, in an effort not only to ensure that disabled children received a free and appropriate education, but also that their education prepared them, to the extent possible, to live independently and become self-sufficient. The IDEA makes it perfectly clear that disabled young people should expect to lead as typical a life as possible, living on their own, supporting themselves, and participating in society as any nondisabled person would.

In order to achieve these goals the IDEA requires all state and local governments to implement procedures for screening and diagnosing disabilities in children. The act mentions many categories of disability, including "mental retardation, a hearing impairment including deafness, a speech or language impairment, a visual impairment including blindness, serious emotional disturbance (hereafter referred to as emotional disturbance), an orthopedic impairment, autism, traumatic brain injury, any other health impairment, a specific learning disability, deaf-blindness, or multiple disabilities."

What do those categories mean? In short, just about any disability can qualify a child for special education under the law if that disability impairs or interferes with the child's ability to learn. If the child has a disability and, because of it, needs special education, that child is considered a "disabled child" under the IDEA. Therefore, the categories listed above are only general ones. Within the categories a number of conditions and diseases may qualify a child for a free and appropriate public school education under the IDEA. An "orthopedic impairment," for example, can include clubfoot, missing limbs, and cerebral palsy. An "emotional disturbance" can include depression, bi-polar disorder, and schizophrenia. "Other health impairments" can include, among other things, attention deficit disorder and attention deficit hyperactivity disorder, asthma, diabetes, sickle cell anemia, epilepsy, and leukemia. A "specific learning disability" includes dyslexia and numerous other conditions. As the list of covered disabilities is extensive, any child who may have a condition requiring special education would be wise to obtain an official diagnosis and consult with local school officials to determine eligibility under the act.

Once diagnosed with a disability, each child must receive an individual assessment of his or her educational needs. The school or school district, working with the child and parents, then develops a plan for meeting those needs. Today, this plan is known as an "IEP," or "Individualized Educational Program." The IEP is a very specific document. By law it must identify the child's disability and explain how it hinders his or her educational progress; state clear, measurable goals for the child's educational progress; detail the services or types of assistance the child will receive; and provide for regular input, assessment, and modification by all participants to the plan. The school must put together an IEP team to perform these functions, which generally consists of the child and parents, a school administrator, the child's special education teachers, and, again by law, at least one of the child's regular education teachers.

In addition to educating disabled children, the school must also provide them with "related services." Under the law, "related services" refers to "transportation and such developmental, corrective, and other supportive services as are required to assist a child with a disability to benefit from special education." These services include those of interpreters and readers, counselors, physical therapists, psychologists, and medical personnel. "Assistive devices" must also be provided. These can include hearing aids or other amplification devices, computers, or other items that help a disabled child learn.

Originally, the IDEA applied only to children from three to twenty-five years of age. It was later amended to include even younger children, in the hope that early intervention would provide even greater educational benefits. Technically, the right to a free and appropriate education continues until a child graduates from high school. However, the 1997 amendments require that a student's IEP consider what will happen upon graduation and plan accordingly for the student's transition from school to work. This kind of transition planning must begin when the child turns fourteen. The transitional plan can include a number of components, such as job training, job placement, continuing post-secondary education, or referrals to assisted living facilities.

In addition, it is important to point out that the IDEA applies even when disabled children have been suspended from or expelled from school. Sometimes a child's disability includes or results in behavioral problems that manifest themselves at school. A school must try to accommodate that student in regular classrooms if possible. If, however, the child is too disruptive to remain in a regular classroom, the school's obligation does not end. The school needs to provide some sort of alternative setting for the child's education, often in the form of an after-school program or an alternative school.

The IDEA applies primarily to public schools; however, the 1997 amendments extended the act in part to private schools as well. Like a public school, if a private school accepts federal funds to assist disabled students, it must meet the general requirements of this act. The school must have an IEP-like plan in place for each disabled student, and it must provide necessary accommodations and services to meet the goals of the act.

Although extremely important, the guarantee of a free and appropriate public education for disabled students is just one component of the IDEA. Other important aspects include the participation of parents as well as educators in the educational plans for the child, the regular assessment and evaluation of those plans, an emphasis on including a child in regular classes and programs where possible (often referred to as "mainstreaming" or placing the child in the "least restrictive environment"), and the ability of the parents to object to an inadequate or inappropriate plan. In fact, parents have extensive rights guaranteeing the careful review of any complaints they might have about their child's IEP.

As a first step, dissatisfied parents can try to work out their differences with school personnel. If that fails, they can request a formal review of their complaint by the state. This review is generally conducted by the state agency that regulates education. It consists of a hearing during which the parents enjoy many of the same due process protections granted to criminal defendants: they have the right to their own attorney; their case must be heard by an objective and impartial decisionmaker or arbiter; they have the right to see the other side's evidence; they can present and cross-examine witnesses; they must receive a written order of decision; and they have the right to appeal. If the state rejects their complaint, the parents are free to appeal that decision by bringing a lawsuit in state or federal court. If the parents prevail in court, they are entitled to recover the attorneys' fees they have expended on their case. Finally, if they wish, the parents can also file a separate complaint with the U.S. Department of Education and ask that agency to investigate their claims.

Few can quarrel with the goals of the IDEA. In adopting this law, Congress declared its support for greater equality and enhanced opportunities for disabled children. The specificity of the act demonstrates that Congress did not offer idle words of support, but rather undertook to create a comprehensive approach to educating and emancipating disabled children. Congress has backed up the act with extensive funding—billions have been spent so far. But special education is expensive, and despite federal and state funding efforts, government has not come close to paying for needed educational services. Consequently, many groups, including the federal government's own National Council on Disability, have called for Congress to increase spending on the IDEA. They have labeled it an "underfunded mandate," which means that Congress has ordered the states to comply with this new law for educating disabled children (the "mandate"), without providing adequate funds to the states so that they can meet their legal obligations. Because of inadequate funding, great numbers of disabled children have yet to benefit from the rights Congress established in passing the IDEA.

The Supreme Court entered the funding debate in 1999, in the case of *Cedar Rapids Community School District v. Garret F.* Garret F. was a disabled student in the Cedar Rapids school system. A motorcycle accident at age four had left him paralyzed from the neck down. Consequently, he was bound to a wheelchair and needed a ventilator to breathe. Because of this disability, he required continuous supervision and care by a nurse, including care during school hours. The school district refused to pay for Garret's nurse, arguing among other things that it could not afford to pay for a full-time nurse for a single student. In a seven to two decision, the Supreme Court held that the care of the nurse was a "related service" required by the IDEA. The school district was therefore responsible for providing Garret's nurse.

The Court acknowledged that the school district had "legitimate financial concerns," but noted that Congress had intended the IDEA to "open the door of public education" to disabled children. The Court implied that Congress, through its lawmaking power, could provide guidance and support to school districts that deal with the exceptional expenses incurred in accommodating children like Garret. Until Congress acted, however, the Court could only follow the law and ensure Garret received his nurse; how to pay for it was a political question, not a legal one, and the Court did not resolve it.

Lack of funding probably explains why so many states have yet to fully implement the IDEA. Despite over twenty-five years of efforts to ensure adequate instruction under the IDEA, large numbers of disabled children remain marginalized in public schools. Some school districts lack a commitment to the act or try to limit the number and types of services they offer to disabled students. Other districts value conformity and ease of administration and resist including disabled students in regular classrooms. Still other districts cannot meet their funding requirements for regular education, let alone for special education. Disgruntled parents have recourse, as described above, but often find the prospect of challenging entrenched school officials to be daunting and costly, not to mention time-consuming. Moreover, the federal government, which has responsibility for overseeing state compliance with IDEA, has not yet put forth enough resources to ensure that the states are regularly meeting their obligations.

While great progress has been made in the education of disabled children, the potential of the IDEA remains unfulfilled. Almost everyone agrees with the IDEA in spirit; the challenge remains to meet and abide by the letter of this law. Disabled students and parents, and indeed all who believe in equal treatment and opportunity, need to remain active in asserting the civil rights that Congress recognized with the passage of this sweeping legislation. Only by bringing pressure to bear on Congress, state governments, and local school districts will the promise of the IDEA become reality for all of our nation's disabled children.

18. Individuals with Disabilities Education Act (IDEA)

Section 1400. Congressional statements and declarations.

(a) Short title. This chapter may be cited as the "Individuals with Disabilities Education Act."

(c) Findings. The Congress finds the following:

(1) Disability is a natural part of the human experience and in no way diminishes the right of individuals to participate in or contribute to society. Improving educational results for children with disabilities

is an essential element of our national policy of ensuring equality of opportunity, full participation, independent living, and economic self-sufficiency for individuals with disabilities.

(2) Before the date of the enactment of the Education for All Handicapped Children Act of 1975:

(A) the special educational needs of children with disabilities were not being fully met;

(B) more than one-half of the children with disabilities in the United States did not receive appropriate educational services that would enable such children to have full equality of opportunity;

(C) 1,000,000 of the children with disabilities in the United States were excluded entirely from the public school system and did not go through the educational process with their peers;

(D) there were many children with disabilities throughout the United States participating in regular school programs whose disabilities prevented such children from having a successful educational experience because their disabilities were undetected; and

(E) because of the lack of adequate services within the public school system, families were often forced to find services outside the public school system, often at great distance from their residence and at their own expense.

(3) Since the enactment and implementation of the Education for All Handicapped Children Act of 1975, this chapter has been successful in ensuring children with disabilities and the families of such children access to a free appropriate public education and in improving educational results for children with disabilities.

(4) However, the implementation of this chapter has been impeded by low expectations, and an insufficient focus on applying replicable research on proven methods of teaching and learning for children with disabilities.

(5) Over 20 years of research and experience has demonstrated that the education of children with disabilities can be made more effective by:

(A) having high expectations for such children and ensuring their access in the general curriculum to the maximum extent possible;

(B) strengthening the role of parents and ensuring that families of such children have meaningful opportunities to participate in the education of their children at school and at home;

(C) coordinating this chapter with other local, educational service agency, State, and Federal school improvement efforts in order to ensure that such children benefit from such efforts and that special education can become a service for such children rather than a place where they are sent;

(D) providing appropriate special education and related services and aids and supports in the regular classroom to such children, whenever appropriate;

(E) supporting high-quality, intensive professional development for all personnel who work with such children in order to ensure that they have the skills and knowledge necessary to enable them to meet developmental goals and, to the maximum extent possible, those challenging expectations that have been established for all children; and to be prepared to lead productive, independent, adult lives, to the maximum extent possible;

(F) providing incentives for whole-school approaches and pre-referral intervention to reduce the need to label children as disabled in order to address their learning needs; and

(G) focusing resources on teaching and learning while reducing paperwork and requirements that do not assist in improving educational results.

(6) While States, local educational agencies, and educational service agencies are responsible for providing an education for all children with disabilities, it is in the national interest that the Federal Government have a role in assisting State and local efforts to educate children with disabilities in order to improve results for such children and to ensure equal protection of the law.

(7)(A) The Federal Government must be responsive to the growing needs of an increasingly more diverse society. A more equitable allocation of resources is essential for the Federal Government to meet its responsibility to provide an equal educational opportunity for all individuals. [. . . To this end, we must recognize that America is becoming a much more racially and ethnically diverse country. We must ensure that disabled minority children are served and, to that end, must recruit more minorities into the service of children.]

(8)(A) Greater efforts are needed to prevent the intensification of problems connected with mislabeling and high dropout rates among minority children with disabilities.

(d) Purposes. The purposes of this chapter are:

(1)(A) to ensure that all children with disabilities have available to them a free appropriate public education that emphasizes special education and related services designed to meet their unique needs and prepare them for employment and independent living; (B) to ensure that the rights of children with disabilities and parents of such children are protected; and (C) to assist States, localities, educational service agencies, and Federal agencies to provide for the education of all children with disabilities;

(2) to assist States in the implementation of a statewide, comprehensive, coordinated, multidisciplinary, interagency system of early intervention services for infants and toddlers with disabilities and their families;

(3) to ensure that educators and parents have the necessary tools to improve educational results for children with disabilities . . . ; and

(4) to assess, and ensure the effectiveness of, efforts to educate children with disabilities.

Section 1401. Definitions.

(3) Child with a disability.

(A) In general, the term "child with a disability" means a child: (i) with mental retardation, hearing impairments (including deafness), speech or language impairments, visual impairment (including blindness), serious emotional disturbance (hereinafter referred to as "emotional disturbance"), orthopedic impairments, autism, traumatic brain injury, other health impairments, or specific learning disabilities; and (ii) who, by reason thereof, needs special education and related services [which are defined below.]

(B) Child aged 3 through 9. The term "child with a disability" for a child aged 3 through 9 may, at the discretion of the State and the local educational agency, include a child: (i) experiencing developmental delays, as defined by the State and as measured by appropriate diagnostic instruments and procedures, in one or more of the following areas: physical development, cognitive development, communication development, social or emotional development, or adaptive development; and (ii) who, by reason thereof, needs special education and related services. . . .

(8) Free appropriate public education. The term "free appropriate public education" means special education and related services that (A) have been provided at public expense, under public supervision and direction, and without charge; (B) meet the standards of the State educational agency; (C) include an appropriate preschool, elementary, or secondary school education in the State involved; and (D) are provided in conformity with the individualized education program [IEP] required under [this act]. . . .

(22) Related services. The term "related services" means transportation, and such developmental, corrective, and other supportive serv-

ices (including speech-language pathology and audiology services, psychological services, physical and occupational therapy, recreation, including therapeutic recreation, social work services, counseling services, including rehabilitation counseling, orientation and mobility services, and medical services, except that such medical services shall be for diagnostic and evaluation purposes only) as may be required to assist a child with a disability to benefit from special education, and includes the early identification and assessment of disabling conditions in children. . . .

(25) Special education. The term "special education" means specially designed instruction, at no cost to parents, to meet the unique needs of a child with a disability, including: (A) instruction conducted in the classroom, in the home, in hospitals and institutions, and in other settings; and (B) instruction in physical education.

Section 1412. State eligibility.

(a) In general. A State is eligible for assistance under this subchapter for a fiscal year if the State demonstrates . . . that it meets each of the following conditions: [(1) It makes a free appropriate public education available to all disabled children age three through twenty-one; (2) it pursues the goal of providing full educational opportunities to them; (3) it seeks out, identifies, and evaluates disabled children; (4) it develops an Individualized Education Program for each disabled child; (5) it instructs these children, to the extent possible, in a regular school environment with non-disabled children; (6) it ensures that evaluation methods and procedures are not racially or culturally discriminatory; (7) it follows the evaluation standards of this act; (8) it maintains the confidentiality of records and information about its disabled children; (9) it provides for a smooth transition for disabled toddlers into pre-school; (10) it allows disabled children in private schools to receive educational services as provided in this act; . . . (16) it establishes educational performance goals and indicators for disabled children; (17) it provides for regular assessment of their progress . . . ; and (20) it allows for public participation in disability education policies set under this act.]

Section 1414. Evaluations, eligibility determinations, individualized education programs, and educational placements.

(b) Evaluation procedures. . . .

(2) Conduct of evaluation. In conducting the evaluation, the local educational agency shall:

(A) use a variety of assessment tools and strategies to gather relevant functional and developmental information . . . , including information related to enabling the child to be involved in and progress in the general curriculum or, for preschool children, to participate in appropriate activities;

(B) not use any single procedure as the sole criterion for determining whether a child is a child with a disability or determining an appropriate educational program for the child; and

(C) use technically sound instruments that may assess the relative contribution of cognitive and behavioral factors, in addition to physical or developmental factors.

(4) Determination of eligibility. Upon completion of administration of tests and other evaluation materials, a team of qualified professionals and the parents of the child . . . shall determine whether the child has a disability. . . .

(d) Individualized education programs.

(1) Definitions. As used in this chapter:

(A) Individualized education program. The term "individualized education program" or "IEP" means a written statement for each child with a disability that is developed, reviewed, and revised in accordance with this section and that includes:

(i) a statement of the child's present levels of educational performance, including (I) how the child's disability affects the child's involvement and progress in the general curriculum; or (II) for preschool children, as appropriate, how the disability affects the child's participation in appropriate activities;

(ii) a statement of measurable annual goals, including benchmarks or short-term objectives, related to (I) meeting the child's needs that result from the child's disability to enable the child to be involved in and progress in the general curriculum; and (II) meeting each of the child's other educational needs that result from the child's disability;

(iii) a statement of the special education and related services and supplementary aids and services to be provided to the child. . . . [The IEP should] advance [the child] appropriately toward attaining the annual goals; [involve the child] in the general curriculum in accordance with clause (i); [provide for the child] to participate in extracurricular and other nonacademic activities; and [afford the child an opportunity to be] educated and [to] participate with other children with disabilities and nondisabled children . . . ;

(iv) an explanation of the extent, if any, to which the child will not participate with nondisabled children in the regular class and in the activities described in clause (iii);

(v) (I) a statement of any individual modifications in the administration of State or districtwide assessments of student achievement that are needed in order for the child to participate in such assessment; [if such assessments are not used, the IEP must explain why and must describe how the child will be assessed.]

(vii) (I) beginning at age 14, and updated annually, a statement of the transition service needs of the child under the applicable components of the child's IEP that focuses on the child's courses of study (such as participation in advanced-placement courses or a vocational education program);

(II) beginning at age 16 (or younger, if determined appropriate by the IEP Team), a statement of needed transition services for the child.

(B) Individualized education program team. The term "individualized education program team" or "IEP Team" means a group of individuals composed of (i) the parents of a child with a disability; (ii) at least one regular education teacher of such child (if the child is, or may be, participating in the regular education environment); (iii) at least one special education teacher, or where appropriate, at least one special education provider of such child; (iv) a representative of the local educational agency who (I) is qualified to provide, or supervise the provision of, specially designed instruction to meet the unique needs of children with disabilities; (II) is knowledgeable about the general curriculum; and (III) is knowledgeable about the availability of resources of the local educational agency; (v) an individual who can interpret the instructional implications of evaluation results, who may be a member of the team described in clauses (ii) through (vi); (vi) at the discretion of the parent or the agency, other individuals who have knowledge or special expertise regarding the child, including related services personnel as appropriate; and (vii) whenever appropriate, the child with a disability.

[SUBCHAPTER III: INFANTS AND TODDLERS WITH DISABILITIES]

Section 1431. Findings and policy.

(a) Findings. The Congress finds that there is an urgent and substantial need (1) to enhance the development of infants and toddlers with disabilities and to minimize their potential for developmental delay; (2) to reduce the educational costs to our society, including our Nation's schools, by minimizing the need for special education and related services after infants and toddlers with disabilities reach school age; (3) to minimize the likelihood of institutionalization of individuals with disabilities and maximize the potential for their independently living in society; (4) to enhance the capacity of families to meet the special needs of their infants and toddlers with disabilities; and (5) to enhance the capacity of State and local agencies and service providers to identify, evaluate, and meet the needs of historically underrepresented populations, particularly minority, low-income, inner-city, and rural populations.

(b) Policy. It is therefore the policy of the United States to provide financial assistance to States (1) to develop and implement a statewide system that provides early intervention services for infants and toddlers with disabilities and their families, [that expands the states' existing] capacity to provide quality early intervention services, and [that encourages] States to expand opportunities for children under 3 years of age who [are] at risk of having substantial developmental delay if they [do] not receive early intervention services.

Section 1432. Definitions.

As used in this subchapter: (1) At-risk infant or toddler. The term "at-risk infant or toddler" means an individual under 3 years of age who would be at risk of experiencing a substantial developmental delay if early intervention services were not provided. . . . ; (4) Early intervention services. The term "early intervention services" means developmental services that are [publicly] provided at no cost . . . to meet the developmental needs of an infant or toddler with a disability in any of the following areas: physical development; cognitive development; communication development; social or emotional development; or adaptive development. . . . (E) [Services to be provided] include: family training, counseling, and home visits; special instruction; speech-language pathology and audiology services; occupational therapy; physical therapy; psychological services; service coordination services; medical services only for diagnostic or evaluation purposes; early identification, screening, and assessment services; health services necessary to enable the infant or toddler to benefit from the other early intervention services; social work services; vision services; assistive technology devices and assistive technology services; and transportation and related costs that are necessary to enable an infant or toddler and the infant's or toddler's family to receive another service described in this paragraph. . . . (G) To the maximum extent appropriate, [these services should be] provided in natural environments, including the home, and community settings in which children without disabilities participate. . . . (5) Infant or toddler with a disability. The term "infant or toddler with a disability": (A) means an individual under 3 years of age who needs early intervention services because the individual (i) is experiencing developmental delays, as measured by appropriate diagnostic instruments and procedures in one or more of the areas of cognitive development, physical development, communication development, social or emotional development, and adaptive development; or (ii) has a diagnosed physical or mental condition which has a high probability of resulting in developmental delay; and (B) may also include, at a State's discretion, at-risk infants and toddlers.

Section 1436. Individualized family service plan.

(a) Assessment and program development. [Each state shall assess] the unique strengths and needs of the infant or toddler and [identify] services appropriate to meet [his or her] needs. [The state shall also assess] the resources . . . necessary to enhance the family's capacity to meet the developmental needs of the infant or toddler. [The state shall provide] a written individualized family service plan [to the infant or toddler's family].

(d) Content of plan. The individualized family service plan shall be in writing and contain (1) a statement of the infant's or toddler's present levels of physical development, cognitive development, communication development, social or emotional development, and adaptive development, based on objective criteria; (2) a statement of the family's resources, priorities, and concerns relating to enhancing the development of the family's infant or toddler with a disability; (3) a statement of the major outcomes expected to be achieved for the infant or toddler and the family, and the criteria, procedures, and timelines used to determine the degree to which progress toward achieving the outcomes is being made . . . ; (4) a statement of specific early intervention services necessary to meet the unique needs of the infant or toddler . . . ; (5) a statement of the natural environments in which early intervention services shall appropriately be provided . . . ; (6) the projected dates for initiation of services and the anticipated duration of the services; (7) the identification of the service . . . who will be responsible for the implementation of the plan and coordination with other agencies and persons; and (8) the steps to be taken to support the transition of the toddler with a disability to preschool or other appropriate services.

[PART A: STATE PROGRAM IMPROVEMENT GRANTS FOR CHILDREN WITH DISABILITIES]

Section 1451. Findings and purpose.

(a) Findings. The Congress finds the following: . . .

(3) Targeted Federal financial resources are needed to assist States, working in partnership with others, to identify and make needed

changes to address the needs of children with disabilities into the next century.

(b) Purpose. The purpose of this part is to assist State educational agencies, and their partners, in reforming and improving their systems for providing educational, early intervention, and transitional services, including their systems for professional development, technical assistance, and dissemination of knowledge about best practices, to improve results for children with disabilities.

19

Americans with Disabilities Act (ADA)

1990

The Americans with Disabilities Act is perhaps the most comprehensive civil rights legislation passed since the famous Civil Rights Act of 1964. At its core, the act aims to prevent discrimination against the disabled and ensure that they live full and independent lives. It targets four major areas: employment; state and local government, including public transportation; public accommodations; and telecommunications. In each area the act outlaws discrimination against the disabled, calls for enhanced access and opportunities, requires certain accommodations for the needs of the disabled, and provides remedies against violators of the act.

Even the definition of a "disabled person" is sweeping: the act applies to anyone who has a "physical or mental impairment that substantially limits one or more major life functions" (such as learning, working, caring for one's self), or has a record of having such an impairment, or who is *perceived* as having an impairment. The act also protects those who associate with disabled persons. The act applies to virtually all public and private employers, public and private schools, all levels of government, and entities engaged in providing public services—whether or not they receive federal funds. In fact, the language of the act closely resembles that of the Civil Rights Act, which identified groups to be protected from discrimination, detailed unlawful types of discrimination, and provided tough remedies against violators. The ADA follows the same framework.

How did Congress, which is often accused of being bogged down and never able to get anything done, manage to pass such sweeping legislation, and by such a wide, bipartisan margin? Answering this question would require a new book; for present purposes, a summary of the major activities behind the act's passage must suffice.

The National Council on Disability prepared a comprehensive report detailing the history of the ADA, the highlights of which are summarized below. In it author Jonathan M. Young identified many factors that contributed to the act's creation and passage. First, the introduction of the act to Congress was well timed. Congress was not a stranger to disability rights laws, having passed among other things the Rehabilitation Act and the IDEA. But passage of an act as comprehensive as the ADA required something more. That something was public and congressional support. At the time the ADA was introduced, the growing disability rights movement had won a number of legislative and public relations victories across the United States. State legislatures, public and private colleges and universities, and even some private businesses were beginning to take steps to make facilities more accessible and to ensure that disabled persons enjoyed some of the same rights as nondisabled persons. People across the nation were becoming more aware of the challenges facing the disabled and more sympathetic to their cause.

In fact, the Civil Rights Act served as a model for people to understand the disability rights movement. Just as it was unfair to judge, exclude, or otherwise discriminate against people based on the color of their skin or on their choice of religion, so too was it unacceptable to treat the disabled as second-class citizens. People across the country, including public officials, had learned much from the civil rights movement two decades earlier, and were now applying that knowledge to the disability movement. Public opinion supported the idea that it was unfair, and even un-American, to judge people by immutable characteristics—that is, by characteristics that a person did not choose and could not change, like skin color. Disabilities began to be viewed as immutable characteristics. Moreover, people began to abandon the idea that disabled persons offered little to society. As the disabled became more active and more vocal in mainstream American life, their contributions became more widely recognized and appreciated.

Along with the changing perceptions of the American people, Young notes that the ADA owes its passage to the leadership of its early key supporters in Congress and the White House. Many, if not most, of the ADA's early advocates were either disabled themselves or had family members with disabilities. Consequently, they had first-hand experience with the challenges faced by the disabled and with the frustration and poor treatment the disabled often faced in undertaking basic life activities. The act's initial sponsor in the Senate was Senator Lowell Weicker (R-CT), a liberal Republican and long-time advocate for the disabled. In the House, the sponsor was Representative Tony Coelho (D-CA), who suffered from epilepsy. When Senator Weicker lost his re-election bid in 1988, Senator Tom Harkin (D-IA) became the chief sponsor in the Senate. Senator Harkin, who had a deaf brother, enlisted the help of Senator Edward Kennedy (D-MA), a powerful advocate of civil rights who was himself well familiar with disabilities through his own experiences and those of his family members.

The early advocates of the ADA knew it had no chance of passing unless it received bipartisan support. For months Senators Harkin and Kennedy worked to convince important Republican senators to support the ADA. Senator Orrin Hatch (R-UT), who had a solid voting record in support of the disabled as well as a brother paralyzed by polio, was a main target. So too was former presidential candidate Robert Dole (R-KS), who was the Senate's minority leader at that time. Senator Dole also was a strong advocate for the disabled, having been permanently disabled as a result of injuries he sustained in the armed services during World War II.

Hatch and Dole, while sympathetic, were not ready to cosponsor the bill until certain changes were made. In fact, Hatch had his office draft an alternative version of the bill, one tailored to the concerns of Republicans. These two bills eventually merged into one, as the Senate Democrats and Republicans began working on compromise legislation. Republicans enlisted the participation of the White House, given that President George Bush (Sr.) would be required to sign any bill that the Congress succeeded in passing. President Bush, who had both children and relatives with disabilities, proved willing to listen. He sent negotiators from his staff and Cabinet to work with the Senate in framing an acceptable bill.

The major sticking points in drafting the legislation were numerous: some considered the bill too expensive to implement and too much of a burden on private businesses; others wanted religious schools and organizations to be excluded from coverage; still others were concerned that the remedies provided under the bill were too strong, particularly the right to sue. To combat these concerns, drafters provided for a gradual implementation of the act's protections, a qualification that protected entities from "undue" financial burdens, a provision that alterations to allow access be required only if "readily available," and limits on when private lawsuits could be filed. The bill stressed the goals of independence and dignity for the disabled, and tried to strike a balance between the rights of the disabled and the concerns of the institutions that would now be forced to accommodate them.

The process of negotiating the ADA took over two years. Senator Weicker and Representative Coelho introduced their version to their respective houses in April of 1988. After nearly a year and a half of debate, the Senate approved its bill on September 7, 1989, by a whopping margin of seventy-six to eight. The Senate had clearly succeeded in drafting a version of the ADA that enjoyed wide bipartisan support. President Bush had endorsed the Senate bill even before the Senate vote was taken.

The House of Representatives, however, proved more difficult for ADA proponents to negotiate. Earlier in the summer of 1989, Representative Coelho had resigned, leaving the task of ushering the bill through the House to others, particularly Representative Steny Hoyer (D-MD) for the Democrats and Representative Steve Bartlett (R-TX) for the Republicans. Before leaving office Coelho and several dozen co-sponsors introduced a bipartisan version of the bill to their colleagues. However, it took eight more months before the House was finally able to vote on its version of the act. During that time representatives received tremendous pressure from their local constituencies both for and against the bill. Business interests feared the costs of the act; disabled advocates demanded its passage. Constituent pressure led to the introduction of numerous amendments to the House version of the bill. These amendments were not sorted out until late May 1990, when the House finally passed its version of the ADA by a vote of 403 to 20.

Given that the Senate and the House had approved different versions of the act, members from both houses met in conference committee to iron out their differences. According to Jonathan Young, two issues proved particularly divisive: the "Chapman Amendment," which would allow employers to prohibit persons with contagious diseases (and particularly HIV and AIDS) from working as food handlers, and the application of the ADA to Congress itself. The second issue was resolved relatively quickly: the conference committee agreed that the Senate and House, as well as its members, could be sued for violating the ADA. The issue of food handling, to the contrary, was resolved only after major negotiating efforts. Ultimately, the conference committee rejected the Chapman Amendment in favor of a compromise submitted by Senator Hatch. The Hatch Amendment rejected a blanket ban on food handling and proposed instead that the Secretary of Health and Human Services compile a list of those communicable and contagious diseases that were transmittable through food handling. Persons with these diseases could be legally prohibited from handling food. In addition, the amendment provided that local food handling ordinances would remain unaffected by the ADA.

With these compromises the final version of the ADA was ready for a vote. It passed resoundingly: more than 90 percent of the members of both houses approved the legislation. President George Bush (Sr.), who had remained an advocate of ADA amidst the congressional wrangling, signed the bill into law on July 26, 1990. Good timing, strong congressional leadership, a supportive president, and a persistent and outspoken disabled community had come together to make the promise of the ADA a reality.

The ADA itself is divided into five main sections, or titles. For young people the most important sections are Titles II and III, which deal with state and local governments and public accommodations, respectively. These titles resemble the Rehabilitation Act, in that they prohibit state and local governments and all types of public accommodations from discriminating against the disabled. But this time the law binds all entities regardless of whether they receive federal funds. Thus, disabled persons, including disabled children, are specifically entitled to equal access to, and equal treatment by, schools, colleges and universities, technical institutes, day-care centers, and "any other place of education." The act also requires schools and any kind of testing or licensing agency to accommodate disabled test-takers by providing, for example, extra time to complete an examination. Both public and private educational institutions are covered by the ADA; because of a legislative compromise, religious-based ones are exempt.

Under Title III disabled persons must have access to grocery stores, shopping centers, and numerous other social service and retail establishments. They can now also expect access to a whole host of social and cultural venues: hotels, restaurants, and bars; convention centers and exhibit halls; stadiums, gymnasiums, and other recreational facilities; movie theaters and concert arenas; museums and galleries; zoos, parks, and playgrounds. Congress spelled out the types of businesses and facilities covered by the ADA in great detail, as shown in the excerpt of the law provided. Under the act existing establishments are required to make structural changes to their facilities to ensure that they are open to the disabled. New establishments must be constructed to accommodate the disabled. Accommodation generally requires not only changes to the architecture of the main facility, but often to related facilities such as telephones and bathrooms.

With respect to state and local governments, the ADA applies to schools, as mentioned above, but also and importantly to virtually all types of public transportation. Accessible public transportation in many ways is key to the overall success of the ADA; without transportation, disabled individuals cannot take advantage of many of their newly gained employment and recreational opportunities. Title II provides that public transit systems, including buses, commuter rail, light rail, and national rail transit providers such as Amtrak, make their vehicles and rail cars accessible to the disabled, either by refurbishing current fleets, purchasing new accessible equipment, or providing appropriate paratransit services. (Access to air travel is covered by a separate law, the Air Carrier Access Act.) Recognizing that accessibility renovations would prove costly, the act stated that transportation providers would not have to suffer "undue" financial burdens; nevertheless, the act also made clear that the transportation options offered to the disabled have to be equivalent to those offered to nondisabled transportation patrons.

A similar standard is also applied to public accommodations: although private businesses are not be expected to undertake excessively costly repairs or renovations, they must make "readily available" changes to their facilities, and the facilities offered to the disabled must be similar to those enjoyed by the nondisabled. Moreover, proprietors often are required to provide assistive devices to accommodate disabled customers. For example, a movie theater should provide some sort of amplification device to someone suffering from a hearing disability. A restaurant may provide a Braille menu to a blind patron, or alternatively may have its staff read the menu. Although the requirements vary, the main purpose remains the same with respect to transportation and public accommodations: to eliminate discrimination against the disabled and especially the routine but insidious discrimination they experience in their daily lives.

Title IV of the act concerns telecommunications for the disabled. The act requires telephone companies to provide assistive devices for the disabled, particularly for hearing- and speech-impaired individuals. It also requires television stations to provide closed captioning for public service announcements. Since the adoption of the ADA, the Federal Communications Commission has issued regulations requiring extensive closed-captioning of new television programs.

Of course, the ADA is not without controversy. Although many agree with the act in principle, just as many have had trouble adjusting to it. For the disabled access and opportunities often seem too slow in coming. For businesses the ADA appears to give disgruntled employees yet another pretext for suing their employers. Proprietors continue to argue that removing structural barriers in their establishments is too costly. And the language of the ADA, which seems so clear on the surface, is often itself a source of controversy.

Indeed, even the definition of a "disability" has proven contentious. The Supreme Court, for example, has determined in recent years that myopia (nearsightedness), hypertension (high blood pressure), and blindness in one eye do not constitute disabilities under the ADA. In 2001, moreover, the Court struck a major blow to the ADA by ruling five to four that state workers could not sue their employers in federal court for discrimination under the act. Although the ADA contains a provision (included in the excerpt) rendering the states subject to suit, the Supreme Court held that this provision violates the Eleventh Amendment, which gives state governments immunity from federal lawsuits. On a more positive note for ADA supporters, however, the Supreme Court recently ruled that the Professional Golfers' Association (PGA) must allow disabled professional golfer Casey Martin to use a motorized golf cart when competing in PGA Tour events. Use of a golf cart, according to the Court, was a necessary and reasonable accommodation to make for Martin, who suffers from a debilitating circulatory disorder called Klippel-Trenaunay-Webber Syndrome, which makes it extremely difficult for him to walk the eighteen holes of a golf course.

Litigation over the nature and extent of the ADA's promises and protections will no doubt continue, as the parties affected by the legislation seek to understand their entitlements and their responsibilities. But while parties argue its details in court, the ADA continues to be a powerful symbol for the rights of the disabled and a powerful tool for obtaining those rights. Taken together, the ADA, the IDEA, and the Rehabilitation Act constitute a major force for ensuring that discrimination against the disabled is eradicated and that the focus of legislative, social service, and educational efforts remains on promoting their dignity and independence. With these three pieces of legislation in place, the next generation of America's disabled children should enjoy new opportunities, ones that, until recently, existed only in the dreams of their predecessors.

19. Americans with Disabilities Act

An Act to establish a clear and comprehensive prohibition of discrimination on the basis of disability.

Section 12101. Findings and purposes.

(a) Findings. The Congress finds that:

(1) some 43,000,000 Americans have one or more physical or mental disabilities, and this number is increasing as the population as a whole is growing older;

(2) historically, society has tended to isolate and segregate individuals with disabilities, and, despite some improvements, such forms of discrimination against individuals with disabilities continue to be a serious and pervasive social problem;

(3) discrimination against individuals with disabilities persists in such critical areas as employment, housing, public accommodations, education, transportation, communication, recreation, institutionalization, health services, voting, and access to public services;

(4) unlike individuals who have experienced discrimination on the basis of race, color, sex, national origin, religion, or age, individuals who have experienced discrimination on the basis of disability have often had no legal recourse to redress such discrimination;

(5) individuals with disabilities continually encounter various forms of discrimination, including outright intentional exclusion, the discriminatory effects of architectural, transportation, and communication barriers, overprotective rules and policies, failure to make modifications to existing facilities and practices, exclusionary qualification standards and criteria, segregation, and relegation to lesser services, programs, activities, benefits, jobs, or other opportunities;

(6) census data, national polls, and other studies have documented that people with disabilities, as a group, occupy an inferior status in our society, and are severely disadvantaged socially, vocationally, economically, and educationally;

(7) individuals with disabilities are a discrete and insular minority who have been faced with restrictions and limitations, subjected to a history of purposeful unequal treatment, and relegated to a position of political powerlessness in our society, based on characteristics that are beyond the control of such individuals and resulting from stereotypic assumptions not truly indicative of the individual ability of such individuals to participate in, and contribute to, society;

(8) the nation's proper goals regarding individuals with disabilities are to assure equality of opportunity, full participation, independent living, and economic self-sufficiency for such individuals; and

(9) the continuing existence of unfair and unnecessary discrimination and prejudice denies people with disabilities the opportunity to compete on an equal basis and to pursue those opportunities for which our free society is justifiably famous, and costs the United States billions of dollars in unnecessary expenses resulting from dependency and nonproductivity.

(b) Purpose. It is the purpose of this [act]:

(1) to provide a clear and comprehensive national mandate for the elimination of discrimination against individuals with disabilities;

(2) to provide clear, strong, consistent, enforceable standards addressing discrimination against individuals with disabilities;

(3) to ensure that the Federal Government plays a central role in enforcing the standards established in this Act on behalf of individuals with disabilities; and

(4) to invoke the sweep of congressional authority, including the power to enforce the fourteenth amendment and to regulate commerce, in order to address the major areas of discrimination faced day-to-day by people with disabilities.

Section 12102. Definitions.

As used in this [act]:

(2) Disability. The term "disability" means, with respect to an individual, (A) a physical or mental impairment that substantially limits one or more of the major life activities of such individual; (B) a record of such an impairment; or (C) being regarded as having such an impairment.

[TITLE I: EMPLOYMENT]

Section 12111–12117. [Prohibits discrimination in employment on the basis of disability and requires employers with fifteen or more employees to provide qualified disabled individuals the same employment opportunities as nondisabled workers.]

[TITLE II: PUBLIC SERVICES]

Section 12131. Definitions.

(1) Public entity. The term "public entity" means (A) any State or local government; (B) any department, agency, special purpose district, or other instrumentality of a State or States or local government; and (C) the National Railroad Passenger Corporation [Amtrak], and any commuter [railroad] authority.

(2) Qualified individual with a disability. The term "qualified individual with a disability" means an individual with a disability who, with or without reasonable modifications to rules, policies, or practices, the removal of architectural, communication, or transportation barriers, or the provision of auxiliary aids and services, meets the essential eligibility requirements for the receipt of services or the participation in programs or activities provided by a public entity.

Section 12132. Discrimination.

Subject to the provisions of this title, no qualified individual with a disability shall, by reason of such disability, be excluded from participation in or be denied the benefits of the services, programs, or activities of a public entity, or be subjected to discrimination by any such entity.

Section 12133. Enforcement.

The remedies, procedures, and rights [provided by the Rehabilitation Act of 1973] shall be the remedies, procedures, and rights this title provides to any person alleging discrimination on the basis of disability.

Section 12134. Regulations.

(a) In General. Not later than 1 year after the date of enactment of this Act, the Attorney General shall [create] regulations in an accessible format that implement [the following requirements].

Section 12142. Public entities operating fixed route systems.

(a) Purchase and Lease of New Vehicles. It shall be considered discrimination for purposes of this Act and section 504 of the Rehabilitation Act of 1973 for a public entity which operates a fixed route [transportation] system to purchase or lease a new bus, a new rapid rail vehicle, a new light rail vehicle, or any other new vehicle to be used on such system, . . . if such bus, rail vehicle, or other vehicle is not readily accessible to and usable by individuals with disabilities, including individuals who use wheelchairs. [The requirement that transportation vehicles be accessible to the disabled includes school buses and vans.]

Section 12143. Paratransit as a complement to fixed route service.

(1) (a) General Rule. It shall be considered discrimination for purposes of this Act and section 504 of the Rehabilitation Act of 1973 for

a public entity which operates a fixed route system (other than a system which provides solely commuter bus service) to fail to provide [comparable] paratransit and other special transportation services to individuals with disabilities, including individuals who use wheelchairs. . . .

(4) Undue financial burden limitation. The regulations issued under this section shall provide that, if the public entity is able to demonstrate to the satisfaction of the Secretary [of Transportation] that the provision of paratransit and other special transportation services otherwise required under this section would impose an undue financial burden on the public entity, the public entity shall only be required to provide such services to the extent that providing such services would not impose such a burden.

Section 12146. New facilities.

For purposes of this Act and section 504 of the Rehabilitation Act of 1973, it shall be considered discrimination for a public entity to construct a new facility to be used in the provision of designated public transportation services unless such facility is readily accessible to and usable by individuals with disabilities, including individuals who use wheelchairs.

[TITLE III: PUBLIC ACCOMMODATIONS AND SERVICES OPERATED BY PRIVATE ENTITIES]

Section 12181. Definitions. . . . The following private entities are considered public accommodations for purposes of this title, if the operations of such entities affect commerce:

(7)(A–L) [a hotel, motel, restaurant, bar, motion picture house, theater, concert hall, stadium, auditorium, convention center, lecture hall, or other place of public gathering; a bakery, grocery store, clothing store, hardware store, shopping center, or other sales or rental establishment; a laundromat, dry-cleaner, bank, barber shop, beauty shop, travel service, shoe repair service, funeral parlor, gas station, office of an accountant or lawyer, pharmacy, insurance office, professional office of a health care provider, hospital, or other service establishment; a terminal, depot, or other station used for specified public transportation; a museum, library, gallery, or other place of public display or collection; a park, zoo, amusement park, or other place of recreation; a nursery, elementary, secondary, undergraduate, or postgraduate private school, or other place of education; a day care center, senior citizen center, homeless shelter, food bank, adoption agency, or other social service center establishment; and a gymnasium, health spa, bowling alley, golf course, or other place of exercise or recreation.]

(9) Readily achievable. The term "readily achievable" means easily

accomplishable and able to be carried out without much difficulty or expense. In determining whether an action is readily achievable, factors to be considered include: the nature and cost of the action needed under this Act; the overall financial resources of the facility or facilities involved in the action; the number of persons employed at such facility; the effect on expenses and resources, or the impact otherwise of such action upon the operation of the facility; the overall financial resources of the covered entity; the overall size of the business of a covered entity with respect to the number of its employees; the number, type, and location of its facilities; and the type of operation or operations of the covered entity. . . .

Section 12182. Prohibition of discrimination by public accommodations.

(a) General Rule. No individual shall be discriminated against on the basis of disability in the full and equal enjoyment of the goods, services, facilities, privileges, advantages, or accommodations of any place of public accommodation by any person who owns, leases (or leases to), or operates a place of public accommodation.

(b) Construction.

(1)(A) Activities.

(i) Denial of participation. It shall be discriminatory to [deny a disabled person] the opportunity . . . to participate in or benefit from the goods, services, facilities, privileges, advantages, or accommodations of an entity.

(ii) Participation in unequal benefit. It shall be discriminatory to [provide a disabled person] a good, service, facility, privilege, advantage, or accommodation that is not equal to that [given] to other individuals.

(iii) Separate benefit. It shall be discriminatory to provide [a disabled person] with a good, service, facility, privilege, advantage, or accommodation that is different or separate from that provided to other individuals, unless such action is necessary to provide [that person] with a good, service, facility, privilege, advantage, or accommodation, or other opportunity that is [equivalent to that given a nondisabled person].

(E) Association. It shall be discriminatory to exclude or otherwise deny equal goods, services, facilities, privileges, advantages, accommodations, or other opportunities to an individual or entity because of the known disability of an individual with whom the individual or entity is known to have a relationship or association.

(2) Specific prohibitions.

(A) Discrimination. Discrimination includes:

(i) the imposition or application of eligibility criteria that screen out or tend to screen out an individual with a disability or any class of individuals with disabilities from fully and equally enjoying any goods, services, facilities, privileges, advantages, or accommodations, unless such criteria can be shown to be necessary for the provision of the goods, services, facilities, privileges, advantages, or accommodations being offered;

(ii) a failure to make reasonable modifications in policies, practices, or procedures, when such modifications are necessary to afford such goods, services, facilities, privileges, advantages, or accommodations to individuals with disabilities, unless the entity can demonstrate that making such modifications would fundamentally alter the nature of such goods, services, facilities, privileges, advantages, or accommodations;

(iii) a failure to take such steps as may be necessary to ensure that no individual with a disability is excluded, denied services, segregated or otherwise treated differently than other individuals because of the absence of auxiliary aids and services, unless the entity can demonstrate that taking such steps would fundamentally alter the nature of the good, service, facility, privilege, advantage, or accommodation being offered or would result in an undue burden;

(iv) a failure to remove architectural barriers, and communication barriers that are structural in nature, in existing facilities, and transportation barriers in existing vehicles and rail passenger cars; and

(v) where an entity can demonstrate that the removal of a barrier is not readily achievable, a failure to make such goods, services, facilities, privileges, advantages, or accommodations available through alternative methods if such methods are readily achievable.

Section 12183. New construction and alterations in public accommodations and commercial facilities.

(a) Application of Term. Discrimination includes:

(1) a failure to design and construct [new housing] facilities . . . that are readily accessible to and usable by individuals with disabilities, except where an entity [such as a builder or contractor] can demonstrate that it is structurally impracticable to meet the requirements of [this act]; and

(2) . . . a failure to make alterations [to buildings], to the maximum extent feasible, that are readily accessible to and usable by individuals

with disabilities, including individuals who use wheelchairs. . . . [T]he entity shall also make the alterations in such a manner that, to the maximum extent feasible, [make] the path of travel to bathrooms, telephones, and drinking fountains readily accessible to and usable by individuals with disabilities. . . .

Section 12184. Prohibition of discrimination in specified public transportation services provided by private entities.

(a) General Rule. No individual shall be discriminated against on the basis of disability in the full and equal enjoyment of specified public transportation services provided by a private entity that is primarily engaged in the business of transporting people and whose operations affect commerce.

Section 12187. Exemptions for private clubs and religious organizations.

The provisions of this title shall not apply to private clubs or establishments exempted from coverage under title II of the Civil Rights Act of 1964 or to religious organizations or entities controlled by religious organizations, including places of worship.

Section 12188. Enforcement.

(a) In General. (1) Availability of remedies and procedures. The remedies and procedures set forth in . . . the Civil Rights Act of 1964 are [available] to any person who is being subjected to discrimination on the basis of disability in violation of this title. . . .

(2) [Types of Relief]. In the case of violations [of this act] . . . injunctive relief shall include an order to alter facilities to make such facilities readily accessible to and usable by individuals with disabilities. . . . Where appropriate, injunctive relief shall also include requiring the provision of an auxiliary aid or service [such as a Braille menu], modification of a policy, or provision of alternative methods, to the extent required by this title.

(b) Enforcement by the Attorney General. The Attorney General shall investigate alleged violations of this title . . . and may commence civil action[s] in any appropriate United States district court.

(b)(1)(B)(2)(A–B). Authority of court. In a civil action, the court [may grant any equitable relief it considers appropriate as well as compensatory damages. It may also,] to vindicate the public interest, assess a civil penalty against the entity in an amount not exceeding $50,000 for a first violation; and not exceeding $100,000 for any subsequent violation. [Punitive damages cannot be awarded.]

[TITLE IV: TELECOMMUNICATIONS]

[Author's Note: The following sections provide for amendments to other laws in the U.S. Code. I have referenced this ADA title by its prior congressional citation (104 Stat. 327 et seq.) and have also included the citations to the affected laws.]

104 Stat. Section 401. Telecommunications relay services for hearing-impaired and speech-impaired individuals.

(a) Telecommunications. The Communications Act of 1934 is amended by adding the following new section [at 47 U.S.C. 225]:

Section 225. Telecommunications services for hearing-impaired and speech-impaired individuals.

(a) Definitions. As used in this section:

(3) Telecommunications relay services. The term "telecommunications relay services" means telephone transmission services that provide the ability for an individual who has a hearing impairment or speech impairment to engage in communication by wire or radio with a hearing individual in a manner that is functionally equivalent to the ability of an individual who does not have a hearing impairment or speech impairment to communicate using voice communication services by wire or radio. Such term includes services that enable two-way communication between an individual who uses a TDD or other nonvoice terminal device and an individual who does not use such a device.

(b) Availability of Telecommunications Relay Services.

(1) In general. In order to carry out the purposes [of this act], to make available to all individuals in the United States a rapid, efficient nationwide communication service, and to increase the utility of the telephone system of the nation, the [Federal Communications] Commission shall ensure that interstate and intrastate telecommunications relay services are available, to the extent possible and in the most efficient manner, to hearing-impaired and speech-impaired individuals in the United States.

104 Stat. Section 402. Closed-captioning of public service announcements.

The Communications Act of 1934 is amended to read as follows [at 47 U.S.C. 611]:

Any television public service announcement that is produced or funded in whole or in part by any agency or instrumentality of Federal Government shall include closed captioning of the verbal content of such announcement.

[TITLE V: MISCELLANEOUS PROVISIONS]

Section 12201.

(a) In General. Except as otherwise provided in this Act, nothing in this Act shall be construed to apply a lesser standard than the standards applied by the Rehabilitation Act of 1973 or the regulations issued by Federal agencies pursuant to such title.

(b) Relationship to Other Laws. Nothing in this Act shall be construed to invalidate or limit the remedies, rights, and procedures of any Federal law or law of any State or political subdivision of any State or jurisdiction that provides greater or equal protection for the rights of individuals with disabilities than are afforded by this Act.

Appendix

Understanding Statute Citations

Each act passed by Congress and signed into law by the president is given a number, called a "public law number" (Pub. L.). This number identifies the new law until it can be included in the U.S. Code, the official publication of federal statutory law. It can take a rather long time for a new law to be processed; a wait of over a year or more is not unusual. (The law is still valid; it just doesn't have a permanent identification number yet.) When the law is finally entered into the U.S. Code, it is assigned to the proper part of the Code, which is arranged by topic, and given a formal citation number. For example, the Fair Housing Act is cited as "42 U.S.C. § 3601 et seq." Translated, the citation means that the law can be found in Title 42 of the U.S. Code, starting at section 3601, and continuing through following sections. ("Et seq." essentially means "and sequential.") If a law is too new to be found in the U.S. Code, I have cited to its public law number instead. Similarly, I have used the public law number to indicate amendments to certain laws should the reader wish to refer directly to those amendments.

Americans with Disabilities Act: 42 U.S.C. § 12101 et seq.

Child Citizenship Act: Pub. L. 106–395

Child Nutrition Act: 42 U.S.C. § 1771 et seq.

Clean Air Act: 42 U.S.C. § 7401 et seq.

Clean Air Act Amendments: Pub. L. 101–549

Early and Periodic Screening, Diagnosis, and Treatment for Children: 42 C.F.R. § 441.56 et seq.

Education for All Handicapped Children Act: See Individuals with Disabilities Education Act

Elementary and Secondary Education Act: The 1994 version of the act, found at 20 U.S.C. § 6301 et seq., has been replaced by the 2002 reauthorization entitled No Child Left Behind Act, cited below.

Fair Housing Act: 42 U.S.C. § 3601 et seq.

Fair Housing Act Amendments of 1988: Pub. L. 100–430

Fair Labor Standards Act: 29 U.S.C. § 201 et seq.

Federal Zero Tolerance Law: 23 U.S.C. § 161

Food Quality Protection Act: Pub. L. 104–170

Fourteenth Amendment: U.S. Constitution

G.I. Bill: 38 U.S.C. § 3001 (This cite is to the current version of the bill, commonly called the "Montgomery G.I. Bill.")

Head Start: 42 U.S.C. § 9831 et seq.

Higher Education Act: 20 U.S.C. § 1001 et seq.

Individuals with Disabilities Education Act: 20 U.S.C. § 1400 et seq.

Intercountry Adoption Act: Pub. L. 106–279

Medicaid: 42 U.S.C. § 1396 et seq.

Military Selective Service Act: 50 U.S.C. Appendix § 453 et seq.

Morrill Act: 7 U.S.C. § 301 et seq.

Morrill Act (Second): 7 U.S.C. § 321 et seq.

National Childhood Vaccine Injury Act: 42 U.S.C. § 300aa–1 et seq.

National School Lunch Act: 42 U.S.C. § 1751 et seq.

No Child Left Behind Act: Pub. L. 107–110

Rehabilitation Act of 1973: 29 U.S.C. § 791 et seq. Section 504 of the Act is now found at 29 U.S.C. § 794.

Residential Lead-Based Paint Hazard Reduction Act: 42 U.S.C. § 4851 et seq.

Safe Drinking Water Act: 42 U.S.C. § 300f et seq.

Safe Drinking Water Act Amendments: Pub. L. 104–182

Social Security Act: 42 U.S.C. § 301 et seq.

School-to-Work Opportunities Act: 20 U.S.C. § 6101

State Children's Health Insurance Program: 42 U.S.C. § 1397aa et seq.

Twenty-sixth Amendment: U.S. Constitution

Uniform Drinking Age Act: 23 U.S.C. § 158 et seq.

CASE CITATIONS

Understanding Case Citations

The official version of each Supreme Court decision is found in the U.S. Reports. Unfortunately, there is an even longer delay in preparing new cases for inclusion in the U.S. Reports than there is in preparing new laws for the U.S. Code. When a case is assigned an official place in the U.S. Reports, it is given a number like those listed below. *Oregon v. Mitchell,* for example, is cited as 400 U.S. 112 (1970), which means that the text of the decision can be found in volume 400 of the U.S. Reports, starting at page 112. The year of the decision is indicated by parentheses. For cases that are too new to have official citations, I have cited them by their Supreme Court case numbers. The case number is the identifying number assigned by the Court to each case it receives.

Adkins v. Children's Hospital: 261 U.S. 525 (1923)

A.L.A. Schechter Poultry Corporation v. United States: 295 U.S. 495 (1935)

Cedar Rapids Community School District v. Garret F.: Case No. 96–1793 (1999)

Dred Scott v. Sanford: 60 U.S. 393 (1856)

Hammer v. Dagenhart: 247 U.S. 251 (1918)

Lochner v. New York: 198 U.S. 45 (1905)

Oregon v. Mitchell: 400 U.S. 112 (1970)

Rostker v. Goldberg: 453 U.S. 57 (1981)

South Dakota v. Dole: 483 U.S. 203 (1987)

West Coast Hotel Company v. Parrish: 300 U.S. 379 (1937)

Zelman v. Simmons-Harris: Case No. 00–1751 (2002)

Selected Bibliography

INTERNET RESOURCES

Congress

web.lexis-nexis.com/universe
Many colleges and universities subscribe to the "Academic Universe" site sponsored by Lexis-Nexis. The highly useful and easily searchable site contains news from major publications dating back up to twenty years; comprehensive legal information including U.S., state, and international laws as well as federal and state judicial decisions; business and medical information; and general reference resources. The "Congressional Universe" contains information about all aspects of Congress, including the current code and agency regulations, bills in progress, congressional publications, testimony before Congress, biographical information about members, voting records, and the like. This site is geared more toward students than to members of the general public. Lexis-Nexis also offers a similar subscription service for members of the legal profession.

www.americaslibrary.gov/cgi-bin/page.cgi
The Library of Congress has created a fun, interactive website for children to learn about U.S. history and government.

www.cq.com
The Congressional Quarterly. Authoritative guide to legislation, policy, and events in Congress. Geared toward scholars.

www.house.gov
U.S. House of Representatives home page, with comprehensive links to members, bills, House history, and more.

www.loc.gov
The Library of Congress online.

www.rollcall.com
Newspaper covering the activities of Congress and Capitol Hill.

www.senate.gov
U.S. Senate home page, with comprehensive links to senators, bills, Senate history, and more.

www.thomas.loc.gov
"Thomas," named after Thomas Jefferson, is the Library of Congress' comprehensive website for legislative information and materials.

The Constitution and United States Code

For discussion of proposed legislation or the status of bills in progress, a student should refer to the House and Senate websites or Thomas. For current legislation several sites offer the U.S. Code. These sites often include federal agency regulations and state codes as well. Perhaps the most current and comprehensive site is that maintained by the Legal Information Institute of Cornell University, which offers information on legislation and a comprehensive site for the Supreme Court. Be aware in reviewing codes that it often takes a year or more for a new law or an amendment to appear in the official U.S. Code. These on-line sites, like the published version of the U.S. Code, will always be somewhat dated as a result.

web.lexis-nexis.com/congcomp
For subscribers, this site on the Lexis-Nexis Congressional Universe allows one to search the U.S. Code, the Code of Federal Regulations, the Federal Register, legislative histories, and so forth.

www.findlaw.com
A comprehensive legal website that addresses topics such as legislation, judicial decisions, and business and consumer legal issues. The site also includes information for pre-law students considering a legal career, links to U.S. law schools, and career and employment information for attorneys. This consumer-oriented site is "one-stop shopping" for students or members of the public who wish to do legal research or to find out more about the law and the legal profession.

www.law.cornell.edu
This comprehensive site is sponsored by the Legal Information Institute at Cornell University. It is oriented more toward scholars, but can be easily navigated.

www.thomas.loc.gov/home/lawsmade.toc.html
The Library of Congress has prepared this accessible, understandable site to explain how a bill becomes a law.

www.uscode.house.gov
The House of Representatives' site for the U.S. Code.

Executive Branch Departments and Agencies

www.cdc.gov
Centers for Disease Control and Prevention. A good source for detailed information about diseases that affect different groups of Americans, including children and young adults. It provides invaluable, if sometimes rather technical, information about lead-based paint hazards, water and airborne disease hazards, potential vaccine side effects, and the like.

http://bhpr.hrsa.gov/vicp/
The home page for the National Vaccine Injury Compensation Program.

www.cdc.gov/ncbddd/kids
"Kids Quest on Disability and Health" is an interactive exploration game for children.

www.cdc.gov/niosh/adoldoc.html
This teen page provides information for working teens about on the job health, safety, and rights.

www.cdc.gov/od/nvpo/vacsafe.htm
The CDC offers this instructive page for parents and children concerned about the safety of childhood vaccines. The CDC works together with the Food and Drug Administration and the Department of Health and Human Services to ensure that children are properly immunized.

www.dol.gov
U.S. Department of Labor. Look here to find out more about the Fair Labor Standards Act and the School-to-Work Opportunities Act.

www.ed.gov
U.S. Department of Education. Comprehensive site for all programs sponsored by the department. Find out more about the Elementary and Secondary Education Act and the Higher Education Act.

www.ed.gov/offices/OSFAP/Students/sfa.html
The department's comprehensive federal financial aid site.

www.ed.gov/offices/OSFAP/Students/student.html
The department offers this site, "Finding Out About Financial Aid," which discusses all of the major federal financial aid programs for college students.

www.epa.gov
Environmental Protection Agency. Find out more about the EPA's efforts to ensure a clean and healthy environment for all Americans. The site includes information about several laws discussed in this book, including the Clean Air Act and amendments, the Safe Drinking Water Act and amendments, the Residential Lead-Based Paint Hazard Reduction Act, and the Food Quality Protection Act.

www.epa.gov/children
EPA Office of Children's Health Protection's interactive website for students and teachers.

www.epa.gov/kids
The EPA's "Explorer's Club" for kids, an interactive website about clean air, clean water, and protecting the environment.

www.fda.gov
Food and Drug Administration. The FDA shares responsibility with other federal agencies to ensure, among other things, that children receive safe and effective medical treatments, including vaccinations, and that they enjoy clean water and air.

www.fda.gov/oc/opacom/kids/default.htm
The Food and Drug Administration maintains this website that includes games for children and information for teens about food and drug safety, vaccines, and other timely information about its regulations and programs.

www.gibill.va.gov
The Department of Veterans Affairs sponsors this website dedicated to the G.I. Bill.

www.ins.gov
Immigration and Naturalization Service. This site answers frequently asked questions about obtaining entry to the United States, maintaining residency, and becoming an American citizen. This site, and the State Department site, offer information about adopting children from overseas, including information about the Child Citizenship Act of 2000 and the Intercountry Adoption Act.

www.niaaa.nih.gov/index.htm
National Institutes of Health's National Institute on Alcohol Abuse and Alcoholism. This site provides information about the causes of and treatments for alcoholism and guidelines for prevention. Among other things, it discusses the research surrounding the Uniform Drinking Age Act and the Federal Zero Tolerance Law.

science-education.nih.gov/homepage.nsf
The National Institutes of Health offers this science education site with materials and activities for children and teens.

www.os.dhhs.gov
U.S. Department of Health and Human Services. This department is responsible for administering numerous public health and welfare programs including Medicaid and Early and Periodic Screening, Diagnosis, and Treatment for Children, the State Children's Health Insurance Program, Head Start, and the School-to-Work Opportunities Act.

www.acf.dhhs.gov/index.html
Many of the above programs are overseen by the Administration for Children and Families, a division of the department.

www.acf.dhhs.gov/programs/hsb
The site of the Head Start Bureau.

www.hhs.gov/kids
The department offers numerous interactive websites for children that are listed at and linked to this site.

www.ssa.gov
Social Security Administration. An excellent website that explains all aspects of the Social Security Program, from its history, to present-day eligibility requirements, to the future challenges facing the system. The site also includes "Youthlink," a fun and informative page for young people, parents, and teachers to learn more about social security.

www.sss.gov
The Selective Service System. This website discusses the history of registration and the draft and lists current registration criteria. Generally, males between the ages of eighteen and twenty-five who reside in the United States must register with the Selective Service. They may do so on-line at this site.

www.state.gov
U.S. State Department. The State Department works with the Immigration and Naturalization Service to facilitate intercountry adoptions.

www.usda.gov
U.S. Department of Agriculture. Learn more about the National School Lunch Act and the Child Nutrition Act.

www.foodsafety.gov/~dms/cbook.html
The USDA's food safety page for children, including a food safety coloring book.

www.usdoj.gov
Department of Justice. The DOJ serves as the federal government's lawyer. It works to enforce federal laws and to defend the government from lawsuits. The easily navigable site is organized largely by topic, including the following that are relevant to this book:

www.usdoj.gov/disabilities.htm
For information on the Americans with Disabilities Act and other legal rights of the disabled, including the Rehabilitation Act of 1973 and the Individuals with Disabilities Education Act.

www.usdoj.gov/discrimination.htm
For information on various types of illegal discrimination, including housing discrimination under the Fair Housing Act.

www.usdoj.gov/immigrationinfo.htm
For information about immigration laws, hearings, and other proceedings.

Other Governmental Sites

www.census.gov/mso/www/educate
This website, offered by the Census Bureau's Marketing Services Office, contains a useful, lengthy list of top federal government websites for children grades K-8 and 9–12. It also includes information about government websites that offer lesson plans for teachers.

www.lbjlib.utexas.edu
Learn more about President Lyndon B. Johnson's "Great Society" programs at the

website for the Johnson presidential library and museum, housed at the University of Texas.

www.supremecourtus.gov
The Supreme Court's homepage. For information about past decisions and pending cases, refer to one of the comprehensive legal websites listed above.

www.whitehouse.gov
Contact the president of the United States at the White House. This site also includes a "kids only" link to whitehousekids.gov, a fun and comprehensive site for young people to learn about American government.

Children's Advocacy Organizations

Often the best place to find the latest information about children's issues, including new programs and pending legislation, is the website of an advocacy group. Hundreds, perhaps thousands, of relevant sites can be obtained by a simple key word search for a specific organization or issue. There are too many to list here. The following organizations are referenced in this book.

www.childrensdefense.org
Children's Defense Fund

www.madd.org
Mothers Against Drunk Driving

www.saddonline.com
National Organization of Students Against Destructive Decisions (also sometimes known as Students Against Drunk Driving)

www.unicef.org
United Nation's Children's Fund

BOOKS

Andrew, John A. III. *Lyndon Johnson and the Great Society.* Chicago, IL: Ivan R. Dee, Inc. 1998.
Berry, Jeffrey M. *The Interest Group Society,* 3rd ed. New York: Longman, 1997.
Bond, James Edward. *No Easy Walk to Freedom: Reconstruction and the Ratification of the Fourteenth Amendment.* Westport, CT: Greenwood Publishing Group, 1997.
Burns, Edward. *IEPs: An Individualized Education Program (IEP) Handbook for Meeting Individuals with Disabilities Education Act (IDEA) Requirements.* Springfield, IL: Charles C. Thomas, 2001.
Califano, Joseph A. *The Triumph and Tragedy of Lyndon Johnson: The White House Years.* College Station, TX: Texas A&M University Press, 2000.
Caro, Robert A. *Means of Ascent,* vol.2, *The Years of Lyndon Johnson.* Reprint. New York: Vintage Books, 1991.

———. *Years of Lyndon Johnson: The Path to Power.* Reprint. New York: Vintage Books, 1990.

Children's Defense Fund. *Poverty Matters: The Cost of Child Poverty in America.* Washington, D.C.: Children's Defense Fund, 1997.

———. *The State of America's Children Yearbook, 2001.* Washington, D.C.: Children's Defense Fund, 2001.

Children's Environmental Health Network. *Resource Guide on Children's Environmental Health.* Emeryville, CA: Public Health Institute, 1997.

Davidson, Roger H., and Walter J. Oleszek. *Congress and Its Members,* 7th ed. Washington, D.C.: Congressional Quarterly Press, 2000.

Davis, Kenneth C. *Don't Know Much About History: Everything You Need to Know About American History but Never Learned.* New York: Morrow/Avon Books, 1999.

Deering, Christopher J., and Steven S. Smith. *Committees in Congress.* Washington D.C.: CQ Press, 1997.

Dodd, Lawrence A., and Bruce I. Oppenheimer. *Congress Reconsidered.* 7th ed. Washington, D.C.: CQ Press, 2001.

Douglas, Paul H. *Social Security in the United States: An Analysis and Appraisal of the Federal Social Security Act.* Beard Group/Beard Books, 2000.

Edmunds, Margaret, and Molly Joel Coye, eds. *Systems of Accountability: Implementing Children's Health Insurance Programs.* Washington, D.C.: National Academy Press, 1998.

Ellsworth, Jeanne, and Lynda Ames, eds. *Critical Perspectives on Project Headstart.* Albany, NY: State University of New York Press, 1998.

Erichsen, Jean, and Heino Erichsen. *How to Adopt Internationally, 2000–2002: A Guide for Agency-Directed and Independent Adoptions.* Fort Worth, TX: Mesa House Publishing, 2000.

Fenno, Richard, Jr. *Homestyle: House Members in Their Districts.* Boston: Little, Brown and Co., 1978.

Fiorina, Morris P. *Congress: Keystone of the Washington Establishment,* 2nd ed. New Haven, CT: Yale University Press, 1989.

Francis, Leslie Pickering, and Anita Silvers, eds. *Americans with Disabilities: Exploring the Implications of the Law for Individuals and Institutions.* New York: Routledge, 2000.

Garraty, Arthur John. *1001 Things Everyone Should Know About American History.* New York: Doubleday & Co., 1992.

Gordon, Michael, and Shelby Keiser, eds. *Accommodations in Higher Education Under the Americans with Disabilities Act.* New York: Guilford Publications, 2000.

Greenberg, Milton. *The G.I. Bill: The Law that Changed America.* New York: Lickle Publishing, 1997.

Hershey, Alan M. *Partners in Progress: Early Steps in Creating School-to-Work Systems.* Princeton, N.J.: Mathematica Policy Research, Inc., 1997.

Hyman, Harold. *American Singularity: The 1787 Northwest Ordinance, the 1862 Homestead and Morrill Acts, and the 1944 G.I. Bill.* Athens, GA: University of Georgia Press, 1986.

Jacobson, Gary C. *The Politics of Congressional Elections.* 4th ed. New York: Longman Publishers, 1997.

Jeffrey, Julie Roy. *Education for the Poor: A Study of the Origins and Implementation of the Elementary and Secondary Education Act of 1965.* Columbus, OH: Ohio State University Press, 1978.

Jehle, Faustin F. *The Complete and Easy Guide to Social Security, Healthcare Rights, and Government Benefits.* Emerson Adams Press, Inc., 2000.

Jennings, John F., ed. *National Issues in Education: Elementary and Secondary Education Act.* Bloomington, IN: Phi Delta Kappa Educational Foundation, 1995.

Kern, Rosemary Gibson. *Medicaid and Other Experiments in State Health Policy.* Washington, D.C.: American Enterprise Institute, 1986.

Kozol, Jonathan. *Amazing Grace: The Lives of Children and the Conscience of a Nation.* Reprint. New York: HarperPerrenial Library, 1996.

Krieg, Frea Jay. *Transition: School to Work.* Bethesda, M.D.: National Association of School Psychologists, 1995.

Lantzy, M. Louise. *Individuals with Disabilities Education Act: An Annotated Guide to Its Literature and Resources, 1980–1991.* Buffalo, NY: William S. Hein & Co., 1992.

Maass, Arthur. *Congress and the Common Good.* New York: Basic Books, 1983.

Mann, Thomas, and Norman J. Ornstein, eds. *Intensive Care: How Congress Shapes Health Policy.* Washington, D.C.: American Enterprise Institute and the Brookings Institution, 1995.

———. *Renewing Congress.* Washington, D.C.: Brookings Institution and American Enterprise Institute, 1993.

Mayhew, David R. *Congress: The Electoral Connection.* New Haven: Yale University Press, 1974.

Miller, Roger LeRoy, Daniel K. Benjamin, and Douglas C. North. *The Economics of Public Issues,* 12th ed. Reading, MA: Addison-Wesley, 2001.

Mott, Lawrie, David Fore, Jennifer Curtis, and Gina Solomon. *Our Children at Risk: The 5 Worst Environmental Threats to Their Health.* New York: Natural Resources Defense Council, 1997.

Oleszek, Walter J. *Congressional Procedures and the Policy Process.* 5th ed. Washington, D.C.: CQ Press, 2001.

Paulsen, George E. *A Living Wage for the Forgotten Man: The Quest for Fair Labor Standards, 1933–1941.* Cranbury, N.J.: Associated University Press, 1996.

Piven, Francis Fox, and Richard A. Cloward. *Poor People's Movements: Why They Succeed, How They Fail.* New York: Vintage Books, 1979.

Rohde, David W. *Parties and Leaders in the Post-Reform House.* Chicago: University of Chicago Press, 1991.

St. John, Edward P. *Public Policy and College Management: Title III of the Higher Education Act.* Westport, CT: Greenwood Publishing Group, Inc., 1981.

Siegel, Lawrence M. *The Complete IEP Guide: How to Advocate for Your Special Needs Child.* Berkeley, CA: Nolo Press, 2001.

Simon, Rita J., and Howard Altstein. *Adoption Across Borders: Serving Children in Transracial and Intercountry Adoptions.* Landham, MD: Rowman & Littlefield, 2000.

Sinclair, Barbara. *Unorthodox Lawmaking: New Legislative Processes in the U.S. Congress.* 2nd ed. Washington, D.C.: CQ Press, 2000.

Taylor, Fred. *Roll Away the Stone: Saving America's Children.* Great Falls, VA: Information International, 1999.

Treanor, J. Robert. *2001 Mercer Guide to Social Security and Medicare.* Louisville, KY: William M. Mercer, 2001.

U.S. Commission on Civil Rights. *The Fair Housing Amendment Acts of 1988: The Enforcement Report.* Washington, D.C.: U.S. Commission on Civil Rights, 1994.

U.S. Environmental Protection Agency. *Environmental Health Threats to Children.* Washington, D.C.: U.S. Environmental Protection Agency, Office of the Administrator, 1996.

Verba, Sidney, Lay L. Schlozman, and Henry E. Brady. *Voice and Equality: Civic Volunteerism in American Politics.* Cambridge, MA: Harvard University Press, 1995.

Vile, John R. *Encyclopedia of Constitutional Amendments, Proposed Amendments, and Amending Issues, 1789–1995*, 3d ed. Santa Barbara, CA: ABC-CLIO, 2001.

Washington, Valora, and Ura J. Bailey, eds. *Project Head Start: Models and Strategies for the Twenty-first Century.* New York: Garland Publishing, Inc., 1994.

Weschler, Henry. *Minimum-Drinking-Age Laws: An Evaluation.* Lexington, MA: Lexington Books, 1980.

Wilson, James Q. *Bureaucracy: What Government Agencies Do and Why They Do It.* New York: Basic Books, 1989.

Witte, Edwin Emil. *The Development of the Social Security Act.* Madison: University of Wisconsin Press, 1962.

Wright, Peter W.D., and Pamela Darr Wright. *Wrightslaw: Special Education Law.* Hartfield, VA: Harbor House Law Press, 1999.

Young, Jonathan M. *Equality of Opportunity: The Making of the Americans with Disabilities Act.* Washington, D.C.: National Council on Disability, 1997.

Zigler, Edward F., and Susan Muenchow. *Head Start: The Inside Story of America's Most Successful Educational Experiment.* New York: Basic Books, 1994.

Index

About the Author

KATHLEEN URADNIK is Assistant Professor of Political Science at St. Cloud State University. She specializes in public law and American government.